Markt- und Unternehmensentwicklung
Markets and Organisations

Edited by
A. Picot, München, Deutschland
R. Reichwald, Leipzig, Deutschland
E. Franck, Zürich, Schweiz
K.M. Möslein, Erlangen-Nürnberg, Deutschland

Change of institutions, technology and competition drives the interplay of markets and organisations. The scientific series 'Markets and Organisations' addresses a magnitude of related questions, presents theoretic and empirical findings and discusses related concepts and models.

More information about this series at http://www.springer.com/series/12561

Julia M. Jonas

Stakeholder Integration in Service Innovation

With a foreword by Prof. Dr. Kathrin M. Moeslein

Springer Gabler

Julia M. Jonas
Nürnberg, Germany

Dissertation Friedrich-Alexander-Universität Erlangen-Nürnberg, 2015

Markt- und Unternehmensentwicklung Markets and Organisations
ISBN 978-3-658-19462-8 ISBN 978-3-658-19463-5 (eBook)
DOI 10.1007/978-3-658-19463-5

Library of Congress Control Number: 2017952535

Springer Gabler

Printed on acid-free paper

This Springer Gabler imprint is published by Springer Nature
The registered company is Springer Fachmedien Wiesbaden GmbH
The registered company address is: Abraham-Lincoln-Str. 46, 65189 Wiesbaden, Germany

Foreword

Service innovation is gaining importance as the distinction between products and services is vanishing and services and tangible products are jointly seen as platforms for value co-creation, in hybrid business models, in cyber-physical systems or digital service offerings. To understand the innovation processes of services as complex and interdisciplinary efforts in organisations and the systems they are embedded in, is accordingly of high relevance for researchers and practitioners. In this context, more knowledge is needed on how to successfully and proactively guide service innovation from idea to implementation, aligning, integrating and motivating multiple involved stakeholders from inside and outside an organisation.

The work of Dr. Julia M. Jonas focuses on stakeholder integration in service innovation in manufacturing and IT firms. Her dissertation explores the roles and modes of stakeholder integration throughout the innovation process of services. She applies a service-dominant logic lens to analyse stakeholder integration as a co-creative process and looks at different stakeholders from inside and outside the core organisation who contribute to path the way of an idea to an implemented service concept.

The book invites the reader to explore stakeholder integration in service innovation. Key questions are: "Which stakeholders from inside and outside an organisation are getting integrated in service innovation, in which mode - passive, reactive, as mutual co-creation or in the mode of proactive initiative? In which stage of the service innovation process are these stakeholders integrated?". Deriving insights about stakeholder integration practice in service innovation, Julia M. Jonas further sheds light on the dynamics of stakeholder integration, to describe what factors affect stakeholder integration and how do stakeholder integration activities such as interdisciplinary innovation effect the work of the stakeholder and its organisational service system.

The thesis has been accepted as a doctoral dissertation in 2015 by the School of Business and Economics at the Friedrich-Alexander University Erlangen-Nürnberg. "Stakeholder Integration in Service Innovation" delivers value for both, practitioners and academics. The book reflects the authors' competence in qualitative research and profits highly from the empathy for industry processes following an engaged scholarship approach. It accesses service innovation in its natural context and reviews and reflects the big picture as well as the relevant details in the complex environment of service innovation.

The work applies service-dominant logic in empirical research and has already received positive response in the service research community. Besides various conference presentations, two studies from the thesis are already published in the academic journals Service Science and International Journals of Technology Management.

This dissertation appeals by its theoretical reach and empirical scope, the fresh methodological approach and the argumentative brilliance by which findings are presented. The book deserves broad dissemination both in the research community and in management practice. It is especially recommended to those with a deep interest in service innovations and the true nature of co-creating them. As a reader you are cordially invited to co-creatively generate your individually perceived value from this reading!

Kathrin M. Möslein

Preface

What processes and activities inside the organisation are necessary for open innovation projects to have impact and to be sustainable? What stakeholders from inside and outside an organisation are needed to enable and guide an innovation concept from idea to market implementation? These questions from practice motivated me to explore stakeholder integration in service innovation and its' dynamics in-depth.

I am thankful and happy that my professor Prof. Dr. Kathrin M. Moeslein at Friedrich-Alexander-University Erlangen-Nuremberg's Institute for Information Systems - Innovation and Value Creation gave me the opportunity and support to align the knowledge and experiences from my studies, including service-dominant logic, and my hands-on work in industry to set up this research project on the roles and modes of stakeholders in service innovation. A big "thank you" to her and to my second supervisor Prof. Dr. Freimut Bodendorf.

Thanks to the departments' joint projects with Fraunhofer IIS and Fraunhofer SCS (e.g. the "Service Factory Nürnberg" including JOSEPHS®), I was provided with the opportunity to engage in exciting and challenging projects in the sphere of user and stakeholder integration, with an interesting research ground, funding and great characters/colleagues to work with.

Special thanks are given to all participants of this research journey - especially to all interview partners and co-creators at Fraunhofer and in the different case companies who have to stay anonymous, unfortunately. This piece of research was brought to life only through your engagement!

Now that the magical moment to print this work has arrived, it is finally time to be somewhat melancholic and have a personal look back at writing this thesis. Hurray!

I feel that going through this dissertation project was like climbing a really impressive mountain: at first, this mountain looked dangerous, but it was so fascinating and pretty that I couldn't resist to start walking towards it. It looked scary in the beginning, but getting warm walking, it could feel like a good trip to do. There were some passages that felt like walking without gaining height. There were passages with rocks and fields of scree where the journey felt like taking two steps forward, slipping one step right back. There were nice views in the sunshine as well as really cloudy passages. In the end, after dreaming about how it would be to actually reach the top of this mountain, after about 3.5 years, the thesis is done. After my Gipfelbrotzeit and a deep breath, it feels like the trip was not too bad after all and I can already look around and speculate about which mountain to climb next. I am really happy that this trip was supported and accompanied by a number of institutions and people.

In the context of several conference presentations, but especially at two doctoral seminars in 2014, at FMM and Reser, I received valuable feedback from senior researchers and PhD student fellows. I want to thank all of them for the interesting discussions and inspiration. Thereby, a special thank you goes to Stephen Vargo, Christian Kowalkowski, David Sörhammar and Kaisa Koskela-Huotari for their feedback, suggestions and sometimes somewhat confusing yet very helpful ideas. I feel grateful for meeting such interesting characters as well as for some really great conference nights out.

Angela and Kathrin: as "drei sehr unterschiedliche Exemplare von Frauen", we had an exciting time together in the past four years. Thank you for always being there for me, for distracting me with diverse other tasks and for sending me home, to go writing, at the same time. I am looking forward to continue our task force! I am pretty sure that we are awaiting more fun, and work, and fun work to do.

Thank you Dominik for pushing me to apply at Wi1 several years ago and for walking next to me. Thank you Katja, Uta, Carlos, Moni, Carolin, Rebekka and the rest of the gang for chocolates, coffees and kind words at any time. Also thanks to my often missed dear friends, and family, in all the different places south and north from here.

Last but not least: Thank you to my mum. Without a clear reason, a long time ago, I was so scared to tell you that I will be doing this crazy academic job. You supported me so much to get this done and to do even more of this in the future! I can be proud because you are.

Overview of contents

Table of contents

Abstract

Service systems as the basis for value creation and service innovation are recently gaining interest in research and practice. In this context, service innovation is understood as the joint efforts of stakeholders in the service system. Research in service innovation has found that the integration of specific stakeholders, such as customers and users or senior management, for instance, brings along a variety of benefits, such as access to tacit knowledge, but also some challenges, i.e. regarding resource allocation. Whereas literature in service innovation has analysed potentials and options for stakeholder integration for specific stakeholder groups in isolation, the potential interrelatedness of stakeholder integration in a systems view has received only little attention in research so far.

It is the aim of this thesis to explore the practices of stakeholder integration in service innovation holistically, from a systems perspective, as proposed by the applied theory lens service-dominant logic. For this purpose, it applies a three step research approach with two single case studies and a multiple case study as its core. In the setting of service innovating IT and manufacturing firms, the thesis analyses which stakeholders are integrated for service innovation, in which mode and in which stages of the innovation process. Moreover, it aims to shed light on the dynamics of stakeholder integration, in particular for mutual integration. This mode of stakeholder integration is, in theory, expected to provide access to tacit knowledge, such as experiences and hidden needs.

The empirical data show that stakeholder integration is, in the majority of cases, implemented as reactive stakeholder integration. Mutual integration is found to be realized foremost with members of the organization, with an emphasis on the early stages of the innovation process. This practice supports the development of unique innovations, network effects and stronger relations of the stakeholders with the innovation project. The thesis further presents examples of how stakeholder integration in service systems includes informal and indirect stakeholder integration. These practices create interdependencies in the service system and support a view on service innovation as a multidimensional process.

The multidimensionality of stakeholder integration in service innovation is contextualised through the exploration of mutual stakeholder integration. It provides evidence on how stakeholder integration is influenced by the surrounding service systems, and on how stakeholder integration creates effects going beyond the scope of the integrated stakeholders. Furthermore, the thesis extrapolates that the resources for the integration of different stakeholder groups have to be balanced, and that service innovation itself has to compete for resources with the everyday product-related business of responsible innovation managers.

Building on these and more findings from exploratory research, the thesis develops a model for stakeholder integration as an interrelated process and derives implications for management and service research. This is followed by an outlook for future research opportunities that originate from the in-depth analysis of the case studies in IT and manufacturing.

List of figures

List of tables

List of abbreviations

B2B	Business-to-Business
CEO	Chief Executive Officer
e.g.	exempli gratia (lat.); for example
et al.	et alii (lat.); and others
etc.	et cetera (lat.); and so forth
FMCG	Fast Moving Consumer Goods
hrs.	hours
i.e.	id est (lat.); that is
IfM	Institut für Mittelstandsforschung
IT	Information Technology
min.	minute(s)
p.	page
pp.	pages
PMM	Project Portfolio Management
PLM	Product Lifecycle Management
R&D	Research & Development
SME	Small- and Medium-sized Enterprises

Part I
Introduction

1 The motivation for this thesis

What decides if a service innovation will be successful, or not? If you ask Google, you will receive a vast variety of answers by search engine optimised innovation consultancies, individual bloggers and multi-national consulting firms: Cross-disciplinary[1], (eco-)systems thinking[2] and "having key stakeholders on board"[3] are amongst the often cited factors that decide whether innovation will develop into a success or a failure. There is a common understanding in practice and research that innovation is a matter of joint efforts - examples such as the integration of various suppliers for the development of the Apple iPod[4] or the R&D team of developers at Thomas Edison's Menlo Park laboratory[5] (Möslein, 2014) demonstrate that innovations are more often developed by "Collective Genius" (Hill et al., 2014; Agarwal & Selen, 2009) than by a lone isolated inventor.

In an increasingly digitalised world with connected systems, it seems like one of the key elements for sustainable innovation to embed innovations into a service system, or to create solutions that are a service system on their own. Thomas Edison was not the first who worked on the development of a glowing thread in a glass bulb. His merit is that he created a whole system to bring light into homes - a value creation system as a solution for the distribution of electricity, including an improved version of the light bulb, power distribution stations and light switches. Examples for service systems for hybrid value creation are the iPhone with iTunes and the Apple AppStore or the smart production sites of Caterpillar Mining with vehicles including technology that allows for driving optimisation and route planning. To build such service systems, to develop optimal system solutions, it is required that all stakeholders of the system have to be part of the service innovation process.

The example of a service system innovation at Michelin, the PAX flat tire innovation, shows how a completely designed and launched innovation can fail, if a

1 http://www.fastcompany.com/3002768/why-innovation-fails (2015-04-06)

2 http://www.forbes.com/sites/frederickallen/2012/03/05/why-great-innovations-fail-its-their-ecosystem/

3 http://www.altitudeinc.com/3-reasons-why-innovation-fails/
https://www.kindlingapp.com/best-practices/why-innovation-programs-fail-2/

4 http://www.macworld.com/article/1163181/the_birth_of_the_ipod.html?page=2
http://archive.wired.com/gadgets/mac/news/2004/07/64286?currentPage=all

5 https://www.thehenryford.org/exhibits/edison/

key service system element was not integrated in the innovation process: when establishing a new solution for car tires that would not go flat after breaking, the innovation management forgot to integrate service garages, as part of the value creation system, into the innovation process. When the new tire was launched in the market, the garages did not have equipment to change the PAX tires when broken. In the innovated service system, they were given a new role for value creation that they could not live up to (Adner, 2012).

As the integration of all stakeholders of a service system is becoming a central aspect for innovation, research has (and is still encouraging to) put focus on the interaction of the various stakeholders who form innovation as a joint effort in service systems (Carlborg, Kindström, & Kowalkowski, 2013) The role of customers and stakeholders outside the organisation for innovation is strongly emphasised in innovation research (Möslein, Neyer, & Rau, 2012; Agarwal & Selen, 2009), yet the interactions with stakeholders have been foremost studied as one-to-one relationships between the firms and the integrated stakeholders.

Nevertheless, I experienced that customer integration activity demands for the parallel integrating of different internal stakeholders, alongside the customer integration process. Before entering the academic world, I worked as a consultant for an open innovation enabler. In this innovation consultancy, we did not only provide support for the open innovation projects of large and medium-sized clients, but also gained insight into the clients' overall innovation processes, innovation culture and daily issues. I want to share some anecdotes from this time, from the context of a large German producer of consumer goods.

For more than four years, the innovation consultancy was working for the R&D department of this firm, in sequential projects for one major project in a specific product unit, but also a couple of smaller projects with other R&D units. Even though the main task for us, as an external service provider, was to guide and assist the integration of customers, users or lead users through different open innovation methods (such as co-ideation workshops, online discussion boards or co-evaluation questionnaires), the team of researchers also had to deal with internal processes and strategic decision making, repeatedly. Questions arising in joint meetings were, amongst others: "When and how can we from the R&D department integrate the marketing department so they will support the project?" "Who from our team or from our organisation should participate in the lead user workshop to support the internal acceptance of the generated ideas?" and "How can we get the purchasing department on board to support the methods in use?"

Due to these issues in the organisation we worked for, it happened for instance that a final presentation of a customer integration project was held twice - once for the key initiators and utilizers of the project and a second time in an adapted version for a broader audience with different internal stakeholders. This experience involved a very nervous manager, who had to trust the consultancy's performance to convince his internal stakeholders; in addition it resulted in additional travel and consultancy costs.

Another time, it happened that the consultancy, as an outsider, found itself caught up in a serious conflict between our client and its purchasing department during a presentation which should have focused on content rather than internal politics. Last but not least, we got used to and welcomed the practice that managers and developers from other R&D departments were included in the project meetings and presentations, because they wanted to learn about the methods in use and the results gained. This may have led to knowledge transfer regarding the content of the open innovation project and the transfer of methodological knowledge as investigated by Krämer (2015), but also to the observation of one or the other heated discussion of the R&D manager with his boss or the responsible packaging manager.

We also experienced that the customer integration activities had unexpected results. In lead user workshops, pioneer users did not only generate new ideas, also new friendships, unique insights into unknown domains and ways of thinking were enabled. However, unexpected twists arose when, for example, the R&D experts from the firm brought up sensitive information about the production of a product that changed the attitude of the lead user towards the brand and his overall product usage behaviour or, for another example, when a new business cooperation between our client firm and the employer of one of the lead users was established as a consequence of the lead users private participation in an innovation workshop.

These anecdotes from my experience in practice show how demanding the integration of internal stakeholders for innovation was in terms of time and effort, in situations when the primary goal was actually to integrate customers. The management of internal and external stakeholders[6], the decision making on when to integrate whom, and to decide which persons should stay out of the process as long as possible, required much attention. It gave the impression that it was one of the factors that impact upon the overall chance of an innovation to pass through the innovation process and enter the market.

Furthermore the anecdotes provide some initial evidence for the interdependencies between different internal and external stakeholders in innovation management. Recent management textbooks and theories in service research suggest that the awareness of interdependencies and of the thinking in systems for innovation is necessary, if not crucial. But where exactly are these interdependencies in service systems that can so strongly determine success or failure of an innovation throughout the innovation process? If we can define which stakeholders should be integrated for an innovation project, how does a manager know what the best timing for integration is? Practices that are formed and guided by experience or routines today, could be improved to reduce the costs, resources, "sweat and tears" as well as the risk of sunk costs for innovation projects that do not reach the market. Here, more insight is needed on which stakeholders have to be integrated, how they should be prioritized and how the different stakeholders in a service system interplay (Möslein, Huff & Reichwald, 2012). As Carlborg et al. (2013, p. 386) formulate it,

> *"in dynamic environments in which technology and market needs change quickly, managing service innovations means not only the ability to design the service concept but also continuously redesigning and adapting new and existing services to address frequent exogenous changes and emerging opportunities. Additional studies thus should focus on processes and gain a better understanding of interactions with the customer as well as other stakeholders in the organization's service ecosystem"* (Carlborg et al. 2013, p. 386)

To understand the interactions of stakeholders in service systems (configurations of people, technology, value propositions and shared information[7]) and the linked processes, we first need to know how stakeholder integration in service innovation is

6 Stakeholders in this thesis are understood as all parties that are potentially affected by or can have effect on a service innovation (project) and can engage as co-developers for service innovation. In a broad understanding, the term "stakeholder" is often linked to interest groups outside an organisation, such as NGO's, media, trade unions etc. This thesis is using the term stakeholder in a narrow sense, in the notion of "actors to be potentially included in the service system of an innovation project". A more detailed explanation will be provided in Part II, chapter 4.1.

7 Definition by Maglio & Spohrer (2008). An explanation will be provided in Part II, chapter 4.1

implemented in organisations. This is why I chose to explore stakeholder integration in service innovation as a process of stakeholder integration in service systems.

To learn about "Who is getting integrated in which mode and in which stages of the service innovation process?" and "What are influence factors on and impacts of stakeholder integration?" I chose the approach of case study research for an in-depth emergence in the field and a high degree of communication with the research subject, managers of service innovation. As an empirical field, organisations that develop services in a setting of manufacturing and IT evolved as interesting, relevant and approachable. Here, the interfaces between service innovation and product-oriented business create the possibility to access valuable narratives from practice.

The theoretic lens for this exploration is the service-dominant logic. This theory includes the increasingly important service system view for business processes and it puts joint reciprocally beneficial value creation between different stakeholders in the centre of organisational behaviour. This theory can seem a bit abstract at first, but it can help to open up a broader view on value creation processes, such as service innovation. Now, after I have given the reader some insights in the reasoning behind the set-up of this thesis, the empirical and theoretical underpinnings for the exploration of stakeholder integration on service innovation will be presented, followed by an outline of the structure of this thesis. This follows the logic of getting closer to, and more interactive with, the research subject, step-by step.

2 The theoretical background and purpose of this thesis

> *"The service development strategy and a formalized development process should enable and secure external and internal learning and the integration of different skills and customer knowledge in the right stage of the service development process."* (Edvardsson, Meiren, Schäfer, & Witell, 2013; p. 38)

Services are regarded as naturally put into action by service systems, working simultaneously and interdependently. Unlike in the traditional product-oriented view of value generation in supply chains where goods are handed over from one unit to the next, to add value to the tangible piece, the service-dominant logic view proposes that the co-creation of value is realized in parallel and interdependent processes (Normann & Ramirez, 1993; Normann, 2001). This theoretical understanding argues that a firm cannot offer ready-made value to the customer, but rather that it can only offer a value proposition that needs to be taken up by the customer (Normann 2001; Vargo & Lusch, 2004). In service systems, the development and fulfilment of a value proposition include a variety of actors and resources functioning together at the same time. This implies that it is the role of the organisation, in the centre of the increasingly fragmented service providing systems, to align internal resources with customers, but also with other external stakeholders, e.g. suppliers and partners (Lusch, Vargo, & Tanniru, 2009; Rondell & Sorhammar, 2010).

As a consequence, value co-creation with customers and other stakeholders might not only be implemented during service delivery, but should also be embedded throughout the innovation process itself, as shown by the introductory citation (Edvardsson et al., 2013; Kindström, Kowalkowski, & Sandberg, 2013). Service innovation is accordingly seen as an organisation-wide, multi-dimensional process (Kindström & Kowalkowski, 2014) that aligns internal and external stakeholders[8], their knowledge and resources as parts of interdependent service systems (Kindström et al., 2013; Lusch et al., 2009; Vargo, 2008). Service innovation even affects various dimensions of a service organisation and the service system it is

[8] In the context of this thesis, stakeholders are *all groups or individuals that can affect, or are affected by service innovations* (adapted from Freeman and Reed, 1983, p. 91). Looking at actor or resource integration prior from an organisational perspective, the word stakeholder is used interchangeably with "actors of service systems".

embedded in (Agarwal & Selen 2011; Kowalkowski, Witell, & Gustafsson, 2013; Maglio, Vargo, Caswell, & Spohrer, 2009; Rubalcaba, Michel, Sundbo, Brown, & Reynoso, 2012; Smith & Fischbacher, 2005; Vargo, Maglio, & Akaka, 2008). This is reflected in the following definition by Lusch (2006) describing the co-creation of service innovation as the participation of customers and other partners "*in the creation of the core offering itself*" (Lusch, 2006; p.284). Service innovation itself is thereby defined with a broad meaning; it includes the development of new and unique services, but also the innovations in the service system, the service delivery process, customer interfaces, the buyer-seller relationship or the role of the customer in the service process (Kindström et al., 2013).

The investigation of stakeholder integration for service innovation, considering both internal and external stakeholders, gained attention in research only recently (Mention & Asikainen, 2012; Neyer, Bullinger, & Möslein, 2009). In the past, research has put high emphasis on the possibilities and practices of stakeholder integration for specific groups, often in isolated cases in service organisations (see e.g. Alam, 2002, 2006a; Carbonell, Rodriguez-Escudero, & Pujari, 2009; 2012; Faullant, Krajger, & Zanker, 2012; Kristensson, Matthing, & Johansson, 2008; Magnusson, Matthing, & Kristensson, 2003; Matthing, Kristensson, Gustafsson, & Parasuraman, 2006; Matthing, Sandén, & Edvardsson, 2004; Skiba & Herstatt, 2012). A variety of scholarly papers show the differences between the integration of specific types of users for service innovation and describe either external (Frow & Payne, 2011; Mention & Asikainen, 2012) or internal stakeholder integration only (Melton & Hartline, 2012). Whilst these research outcomes create valuable insights for particular external actors in the service system, research considering the co-existence and the interdependence of external stakeholder integration with the internal innovation management of the organisation (Perks & Riihela, 2004) from a service system perspective is only recently developing (Carlborg et al., 2013; Smith & Fischbacher, 2005).

Kindström et al. (2013) as well as Agarwal and Selen (2009, 2011) have researched the management of multi-dimensional service innovation within organisations. Perks, Gruber and Edvardsson (2012) as well as Schleimer and Shulman (2011) have contributed to this with their work which includes the collaboration between internal and external stakeholders, in specific service innovation contexts. Taking the strong notion of service delivery and service innovation with various interdependent stakeholders into account, more in-depth knowledge on stakeholder integration as an organisation-wide process in its natural real life setting is needed (Mattson, 2010; Ettlie & Rosenthal, 2011; Rusanen, Halinen-Kaila, & Jaakkola, 2014), especially in business-to-business settings, and industries other than core service organisations (Carlborg et al., 2013; Ostrom, Bitner, Brown et al., 2010).

Knowledge of the management and design of stakeholder integration is gaining relevance for the practice of organisational service innovation, since the integration of stakeholders from inside and outside the organisation is being discussed as a necessary and rewarding practice. However, little guidance exists on how to manage the stakeholders in the innovation. For service innovation, the coordination and facilitation of exchange between the different actors (across organisational units and external stakeholders) in service systems may be seen as a major management task (Gottfridsson, 2012; Schilling & Werr, 2009). However, the active framing of internal and external stakeholder integration is also explicitly demanded in the context of manufacturing firms where service and product innovation should be aligned processes (Carlborg et al., 2013)[9].

The service system view of the service-dominant logic adds the notion of interdependencies and multi-dimensionality to stakeholder integration for service innovation as an organisational challenge. Still, there is little knowledge on the co-existence of inter- and intra-firm collaboration and their eventual reciprocal influences (Perks & Riihela, 2004; Payne, Storbacka, & Frow, 2007; Schleimer & Shulman, 2011). This is why more in-depth knowledge on service innovation in practice is needed, especially in respect to the roles and modes of stakeholder integration throughout the stages of the innovation process, to successfully coordinate knowledge integration and to manage both internal and external stakeholders in interdependent systems throughout the innovation process (Tossavainen, 2013; Kindström et al., 2013; Möslein, Huff, & Reichwald, 2012).

To gain a better understanding of stakeholder integration in service innovation and the dynamics resulting from its proposed multi-dimensionality, this thesis aims to develop a clearer picture of stakeholder integration practice. In a three-step approach, it seeks to show which stakeholders are integrated in which mode and in which stage of the service innovation process. It aims to create a thorough understanding of the dynamics of stakeholder integration and aims to explore the

---

9 This is even discussed in other research domains, such as open innovation. The collaboration with external stakeholders (Ollila & Elmquist, 2011; Chesbrough, 2010), puts forward a need to actively balance openness and closedness of innovation processes.

research question: "What factors affect the integration of stakeholders in service innovation and what effects come along with mutual stakeholder integration?"

The overall purpose of this doctoral thesis is thereby to explore and understand stakeholder integration in more depth. By the application of an open research approach, this piece of research aims to gain an understanding of the practice and dynamics of stakeholder integration for service innovation, as one of the first steps on the research journey towards more knowledge of innovation in complex service systems. By clarifying the rationales and dynamics of stakeholder integration practice, it aims to explain the factors of service innovation complexity, as a basis for the conscious design and balanced implementation of stakeholder integration throughout the service innovation process.

Contributing to literature on service innovation, the thesis seeks to contribute to scholarly research by evidencing and exemplifying the multi-dimensionality of stakeholder integration in service innovation. The thesis aims to add more details to the current perception of service innovation processes and related stakeholder integration.

3 Structure of the thesis - a three step approach

To tackle the presented research objectives, this thesis is set up as a three-step approach that moves from an outside look on the topic to an interactive exploration of stakeholder integration in service innovation. The introduction, the background and motivation for this dissertation as well as the methodology have already been presented. This chapter describes the structure of the thesis and is followed by the research design of the thesis in Part II and the theoretical underpinning of this work in Part III. This section elaborates on the service dominant logic and its understanding of service innovation in service systems. The subsequent three core building blocks of this thesis in Part IV, V and VI are: "a passive look from outside", "the reactively engaged exploration of case studies" for an organisational management perspective; and finally "the mutually engaged exploration of a case study on internal stakeholder integration" for a participant's perspective. These blocks build upon each other and, step-by-step, reduce the distance to the phenomenon under research. It develops from an external and passive observation of stakeholder integration towards a dialogical interactive engagement with the research subject, as illustrated in Figure 1.

After summarizing the case studies of Part V and VI, the thesis illustrates the affecting factors and effects of stakeholder integration in a derived model of stakeholder integration. Further, it provides theoretical and practical implementations in Part VII and concludes with an outlook for further research.

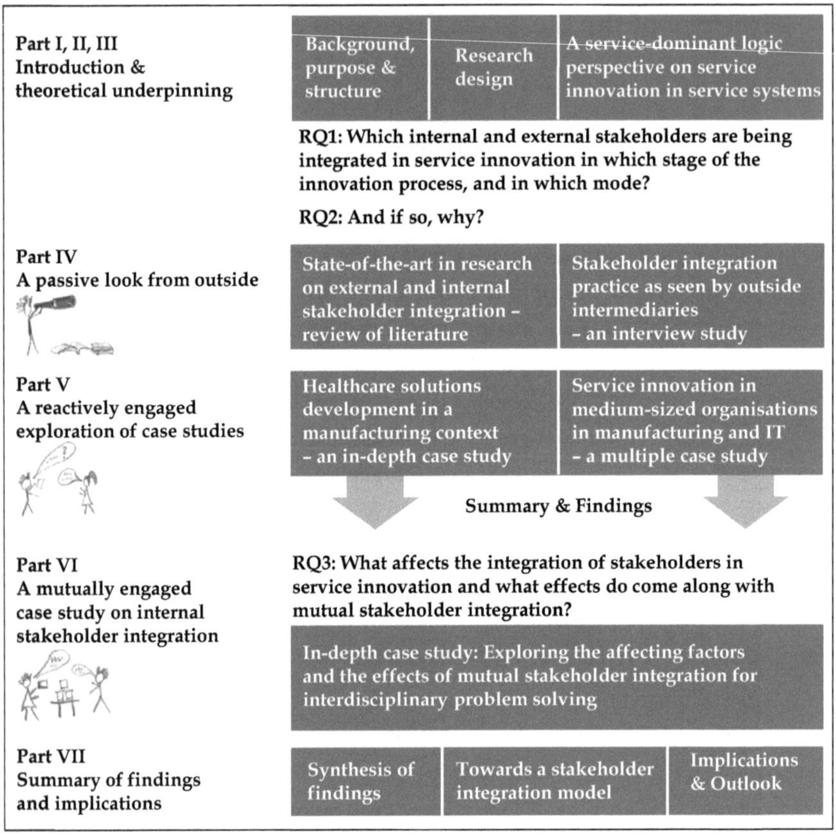

Figure 1: The structure of this thesis to approach stakeholder integration in service innovation

The three core Parts IV, V and VI and their research approaches are described in more detail in the following paragraphs.

3.1 A passive look from outside

Parts IV represents a look from outside on the topic of stakeholder integration in service innovation. In this part, a literature review of state-of-the-art service research on stakeholder integration provides a fundament of current views and findings about the topic. Additionally, a pre-study on stakeholder integration practices with central European service innovation intermediaries (innovation enablers and consultancies) gives insights into stakeholder integration practice from the outsiders' perspective.

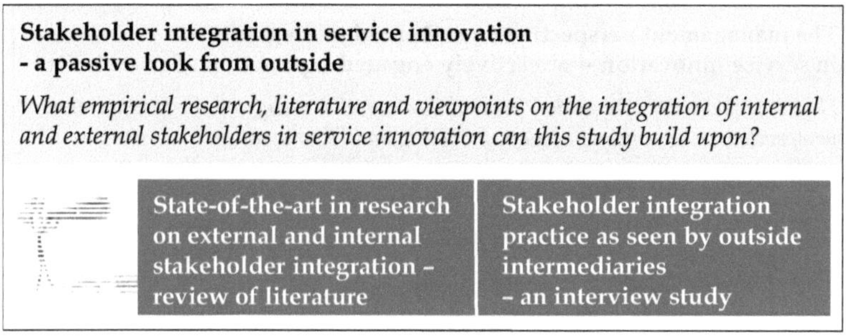

Figure 2: Visualization of Part IV - a passive look from outside

3.2 Reactively engaged exploration from a management perspective

Part V presents explorative case studies in IT and manufacturing organisations as an approach of reactive exploration of stakeholder integration. Following guidance by Eisenhardt (1989), first an in-depth case study is implemented to search for patterns regarding modes of stakeholder integration; following this, confirmation is sought through a second multiple case study. The first, in-depth, case study is concerned with the IT service development at a healthcare appliance manufacturer and examines stakeholder integration in a multi-national matrix organisation. The second, multiple case study relates to medium-sized organisations in manufacturing and IT; it expands the findings from the first case and creates an understanding of stakeholder integration practice in organisations that can be considered as belonging to the typical German "Mittelstand". Both case studies explore the stages, modes and motives for the integration of identified stakeholder groups.

The findings of this part show that external stakeholders, like partners or customers and users, are often integrated in a reactive mode. The same applies for customer contact employees. For the stages idea generation and development, mutual integration of internal stakeholders is found to be a common practice. It is reported that the combination of internal knowledge from different disciplines creates potential for competitive advantage from innovations that cannot be copied.

Furthermore the explorative character of the case studies generated findings about interdependencies and also the indirect nature of stakeholder integration in service innovation. The evidence from the case studies puts forward how strong impact of resource limitations on stakeholder integration for service innovation is.

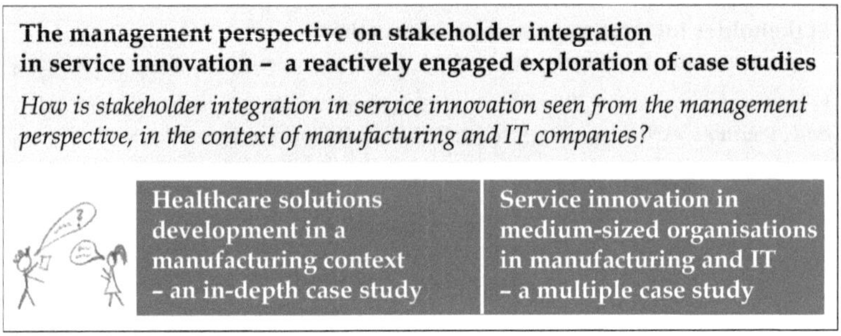

Figure 3: Visualization of Part V - a reactively engaged exploration of case studies

3.3 Mutually engaged exploration with a service systems view

Part VI takes up the learnings which demonstrate the interdependence of service innovation in service systems, the difficulties that come along with setting-free and balancing resources, as well as the fact that mutual integration creates superior offerings. The in-depth case-study analyses the initiation of an internal cross-functional interdisciplinary innovation workshop. More specifically it investigates the research questions "What factors affect a stakeholder integration activity such as an internal co-creation workshop?" and "What effects does mutual stakeholder integration have?" This case study has an interactive character and engages with the research subject through participatory observations. Findings show that affecting factors as well as the effects of mutual stakeholder integration can be observed on the individual level of the project manager (integrating party), the participants of the workshop (integrated party) and the service systems that these actors are embedded in.

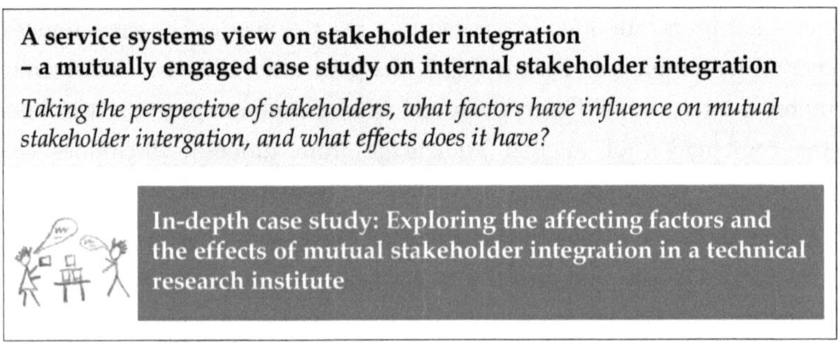

Figure 4: Visualization of Part VI - a mutually engaged case study on internal stakeholder integration

From the findings of the case studies in Part IV and V, a model for stakeholder integration is detailed in the final section; subsequently, implications for theory and management are derived and an outlook for further research is given at the end of this thesis, in Part VII.

Part II
Research design

The following section will present the research design of this thesis, to explain how this thesis approaches the research questions "Who is getting integrated, in which mode, and in which stage of the service innovation process?" and "What are affecting factors for stakeholder integration and what effects does stakeholder integration have?". First, it will introduce the constructivist research paradigm as the basis for the chosen research design, case study research, in chapter 1. Second, the case study approach and the reasons for choosing this research method will be described in detail in chapter 2. Finally, chapter 3 of this section will introduce the reader to the engaged scholarship approach. This understanding of interchange between the researcher and the research subject underlies the empirical work of the thesis. It supports the constructivist understanding of research which views the world as co-constructed in its nature.

1 Research methodology

This thesis is asking "how" and "why" questions to understand and partly interpret the studied phenomenon of stakeholder integration in service innovation. Hereby the researcher is following the constructivist paradigm[10] (Guba & Lincoln, 1994) that can be shortly summarized as research to reveal, portray and understand phenomena within their complex context (Tronvoll, Brown, Gremler, & Edvardsson, 2011). According to Tronvoll et al. (2011), this dynamic view of the world reflects the character of services as "*processes, deeds, and performances created in dynamic interactions*" (Tronvoll et al., 2011, p. 576). Since this thesis works with the service-dominant logic lens that advocates the value creation as a process of co-creation by various actors and resources (Vargo et al., 2008), the constructivist paradigm fits with the nature of the applied theory and research subject.

In more detail, the constructivist paradigm is characterized by a relativist ontology, describing a view of the world as socially and experimentally constructed and co-constructed (Guba & Lincoln, 2005). This implies that there are subjective and

10 Constructivism and interpretivism are sometimes used interchangeably since they show the same roots and share the aim for understanding when studying social phenomena, taking the perspective of the people and phenomena under research. Still, interpretivism is has a stronger focus on creating an interpretation that is valid for more than just the phenomenon in focus of research. (Lee & Baskerville, 2003)

local "truths" for individuals and groups (Guba & Lincoln, 1994; Wahyuni, 2012). Within constructivism, the researcher is searching for the meaning of these subjective experiences and individual meanings that are given to the studied complex situations (Creswell, 2014). It includes that the social realities, based on human perspectives and experiences, may change over time and with the experiences of people[11] (Guba & Lincoln, 1994; Wahyuni, 2012). In constructivism, the nature of relationships between the researcher and the objects of investigation (epistemology), is characterized by interactivity, happening in an on-going process of conducting research and gaining understanding (Guba & Lincoln, 1994). Accordingly, in constructivism, the research methodology has to be dialectical and dialogical. This is why case studies are applied as a research approach in this thesis. They reflect the importance of context and seek to create a deep understanding of the research objects' perceived reality. In case study research, the aim is to inductively develop patterns and meaning throughout the research process (Creswell, 2012).

2 Case study research

Case studies, as a qualitative explorative method, are chosen as an appropriate research approach to investigate the rather new and contextual research topic "stakeholder integration in service innovation". Case studies as a research method are suitable for the research questions of this thesis for a number of reasons. First, the research in focus is about discovering and exploring the new, and to develop empirically grounded theory (Yin, 2014, p. 16). In such a new and contextual research topic, openness is required; this is to avoid a priori categorisation of empirical data. Second, case study research fits well with the desire to understand complex social phenomena, as stated by Eisenhardt and Graebner (2007) and Yin (2014). Miles, Huberman and Saldaña[12] (2013) as well as Flick (2014) suggest that case studies are a

[11] Guba and Lincoln (1994) refer to constructivism's relativism to include a change of realities over time, which is not in the original core of the constructivist paradigm. Relativism is criticized because of accepting such a large variety in realities that deriving patterns and conclusions might no more be possible as cases stand for themselves only.

[12] The guidelines for qualitative data analysis in Miles et al. (2013) work do not agree with the constructivist approach taken in this thesis. Accordingly only selected aspects of the authors' guidelines for data analysis and some general aspects about case study research are referred to, as they are in line with the common understanding of qualitative research.

suitable tool to access real life experiences. They allow reflection on practices and subjects in real life interactions. Thereby, the holistic and meaningful characteristics of real-life events can and should be captured by the researcher. Third, the research subject is of a process nature. This is why, especially in research on networks and relationships (Dumbach, 2014; Halinen & Törnroos, 2005; Perks et al., 2012), case studies are the chosen approach to access data and to gain insights into processes (Symon & Cassell, 1999).

Following a constructivist comprehension of research, the case study design of this thesis follows an inductive and abductive approach to case study research rather than a deductive approach[13]. Building upon the richness of the empirical data, the aims of the applied case study approach are oriented towards theory building and the re-defining of theory. For this purpose, Eisenhardt (1989) proposes a strongly inductive view on case study research, relating to grounded theory. The closeness of Eisenhardt to grounded theory implies collecting data without any or at least little knowledge about the literature in the research field. The present work refrains from such a total distance from literature and favours the line of argumentation by Siggelkow (2007). He advises against the conduction of case studies which are too strongly oriented towards grounded theory and encourages researchers not to disregard existing literature in the field of research. To include existing theory can contribute to the research because, as he puts it, "an open mind is good, an empty mind is not" (Siggelkow, 2007, p.21).

To pursue the exploration of practice in stakeholder integration in service innovation and the enhancement of theory from empirical research, this thesis is combining the advantages of single and multiple case studies, as recommended by Yin (2014). The first case study aims to create an in-depth understanding of stakeholder integration in service innovation in the context of healthcare solutions. This is followed by a second, multiple, case study in a broader context, to confirm, to disconfirm, to refine and to extend the findings from the first case study (Eisenhardt, 1989). Part VI takes up the findings from these previous case studies and aims to understand the dynamics of stakeholder integration in service innovation in even

[13] The most prominent authors in case study research (Spring and Santos, 2015) are Eisenhardt and Yin. Eisenhardt (1989) is relating case study research to grounded theory (proposing that theory building through case studies should happen with as little theory and no hypothesis), whereas Yin (2014) stands for a deductive understanding of case study research. Both authors offer widely accepted guidelines for case study research, fostering validity and quality that are similar on an operational level for data collection, but imply different approaches for data analysis and derivation of research findings.

more depth. The applied approach of an in-depth case study allows to take the perspective of the integrated stakeholders, for a comprehensive, service systems view of mutual stakeholder integration in service innovation (Swanborn, 2010).

Throughout all cases, data collection is primarily based on interviews, supported by documents and observations. This triangulation of data sources (Flick, 2014) helps to verify and confirm interview propositions (Creswell, 2012; Yin, 2014). The case analysis follows the guidelines given by Eisenhardt (1989) and Yin (2014), fostering validity and quality of case study research[14]. An overview of all cases and the respective data collections and analyses will be provided in detail in the respective chapters.

3 The engaged scholarship approach

> *"Instead of viewing organizations and clients as data collection sites and founding sources, an engaged scholar views them as a learning workplace (idea factory) where practitioners and scholars co-produce knowledge on important questions and issues […]"* (van de Ven, 2007; p.7)

In a constructivist approach to research, it is recognized that research is not a distant and anonymous procedure, but a process of social interchange between the researcher and the subject of interest (the interviewee). The above quote clarifies that, in engaged scholarship, researchers and research subjects are entering an interchange that can be influencing what is being studied, what knowledge can be derived from the communicative process, and which explanations for the research phenomenon will be given. Research as processes of social interchange, i.e. communication, is thereby seen as a part of the ongoing social construction of the world (Flick, 2014). The "engaged scholarship approach" as a concept of interplay and a joint learning

[14] Spring and Santos (2015) criticize the strictness of the provided guidelines by Yin (12014) and Eisenhardt (1989) as they do not allow for flexibility and adaption of cases depending on the revealed observations and individual circumstances. In the context of this thesis, the level of case analysis is "service innovation project". Thus, the cases are identified and developed in the process of data collection, allowing for a higher degree of adaptability, called "casing" by Spring and Santos (2005) and Ragin (1992) case development with the possibility to adapt in data collection and framing) rather than case definition in advance. This approach helps to avoid the risk of finding something *"in which the evidence does not address the initial research question"* (Yin, 2014, p.29).

process between the researcher and the subject of study has been coined by Andrew van de Ven (2007)[15]. The engaged scholarship approach defines the process of empirical research as

> *"a participative form of research for obtaining the different perspectives of key stakeholders (researchers, users, clients, sponsors, and practitioners) in studying complex problems. By involving others and leveraging their different kinds of knowledge, engaged scholarship can produce knowledge that is more penetrating and insightful than when scholars or practitioners work on problems alone."* (van de Ven, 2007; p.9)

Thereby, van de Ven (2007) differs between four alternative forms of engaged scholarship: "basic science with stakeholder advice", "policy/design science evaluation research for professional practice", "co-produce knowledge with collaborators" and "action/intervention research for a client" (see Figure 5).

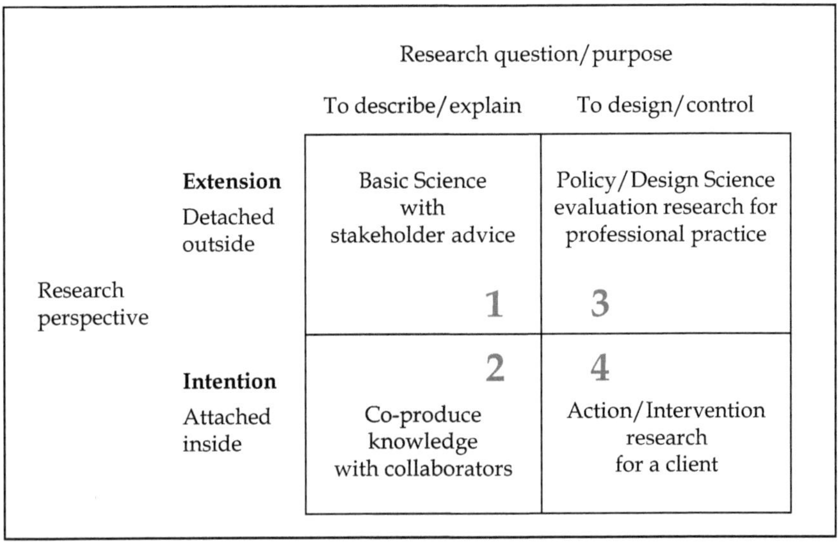

Figure 5: Alternative forms of engaged scholarship (adapted from van de Ven, 2007; p.27)

15 Mohrmann and Lawler (2011) call this "useful research", creating insights for both, scholars and practitioners. Möslein (2005) refers to co-production of management knowledge between "applied researchers" and practitioners.

The first form of engaged scholarship "basic science with stakeholder advice" (top left in Figure 5) is close to traditional social science, with the addition that researchers give advice and feedback in the research process. The empirical work of this thesis is conducted in line with this approach. It considers the mutual influence of the researcher and the subject of interest; however the researchers keep an outside view and stay out of organisational processes.

The interviews and case studies in Part IV and V are conducted in an active style, in relatively open conversations supported by interview-guidelines, as proposed by King (2012). This interview style can allow for interchange between the involved parties (King, 2012) and may include thought-provoking impulses on both sides[16].

The in-depth case study in Part VII (the analysis of mutual integration of internal stakeholder in a co-creation workshop) has a stronger action research character and includes conscious counselling and "joint forces" between researcher and the researched organisation. Still, even here, the data collection with interview guidelines and meeting protocols remains outside the organization. Accordingly, even this study is characterised as "informed basic research" in van de Vens' (2007) framework (this equates with "basic research with stakeholder advice" in box 1 on the top left of Figure 5).

16 According to King (2012), this is a characteristic of interviews in constructivist qualitative research, per se. He outlines that an inter-personal relationship process is part of the research process since "*the interviewee is seen as a 'participant' in the research, actively shaping the course of the interview rather than passively responding to the interviewer's pre-set questions*" (King, 2012, p. 11).

Part III

The service-dominant logic perspective on service innovation in service systems

After the presentation of the research design and structure of this thesis, this third part of the thesis presents the theory lens to be applied, the service dominant logic. First, to create a shared understanding of the concept "service innovation", chapter 1 introduces the three research streams in services: the assimilation, demarcation and synthesis approach. Next, the service-dominant logic is introduced, as a theory lens to look at service innovation embedded in service systems in chapter 2. Chapter 3 will present and contrast the core elements of similar theoretic concepts that include co-creation as a paradigm. Going into more depth, chapter 4 will present the understanding of service innovation and stakeholder integration in service systems from the service-dominant logic perspective.

1 Approaches to service innovation

Service as a research domain is perceived as a broad field under constant development (Ostrom et al., 2015). With different approaches from different schools developing over time, the understanding of service innovation in service research is highly dependent on the underlying research approach (Ordanini & Parasuraman, 2010). A variety of scholars have reviewed the development of research in services and service innovation (Menor, Tatikonda & Sampson, 2002; Edvardsson, Gustafsson & Roos, 2005; Lusch & Vargo, 2014; Vargo & Lusch, 2007; Spring & Araujo, 2009; Janssen, Castaldi, Alexiev, 2014; Droege, Hildebrand, & Forcada, 2009). Shortly summarized, the evolution and parallel development of service research can be described as the journey from seeing "services as products", to perceiving "service as value creation" (Wetter-Edman, 2014).

This statement refers to the fact that research on services was first established in relation to and in contrast with products (Parasuraman, Zeithaml, & Berry, 1985; de Brentani, 1995; Wetter-Edman, 2014). In the assimilation approach, research builds upon knowledge in the field of product innovation and defines service innovation from theories and concepts developed in the manufacturing context (Droege et al., 2009; den Hertog, 2010). Service innovation research applying this assimilation approach is foremost looking at technology (de Vries, 2006; Djellal et al., 2013) and its drivers for service innovation (Droege et al., 2009).

The demarcation approach[17] puts emphasis on the differences between products and services (Droege et al., 2009). This view frames services according to the IHIP paradigm - as intangible (cannot be touched), heterogeneous (cannot be standardized), inseparable (in terms of production and consumption), and perishable (cannot be inventoried) (Parasuraman, Zeithaml, & Berry, 1985; Lusch, Vargo, & Wessels, 2008). In the demarcation approach, special emphasis is given to the distinctive organisation of service innovation, where no R&D department is in charge of innovation (Djellal, Gallouj, & Miles, 2013; Nijssen et al., 2006; Gottfridsson, 2010) and innovation management in services has a less formalized character (den Hertog, 2010). Findings and implications from empirical studies in the demarcation stream are that the intangibility of services makes it more difficult to communicate and protect ideas in service innovation (Witell, Gustafsson, & Johnson, 2014). Since services are seen as the provision of "pre-requisites for service" only (Edvardsson & Olsson, 1996), service innovation has to take into account the credence attributes of service and its dependence on experiences. Services cannot be evaluated before purchase and experience; their process character presumes customer knowledge regarding the (new) process of service co-creation (Johnson, Anderson, & Fornell, 1995; Witell et al., 2014).

Due to the interactive character of services, service innovation implies the creation of a change in the role of the customer (Michel, Brown, & Gallan, 2007; den Hertog, 2010) and in the skills required from the customer contact employees (Nijssen et al., 2006). Accordingly, Shostack (1984) proposes that the alignment of customers, customer contact employees and the operational processes for service delivery create the basis for successful service innovation. Similarly, Alam (2006a) proposes that the inseparability characteristic of service, and the resulting interaction of service provider and customer, implies that service innovators should interact with customers and customer contact employees during the service innovation process.

In assimilation and in demarcation approach, service innovation is defined according to specific elements; service innovation is conceived as a new or significantly improved service, the new organisation of processes or the way how a service is delivered, for instance through a new technology support system (Thether, Hipp, & Miles, 2001; Schilling & Werr, 2009; Droege et al., 2009).[18] Both approaches are criticized heavily: Rubalcaba et al. (2012) and Ordanini and Parasuraman (2010)

---

[17] The demarcation approach is called "differentiation approach" by Djellal, Gallouj and Miles (2013)

[18] For a thorough review of service innovation as seen by a variety of different authors, see chapter 4.1 in Schilling and Werr's (2009) literature review.

put forward that the assimilation approach does not offer a true reflection of service innovation in reality. It is discussed that the demarcation approach creates a picture of services being somewhat inferior to products, as it focusses merely on what services are not (Vargo & Lusch, 2007) and sees customers and other external stakeholders as "*executors of tasks*" (Ordanini & Parasuraman, 2010; p. 6).

The synthesis approach, as first established by Gallouj and Weinstein (1997; see also Droege et al., 2009) integrates the perspectives of manufacturing and service industries. This approach proposes that manufacturing innovation and service innovation may be parallel processes in the same organisation and thereby tries to understand and learn from innovation practices dependent on their specific firm or management settings (den Hertog, 2010). It is applied for instance in the context of collaboration (Schleimer & Schulman, 2011) or innovation capabilities (Janssen et al., 2014). Whereas the synthesis approach was originally developed to reflect a world of product-service combinations and parallel developments (den Hertog, 2010), it also strongly relates to a view on service innovation that is based on the application of competences in deeds, processes and performances as put forward by the service-dominant logic (Ordanini & Parasuraman, 2010).

Being strongly linked to the synthesis approach, or even being labelled as the latter, the service-dominant logic is a theory describing service as the basis of all economic exchange. It constitutes a shift from thinking in "value production outputs" (i.e. tangible products) to thinking of value creation as a process between actors that engage in a service-for-service exchange (that is, the application of knowledge and skills from both actors in value co-creation; for example the competences to design and build a car as a firm and the abilities to purchase, drive and utilize a car as a customer). Its fundamental elements are that *value co-creation* is happening through *resource integrating actors* in *service systems*. The core of the service-dominant logic will be described next, followed by a specification of its elements in the light of service innovation.

2 The service-dominant logic

"Service, the application of competences for the benefit of another, is the fundamental basis of exchange." (Vargo, Lusch, & Akaka., 2010; p. 134)

The service-dominant logic is a theory of exchange in economies which shifted the focus from the transfer of tangible goods to the process of service exchange (Lusch, 2006). This new perspective on economic exchange as value co-creation (Edvardsson et al., 2005; p.118; Grönroos & Ravald, 2011) was coined as the service-dominant logic by Vargo and Lusch in their paper in the Journal of Marketing in 2004. It aligns previous work by, amongst others, Normann and Ramirez (1993), Normann (2001) Grönroos (1994; 2000) and Gummesson (1995). Service-dominant logic provides an understanding of economics as service-for-service exchange and value-in-use (see quote above by Vargo et al., 2010). It thereby replaces the traditional idea of value exchange, which highlights the transfer of tangible goods[19]. This means that business processes are not understood as "selling things to people", but as "serving the exchange partners' needs" (Lusch & Vargo, 2014, p.11).

Building upon ten foundational premises[20], the service-dominant logic proposes that value is always co-created with the customer (foundational premise 6), that value can only be determined by the beneficiary, uniquely and phenomenologically (foundational premise 10) and that firms cannot deliver value, but only offer value propositions (foundational premise 7), which have to be taken up by a value co-creator (Vargo & Lusch, 2004; Vargo et al., 2008). In service-dominant logic, service is defined as the *"application of competences (knowledge and skills) for the benefit of another entity or the entity itself"* (Lusch & Vargo, 2014; p. 12; see also Vargo & Lusch, 2004).

After the first publication in 2004, service-dominant logic has evolved at a fast pace and it has changed its focus from value co-creation with customers to a view of value co-creation in service systems (Vargo & Akaka, 2012; Vargo & Lusch, 2015). This refined view considers value co-creation as the resource integration of actors in

---

[19] For a more detailed elaboration of the historical background and a confrontation of goods- versus service-dominant logic the article "On value and value co-creation: A service systems and service logic perspective" by Vargo, Maglio, & Akaka, (2008) is recommended.

[20] See Annex B

service systems (Lusch & Vargo, 2014), described as *"interactive configurations of mutual exchange"* (Vargo et al., 2008; p. 145).

As shown in Figure 6, the service-dominant logic views value creation in service systems occurring through reciprocal and mutually beneficial relationships between an organisation and the customer. Indeed, value creation is seen as a *"combined effort of firms, employees, customers, stockholders, government agencies, and other entities"* (Vargo et al., 2008; p. 148) involved in the exchange process (Vargo et al., 2008; Normann & Ramirez, 1993). Thereby, service systems are regarded as more than networks of people, but rather as systems of connected resources including people, technology and knowledge (Vargo & Lusch, 2011). Service systems as value creation spaces exist on a micro, meso or macro level - individuals, firms/organisations or an economy actively applying resources for mutual benefit (Vargo et al., 2008). Thereby, value co-creation is embedded in permeable service system structures which include even indirect stakeholders (Lusch & Vargo, 2014).

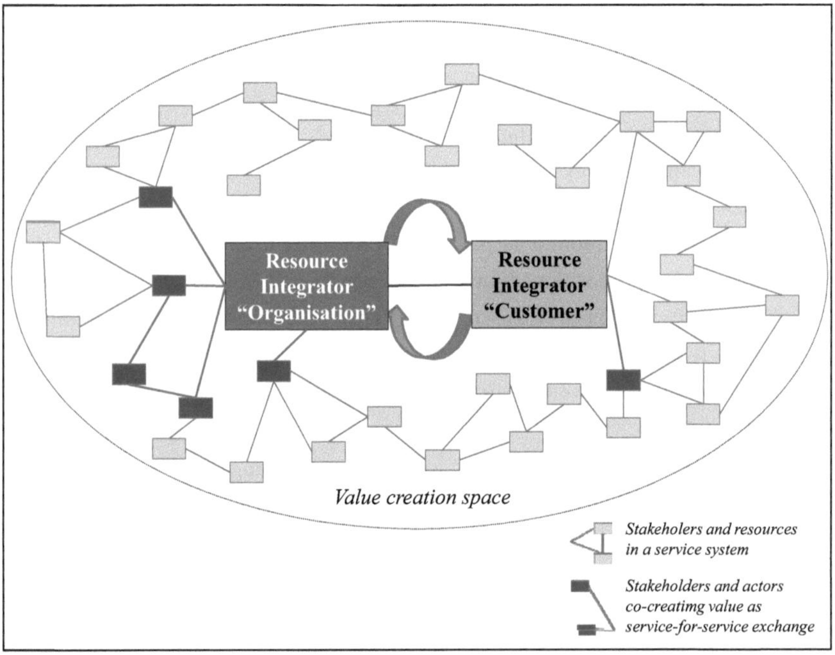

Figure 6: Value co-creation in a service system (based on Lusch & Vargo, 2014; p. 162)

In more recent publications on service-dominant logic, Vargo and Lusch introduced the concept of "service eco-systems" in replacement of service systems (Lusch & Vargo, 2014; Vargo & Akaka, 2012; Vargo, Wieland, & Akaka, 2015). Continuing from the idea of interdependent systems for value co-creation, the term "service eco-system" adds the elements of self-adjustment and self-containment to the service system concept (Lusch & Vargo, 2014; Vargo & Akaka, 2012). Service in eco-systems is described as a constantly evolving process, where the actors in the service eco-system are interacting and (re-)creating their system. This includes the idea that all actors and resources in a service system are guided and influenced by shared institutions[21], and that institutions (the shared rules, norms and thinking of these groups) guide the organizational behaviour and decision making (Edvardsson, Kleinaltenkamp, Tronvoll, McHugh, & Windahl, 2014; Vargo, et al., 2015).

Furthermore, Stephen Vargo and Robert Lusch (Vargo & Lusch, 2014) integrated the aspect of value creation in triads from the actor-network theory to service-dominant logic. The existence of connections that go beyond the reciprocal exchange between two resource integrators in dyads (the firm and the beneficiary as shown in Figure 6), is inherent in network theory, especially in the context of social exchange (Havila, Johanson, & Thilenius, 2004). Triads are seen as the smallest unit of service systems, reflecting the complexity of resource integration actions in service systems, as well as indicating that there might be indirect or unbalanced interactions (Vargo & Lusch, 2014).

To summarize, the service-dominant logic proposes that value is co-created through different actors across different service systems by contributing their resources, skills and knowledge. For service innovation, the alignment of the different actors in the service system is necessary. In particular customer integration is emphasised, as customers have to take up a value proposition and determine the value of a service. This is why co-creation of service innovation is defined as the participation of customers and other partners *"in the creation of the core offering itself"* (Lusch, 2006; p.284). Moreover, service innovation in service systems is characterised by complexity and guided by the institutions of the different actors.

[21] According to Scott (2001), institutions are the humanly devised rules, norms, and meanings that enable and constrain human action (Vargo et al., 2015; Vargo and Lusch, 2011; Edvardsson, Tronvoll, & Gruber, 2010). In the context of service-dominant logic, institutions are closely linked to service innovation as innovation. The simultaneous maintenance, disruption and change of institutions – the modification of "the way things are done" - through the actors in a service system are regarded as necessary facilitators for innovation (Vargo et al., 2015; Vargo & Akaka, 2012).

Service-dominant logic itself was not developed in isolation from other research streams which include different notions of the service-dominant logic. Similar concepts have been presented earlier, were developed in parallel, or are correlated to thinking in terms of service exchange and service systems. This is why, after this introduction of the service-dominant logic, the core concepts of the service-dominant logic will be contrasted with and enriched by some closely related research streams in the next section. First, the co-creation as a paradigm, including the Nordic school of service logic, will be introduced. Then, Open (Service) Innovation and the user active paradigm will be presented to demarcate them from service-dominant logic. After an introduction to the related view on service innovation from the resource-based view and resource dependency theory, a summarizing overview of these five related concepts will be given.

3 Co-creation as a paradigm

Vargo and Lusch do not discuss value co-creation isolated from other research (2004, 2008, 2011; Lusch & Vargo, 2014). Service-dominant logic is closely linked to service logic and to the co-creative paradigm. All three concepts are building upon similar anchorings and are constantly developing intertwined, parallel and in reference to each other.

The service logic of the Nordic School features the same core ideas as service-dominant logic; it views value generation as a process happening through the activity of and the interaction with the customer (Grönroos, 2008). Though, in the understanding of service logic, the firm can get involved with the customers' existing value creation process and provide the customer with the necessary resources for the facilitation of value creation. This way, the firm becomes *"a value co-creator with its customers"* (Grönroos, 2008; p. 298), different to the service-dominant logic view where the firm is creating value propositions for the customer to take them up. Whilst these two logics differ in this firm- versus customer-centricity aspect, both logics agree on the concepts of "value co-creation with the customer", "value in use", "value propositions" and the system and network aspects of service[22]. Grönroos and Gummerus (2014) add that value co-creation is characterised by direct interactions between the relevant actors in a service system. They define co-creation as

> *"the process of creating something together in a process of direct interactions between two or more actors, where the actors' processes merge into one collaborative, dialogical process."* (Grönroos & Gummerus, 2014; p.209)

Different to service-dominant logic, this definition implies that the exchange processes of actors in service systems have to be direct and bidirectional.

A noteworthy aspect for service innovation is that, in the customer-centric view of the service logic, service providers should start with the customers' value creation processes and align their own business processes with that of the customer (Payne et al., 2007). Payne et al. (2007) propose that service innovation is an outside-in process, starting at the customer, to support the customer for better value creation. Service innovation from a service logic perspective accordingly includes: the review of opportunities for co-creation and value generation, planning, testing and prototyping of service innovation with customers: the implementation of customer solutions and management of customer encounters.

The co-creation of value as described in service-dominant logic and service logic are at the core of the so called co-creative paradigm (see for instance Kowalkowski, Persson Ridell et al., 2012). The co-creative paradigm describes the joint creation of value through the exchange of knowledge and resources between the customer and the organization. This happens as engagement with interaction platforms in the context of experiences (Ramaswamy & Gouillart, 2010; Perks et al., 2012). According to the work of Normann and Ramirez (1993), Prahalad and Ramaswamy (2004a, 2004b) and Ramaswamy and Gouillart (2010), who laid the foundation of the co-creative paradigm (Kowalkowski, Persson Ridell et al., 2012), it is argued that a firm cannot offer ready-made value to the customer, but only offer value propositions. Value generation happens only when the customer takes up this value proposition and co-creates value for itself (Normann & Ramirez, 1993). For

[22] For a detailed understanding of conceptual and semantic differences in service logic and service-dominant logic, the lecture of three papers is recommended: Grönroos and Voima (2012) and Grönroos and Gummerus (2014) both provide an in-depth comparison and synthesis of the concepts and terms in service logic and service-dominant logic, from their perspective. Vargo and Lusch (2015) present the evaluation of service-dominant logic in the decade since the publication of their seminal paper in 2004 and discuss the arguments brought forward in the latter two papers from the Nordic school of service logic.

service innovation, Prahalad and Ramaswamy (2004a, 2004b) suggest to establish a resource-intensive, ongoing dialogue with the customer as mutual problem solvers.

Only by integrating the customer as a source for knowledge can firms develop solutions that really meet the needs of the customer. As customer knowledge is difficult to tap, Chesbrough (2003; 2010) and Ramaswamy and Ozcan (2014) propose creating platforms for customer engagement that allow interactive exchange with the customer for co-creation, in the early fuzzy stages of innovation as well as in the later stages, for instance through online innovation contests or toolkits and other individualisation options for engagement and interaction with the firm.

In a similar vein, the user-active paradigm builds upon the need to integrate the latent needs of the customer. The "sticky information" about customer needs is, according to the elaborations of von Hippel (1994; 2005), difficult to transfer. Yet there are users that innovate for themselves to satisfy their unmet needs. These users with urgent or special needs develop and provide services not for co-creating value with the firm, but for themselves with their own resources. The user-active paradigm suggests that firms may observe and screen these user innovations and transfer them into their own context, or invite the user with special needs to co-create innovations together.

In the context of resource dependency theory (Carbonell et al., 2009), the knowledge management and the learning perspective on service innovation (Gottfridsson, 2010, 2012; Hargadon, 1998; Leiponen, 2005; Schilling & Werr, 2009), services are enabled through the interactive value creation between different actors in a service system. Service innovation is described as an interactive exchange between stakeholders as an open process in which actors co-create value for themselves and others, by sharing information (Gottfridsson & Stålhammar, 2014). According to this view, the required knowledge for service innovation is created in, or gathered through, interpersonal exchange inside the organisational structures, but also with externals who add to service innovation with their knowledge, perceptions and perspectives (Gottfridsson & Stålhammar, 2014; Gottfridsson, 2010). In this understanding of service innovation, idea generation is seen as a process of problem solving and knowledge exchange (or collection). As service innovation requires the combination of actors with different types of knowledge, external stakeholders such as customers are needed to increase the knowledge and competencies of the internal innovation team (Leiponen, 2005).

Table 1: Views on co-creation for service innovation in five different scientific concepts

Co-creation for service innovation		
Domain	**Proposition**	**Role of the customer**
Service -dominant logic	*"The customer is always a co-creator of value: There is no value until an offering is used - experience and perception are essential to value determination"* (Vargo & Lusch, 2006;p.44); only the beneficiary of a service can determine the value (Vargo et al., 2008); service innovation has the goal of increasing the value offered, for all parties involved.	The customer can engage as a co-creator of service innovation (=value propositions) throughout the innovation process to create superior value propositions for the customer and the service provider (Payne et al., 2007).
Service logic	The basic assumptions are very similar to the service-dominant logic. The main difference is a customer-centric perspective to value creation that entails the firm becoming a value co-creator with the customer (Grönroos, 2008, Grönroos & Gummerus, 2014).	The customer is central and regarded as the creator of value. The firm aligns its business process with those of the customer and propose possibilities to make his/her value creation better or easier (Grönroos, 2008; Grönroos & Gummerus, 2014; Payne et al., 2007).
Open (Service) Innovation	Knowledge and resources are spread all over the world; outside-in knowledge tapping is pursued to create better offerings, inside-out openness allows for economies of scale (Chesbrough, 2010); value creation is best achieved through engagement and experiences that enable value co-creation (Ramaswamy & Ozcan, 2014).	Customers should be integrated in service innovation to access their tacit knowledge. Firms must learn about their customers by data collection as well as by offering them platforms for feedback and participation in innovation (Chesbrough, 2010).
User-active paradigm	Service innovation is not always generated by firms, but also by users with unsatisfied needs (Lüthje & Herstatt, 2004).	Users are innovators - developing and providing themselves services (Oliveira & von Hippel, 2011); they serve their own needs best themselves as sticky information is costly to transfer (von Hippel, 1994; Lüthje, Herstatt, & von Hippel, 2006).
Resource-based view and resource dependency theory	Service innovation depends on the accessible resources of the organisation, especially people's skills and knowledge (Edvardsson, Gustafsson, Johnson, & Sanden, 2000). Service innovation happens in networks for knowledge and idea exchange (Gottfridsson, 2012; Schilling & Werr, 2009; Syson & Perks, 2004).	Customers are seen as resources of knowledge which can be accessed to increase the competencies of the organisation for service innovation. Customer integration strives for feedback, perspectives and learning from exchange (Leiponen, 2005; Gottfridsson, 2010; Gottfridsson & Stålhammar, 2014).

All five presented approaches to co-creation for service and service innovation are summarized in an overview in Table 1. Hereby, the different views regarding exchange with the customer are stressed to enable a sharp distinction between the interrelating concepts.

4 The service-dominant logic view on service systems and stakeholder integration

Focussing on the service-dominant logic and its immanent service system approach which has been developed in the past decade (Vargo & Lusch, 2015), this chapter will first introduce service systems and their definitions, and secondly shed light on stakeholder integration in the context of the theory.

4.1 Service systems in service innovation

> *"The ethos of services is interactivity and services, by their very nature, are developed and consumed as a process with a multiplicity of actors. The innate characteristics of services exacerbate the complexities of such interactions. Interactions are difficult to anticipate or plan, standardise and control. Such characteristics point to the value of harnessing and managing interactivity through inter-personal and inter-organisational relationships throughout the service development process."* (Syson & Perks, 2004; p. 256)

As already pointed out in the context of the previous two chapters, service-dominant logic views value co-creation and service innovation as embedded in service systems. In the past decade, scholarly research has contributed from different angles to elaborate on a service systems view in the context of service innovation. Networks[23] (Fenton & Pettigrew, 2000; Perks et al., 2012; Rusanen et al., 2014; Syson & Perks, 2004), value constellations (Kowalkowski et al., 2013; Normann & Ramirez, 1993),

---

[23] Networks, as defined by Fenton and Pettigrew (2000), *"arise from an interdependence of individual lines of action"* (Fenton & Pettigrew, 2000; p.19). Whilst networks often refer to actors in the network as roles, authority and relationships, systems include more than people but also non-human resources of the organisation. Nevertheless, Obstfelds (2005) definition of networks includes social connections between people and the ideas and resources of people that can be combined for innovation.

value networks (Lusch et al., 2009), and eco-systems (Vargo & Akaka, 2012) are terms being used to highlight the relational aspects of service innovation, regarding actors and resources as interdependently connected by the actions in a system (as illustrated by the above quote by Syson and Perks). The different terms may sometimes be used interchangeably or to stress slightly different aspects of systems. E.g. when analysing networks, a more stable picture of actors in their roles, authorities and relationships is communicated (Fenton & Pettigrew, 2000). Service eco-systems stress the flexibility and viability of systems. Eco-systems are defined as loose and wider organisms (Perks et al., 2012; Vargo & Lusch, 2011) whilst service systems are used in the context of organisations or parts of an organisation. Overall, the definitions have in common that they inherit the idea of multiple stakeholders connected through their interactions, and imply some interdependent dynamics.

Maglio and Spohrer (2008) provide a widely accepted consensus of service systems[24]: these are defined as the dynamic *"value co-creation configurations of people, technology, value propositions connecting internal and external service systems, and shared information"* (Maglio & Spohrer, 2008, p. 18). Seen in this light, service systems can be individuals, groups, business units, organisations, firms, cities, nations or government agencies -configurations that exchange with others as they apply resources, for the benefit of others and/or themselves (Maglio & Spohrer, 2008; Vargo et al., 2008). Not only are service systems connected through the exchange of value, they are also "parts of each other". That is, a service system such as a business unit is part of a larger service system, for example the firm it belongs to (Chandler and Vargo, 2011)[25].

This interconnected service system view on innovation includes the concept that service innovation on a micro level may have effects on other levels, e.g. in its core service system, other service systems (e.g. the service systems of integrated stakeholders, such as suppliers or customers) or the broader service systems it is embedded in (e.g. the department, business unit or the overall organisation). Inherent in this service system view is the understanding that service innovation is a multi-

24 see e.g. Böhmann, Leimeister, & Möslein, 2014; Vargo & Lusch, 2015; Vargo et al., 2008; Barile & Polese, 2010; Edvardsson, Tronvoll, & Gruber , 2010; Ng, Maull, & Yip, 2009.

25 Chandler and Vargo (2011) conceptualise service ecosystems as having a micro, meso and macro level. Micro level service systems are e.g. households and organisations, meso level service systems are service systems such as industries or brand communities and macro level service systems are overarching, e.g. nations, cultures or global markets. To learn more about the relations between ecosystem, institutions and innovation, read Vargo & Lusch (2015) or the paper "Innovation through institutionalization: A service ecosystems perspective" by Vargo, Wieland & Akaka (2015).

dimensional process, which is broadly supported in service research today (Agarwal & Selen, 2011; Kindström et al., 2013; Maglio et al., 2009; Rubalcaba et al., 2012; Smith & Fischbacher, 2005; Vargo et al., 2008).

4.2 Stakeholder integration for service innovation in service systems

This multi-dimensionality in service systems implies that service innovation has to align internal and external stakeholders for service innovation (Kindström et al., 2013; Lusch et al., 2009; Vargo 2008). Both, internal and external stakeholders are actors in the service system of a specific service and engage in the co-creation of value and value propositions (i.e. service innovation) with their personal engagement and experiences (Ramaswamy & Gouillart, 2010). Thereby, individual stakeholders exchange and gather knowledge and ideas in an iterative process (Gottfridsson, 2012; Schilling & Werr, 2009; Syson & Perks, 2004).

The integration of stakeholders in service systems is, according to a recent literature stream in service-dominant logic, influenced by the institutions (the shared rules, norms and thinking that guide organisational behaviour) of a service system (Edvardsson et al., 2014; Edvardsson & Tronvoll, 2013; Vargo et al., 2015). The shared institutions in a service system govern the stakeholders' actions, intentions and motivations as well as they influence their decision making in systems, such as an organisation, a unit, a team or a professional group of an organisation. Accordingly, stakeholder integration in service systems can be influenced by the shared or divergent institutions of the individual stakeholders of a service innovation process (Edvardsson et al., 2014). As institutions are not only shaping, but also reciprocally being shaped by the actions in the service system, stakeholder activities can also adjust or even create new guidelines of behaviour (institutions) in the service system. This view is in line with established research outside the service-dominant logic context, e.g. by Stevens and Dimitriadis (2005) who elaborate that service innovation can resemble organisational learning, in the sense of institutionalizing change.

The organisation as a service system can be regarded as a complex service system with sub-systems on its own right. For the management of stakeholder integration in service systems, the different departments, disciplines and functions constitute stakeholder groups that potentially have to be considered for integration (Carlborg et al., 2013; Kowalkowski et al., 2013). This is due to the fact that service innovations directly affect the organizational structure, communication networks, working processes and the internal stakeholders' daily work (Bessant, von Stamm,

Möslein, & Neyer, 2010; Stevens & Dimitriadis, 2005). Accordingly, those units that design service innovations and those that implement and deliver service innovation should create aligned processes (Payne et al., 2007).

A look at service innovation literature shows that this coordination and facilitation of exchange between the different stakeholders of a service system with embedded institutions is seen as a major management task (Gottfridsson, 2012; Schilling & Werr, 2009). The practical challenges coming along with stakeholder integration in service systems for service innovation are interdisciplinary, a dynamic environment (Akama, 2009) and, especially in service innovation in a manufacturing context, a limited exchange of knowledge between different units of the company, because of different understandings, engagement and procedures (Kowalkowski et al., 2013), to name just a few. In the next section, the detailed literature review of empirical research on stakeholder integration, with its challenges and benefits, will provide a fundament for the in-depth exploration of stakeholder integration in service systems that applies the presented theory lens of service-dominant logic.

Part IV
Stakeholder integration in service innovation – a passive look from outside

Leaving behind the "foundation" part of this thesis with the presented research design and its underlying theory lens, the next chapter is concerned with the research topic "Which stakeholders are getting integrated, at what stage of the innovation process and in which mode?" from an outside perspective. This look from outside describes the state-of-the art in service research on stakeholder integration in service innovation. It will first shed light on the field of interests and findings in present empirical research as a fundament for the further exploration of the topic. Second, it will present existing frameworks for stakeholder integration and derive a consolidation of frameworks on the modes of stakeholder integration. Following this, in the third chapter, a pre-study presents the outside view on stakeholder integration practice, as seen by service innovation intermediaries. This will provide a first idea of stakeholder integration, integrated groups as well as the mode of integration in the respective stages of the innovation process

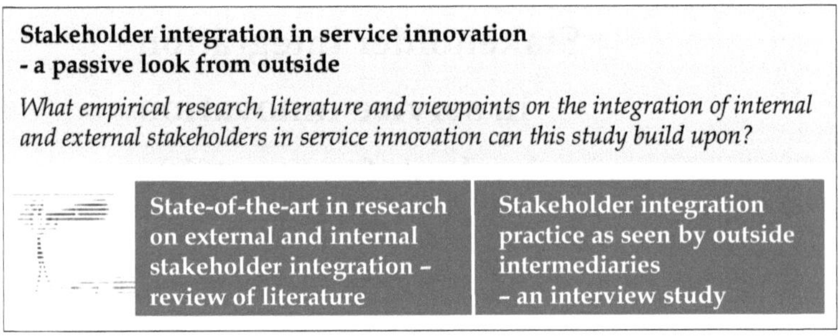

Figure 7: Part IV - a passive look from outside

1 State-of-the-art of research on external and internal stakeholder integration - review of literature[26]

To start with, this chapter defines the concept of a "stakeholder" and then reviews existing empirical research on stakeholder integration in service innovation. First, research on external stakeholders will be presented in detail, followed by research on internal stakeholders. For external stakeholders, the role of customers as a major subject of research in the field will be outlined; then research on lead users and trusted customers as well as further external stakeholders (such as partners and suppliers) will be presented. For the introduction to research on internal stakeholders, the order of presentation will start with the core innovation team, followed by experts and employees from other functions, senior management and finally customer contact employees. Chapter 1.4 summarizes the key insights from this literature review.

1.1 Stakeholders in service innovation

The term "stakeholder" was originally coined by Freeman and Reed in 1983 as "*any identifiable group or individual who can affect the achievement of an organisation's objectives or who is affected by the achievement of the organisation's objectives*" (Freeman & Reed, 1983; p.91). Stakeholders are accordingly different parties, units and persons in the organisation as well as parties, units and persons from the environment around the organisation that have a relationship with the organisation. Stakeholders are groups who can potentially be affected by a service innovation, or who can potentially be

[26] Building blocks of this part are based on the papers Jonas et al. (2013), Jonas et al. (2014a), Jonas et al. (2014b), Jonas & Roth (2017) and Jonas et al. (2015). See Annex A.

engaged in the service innovation process[27]. Literature in service (innovation) research distinguishes between internal and external stakeholders. Internal stakeholders named in service innovation literature are, amongst others, customer contact employees, senior management and experts/other functions, while external stakeholders referred to in the literature are customers, suppliers and partners, universities, competitors and consultants (Rusanen et al., 2014) [28].

In the original description of stakeholders by Freeman and Reed (1983), it was argued that it is the role of the senior management board to map and evaluate stakeholders in the organisation. Only slightly differently, literature about stakeholder integration in service innovation and even in stakeholder theory proposes that the integration of stakeholders is a management task. To steer stakeholder integration managers decide who deserves or requires attention, and who does not (Hart, 1995; Mitchell, Agle, & Wood, 1997; Smith & Fischbacher, 2005)[29]. In the context of this thesis, stakeholder integration is seen as a managerial mapping task and involves decision making about their integration, depending on the managers' perception of which relevant stakeholders may be involved in or be affected by a service innovation project (Smith & Fischbacher, 2005). Driessen and Hillebrand (2013) propose that management develops the capabilities to identify

27 In their recent book, Lusch and Vargo (2014) clarify their understanding of stakeholders as those parties that are part of the service system but not actively co-creating value. In their view, stakeholders are those actors in the service system who are directly connected to the value co-creators and (only) affected by the activities of value co-creation. In this thesis, their understanding of stakeholders is not shared: from the organisational perspective of innovation, all parties that are potentially affected by a service innovation (project) are stakeholders that can engage as co-developers for service innovation (the process of forming and designing value propositions). This involves even indirect stakeholders and stakeholders that can potentially make a contribution to innovation. Actors of the service system that are not directly but indirectly integrated in service innovation are referred to as indirectly integrated stakeholders. This is based on the perception that "helping" for value co-creation cannot and should not be excluded from value co-creation, but is to be seen as part of value co-creation in a complex system. This view of value co-creation is supported by Grönroos and Voima who conclude that "*everything is value co-creation and everyone co-creates value*" (Grönroos & Voima, 2012, p. 144).

28 A different approach to cluster stakeholders from inside and outside the organisation is proposed e.g. by Neyer et al. (2009) in an open innovation context: With a sociotechnical systems perspective, they differentiate between core inside innovators, peripheral inside innovators and outside innovators and suggest to balance the integration of the three groups of innovators, when pursuing a strategy towards open innovation.

29 In their paper on the concept of network centrality, Smith and Fischbacher (2005) provide empirical insight on projects where stakeholders are considered to be salient or given power in the centre of the service innovation project system by management. The same idea was described by Hart (1995) who refers to the degree in which the voice of stakeholders is incorporated in the organization's decision processes. To make the voice of the customer heard amongst those of the many other stakeholders involved in the service innovation process is stressed as a challenging task for managers (Smith & Fischbacher, 2005).

stakeholders and their issues, to manage and guide the stakeholder interests through the course of the innovation process. Through learning and capability development, gained through practice, the learning process of innovation managers can later result in adaptions, changes of innovation processes[30]. This makes clear that for the management of stakeholders and their integration, both meanings of the term "management" apply: the organisation of stakeholder integration with decisions about the design of stakeholder integration, and the leadership of integrated stakeholders requiring soft skills with a feeling for timing and communication (Möslein, 2005).

Stakeholder integration is emphasised especially in the early stages of service innovation. The idea screening and idea generation phase determines the further innovation process and outcome, thus stakeholder integration is needed to reduce uncertainty in these early innovation stages, as Alam (2006a) and Perks and Riihela (2004) point out. A key role is given to the stakeholder group "customers" since they are regarded as the *"experts on their own experiences"* (Bettencourt, 2010; p.xx).

1.2 Literature on external stakeholder integration

There are a number of reasons why customers and users as an external stakeholder group have received great attention in service innovation literature: the customer is seen as the co-creator of value in service-dominant logic and service logic, the customer is perceived as the decision maker about service quality in the SERVQUAL[31] model and constitutes the overall aim of business actions in customer orientation literature, to name just a few. Accordingly, this review of literature on stakeholder integration in service innovation starts with the strong stakeholder group "customers and users".

---

[30] This change of innovation management processes resembles an adaptation of the institutions that guide resource integration, as conceptualized in a current literature stream aligning service-dominant and institutional logics. For further reading, the interested reader may consider the papers "Institutional logics matter when coordinating resource integration" by Edvardsson et al. (2014) or the article by Vargo and Akaka (2012) "Value Cocreation and Service Systems (Re)Formation: A Service Ecosystems View".

[31] SERVQUAL is a service quality model developed by Parasuraman et al. in 1985 to better understand and measure the quality of a service in ten elements. The model highlights the expectations and experiences of the customer as the key element for service quality and its improvement.

1.2.1 Customers and users[32]

> *"It's only by knowing what customers need that companies can engage in meaningful new service creation."* (Bettencourt, 2010; p.xx)

Customer integration in service innovation is understood as a critical issue for the success of a new service (Alam, 2006b; Carbonell et al., 2009; Matthing et al., 2004). Accordingly, high emphasis is put on customer needs; they are regarded as the fundament of meaningful new service innovation (Bettencourt, 2010; Michel et al., 2007). It is only by the integration of the wishes and especially the latent needs or tacit knowledge of customers and users, that the aim (or outcome) of the service innovation can be achieved - this is the satisfaction of the customer's unmet needs (Bettencourt, 2010; Chesbrough, 2003; von Hippel, 1994; Ramaswamy & Gouillart, 2010). Consequently, it is argued that customer information is needed to provide a more accurate and complete assessment of customers' needs, especially in the context of organizations with multiple products and units (Payne et al., 2007). As authors in service innovation research propose, information from customers can contribute to the development of differentiated and superior services (Alam, 2002; Carbonell et al., 2009; Witell et al., 2014).

According to the definition by Narver, Slater and MacLachlan (2004), customer needs vary on a continuum from easily communicable *expressed needs* to unacknowledged *latent needs*. Latent needs are needs that the customer is not conscious of. They can only be observed in their specific social context or may become evident in the context of unsolved problems. This customer knowledge is called "sticky information" as coined by von Hippel (1994) or tacit knowledge (Nonaka & Tekeuchi, 1995; Leiponen, 2005; Antorini & Muñiz, 2013; Lundkvist & Yakhlef, 2004). To gain access especially to the customer's latent needs, the joint development of service innovation with the customers as active collaborators is required (Gustafsson, Kristensson & Witell, 2012; Kristensson et al., 2008; Prahalad and Ramaswamy, 2004a; Witell, Kristensson, Gustafsson, & Löfgren, 2011). This means foremost that customers, as "experts in their own experiences" (Steen, Manschot, & Koning, 2011; Sangiorgi, 2011) become part of the service innovation process through personal engagement - by sharing their own experiences with the service of the respective

[32] When talking about customers, this thesis refers to customers, consumers, business clients or users, if not specified explicitly in context. Literature often uses the different terms interchangeably or without demarcation, except for lead users that will be presented more in detail in the upcoming section.

company, by bringing in their ideas or by evaluating concepts (Alam, 2002; Lee, Olson, & Trimi, 2012; Ramaswamy & Gouillart, 2010; Vargo & Lusch, 2004). This mutual engagement for service innovation is characterized by exchange on an equal footing and a high degree of communication between the two parties (Gustafsson et al., 2012; Kristensson et al., 2008).

A variety of empirical studies, applying qualitative and quantitative research methods, have studied the effects of customer and user integration in natural practice as well as in experimental settings. Empirical findings indicate that the integration of customers leads to more successful innovations (Carbonell et al., 2009). In more detail, it is shown that service innovation including customer integration better answers the customers' expectations (Melton & Hartline, 2010; Sandström, Magnusson, & Kristensson, 2009) and accordingly creates a better fit for the customer needs (Witell et al., 2014). Customer integration in service innovation improves the effectiveness of service innovation (Magnusson et al., 2003; Matthing et al., 2006; Martin & Horne, 1993; Ngo & O'Cass, 2013) and generates a higher profit of new services (Witell et al., 2014) as well as a higher speed to market (Carbonell et al., 2009; Fang, 2008; Alam, 2006a) and higher technical quality (Carbonell et al., 2009).

Furthermore, it has been identified that users can be more innovative than experts or R&D personnel, if given the right opportunities (Kristensson, Gustafsson, & Archer, 2004; Magnusson et al., 2003; Kristensson, Magnusson, & Matthing, 2002; Kristensson et al., 2004; Magnusson, 2003). However, some authors link the integration of customers for idea generation to incremental innovation only, as a literature review by Lundkvist and Yakhlef (2004) shows.

The research findings at hand cannot create a common picture regarding the stages of integration for customers. Some authors argue that customer integration can be implemented in all stages of the service innovation process (Carbonell et al., 2009). Carbonell et al. (2009) found in their empirical study that positive effects of customer integration (speed to market and technical quality) are independent of the stage of integration. Other authors put a high emphasis on the early stages of the innovation process (e.g. Alam, 2006a; Gruner, & Homburg, 2000). Alam (2006a) proposes that customer integration is more effective, the earlier it is implemented in the service development process. In his study of financial service development, idea generation and concept evaluation have been found to be the most intense stages of customer integration. Also Gruner and Homburg (2000) argue in their research that customer integration is best implemented in the early phases.

Alam (2006a) further observed that customer integration leads to best results when customers are integrated as equal partners in a development team. Indeed, additional empirical research by Gustafsson et al. (2012) has shown that direct exchange and interaction can improve the results of customer integration. According to their study, spending more time communicating with the customer creates access to context specific "sticky information"; furthermore the fit between needs and possible solutions can be validated in a better way.

According to the elaboration of Gruner and Homburg (2000), customer integration is not advised in the later phases of the innovation process. Here, the developed concepts are becoming technically complex, and customers cannot be expected to provide solutions for technical issues (Gruner & Homburg, 2000). Witell et al. (2014), on the other hand, suggest that customers can provide feedback for new services much better after they have been developed to a certain degree of maturity. Therefore, customer integration should be implemented in the stages "concept development" and "design". At these stages, customers can contribute with adaptions of the service concept most substantially and profitably. When implemented during testing and launch, Witell et al.'s (2014) empirical work found that customer integration has a minor effect on the profitability of service innovation.

Referring to resource dependency theory, Carbonell et al. (2009) suggest that information on customer needs and user experience can be regarded as essential resources for service innovation, and yet their integration is needed to secure access to customers' knowledge. As customer knowledge is "sticky information" (von Hippel, 1994), firms can find it difficult to identify, understand and adopt knowledge about the value co-creation process of customers (Witell et al., 2014).

Even though customer integration during service innovation is understood to be critical for market success, practice does not reflect the importance it is given to in theory (Matthing et al, 2006; Martin & Horne, 1995). This may be due to the lack of understanding how to integrate customers (de Brentani & Ragot, 1996; Matthing et al., 2006) or because it can be difficult to identify customers as external stakeholders "*that are likely to be the most helpful*" (Matthing et al., 2006, p. 289; see also Nambisan 2002; Alam, 2006a). To obtain customer information causes extra workload and demands more resources in time and money (Lilien, Morrison, Searls, Sonnack, & von Hippel, 2002; Witell et al., 2014), whilst it can remain unclear how to extract tacit knowledge from the interaction with customers (Berger, Möslein, Piller, & Reichwald, 2005; Mention & Asikainen 2012).

Another challenge for customer integration is the willingness and commitment of customers and users. Nordin and Kowalkowski (2010) and Smith and Fischbacher (2005) indicate that customers might not be able or willing to articulate their needs, in a B2B context. Alam (2006a) affirms this practical challenge - he found from his empirical studies in the context of financial services that there might be a lack of commitment from the customers who cannot clearly see a benefit in the innovation activities for themselves. Additionally, Alam (2006a) identified that customer integration may lead to over-customisation, at least in B2B settings.

The identification and engagement of different customer and user groups is discussed as a critical issue in service research. Experienced or inexperienced customers, users, lead users or non-users of a service are explored as special types of customers in service innovation (Edvardsson, Gustafsson, Kristensson, & Witell, 2010). Carbonell, Rodriguez-Escudero and Pujari (2012) and Matthing et al. (2006) demonstrate that the integration of different, specific types of customers and users has effects on the outcome of service innovation. Whilst, for instance, lead users can contribute with novel ideas, the integration of close customers increases speed to market and supports access to critical information (Carbonell et al., 2012).

1.2.2 Special customers and users: lead users and trusted customers

Lead users, as a special type of stakeholder in the group of customers and users, have been given special attention in the context of service innovation since they are perceived to have a *"strong well developed set of needs and a willingness to participate in fulfilling those needs"* (Matthing et al., 2006; p. 289). Lead users, with their special needs going beyond average customers' needs and their willingness to find solutions for their problems (von Hippel, 1986), are expected to be *"a window into the future"* for service innovation (Slater & Narver, 1998; p. 1003). Whereas lead user innovation is predominantly connected to the creation of tangible goods and IT (see for instance Lüthje et al., 2006; Lüthje & Herstatt. 2004; Lilien et al., 2002; Urban & von Hippel, 1988; von Hippel, 1986), there is still a number of studies that investigate lead user innovation and the benefits of lead user integration in service innovation. Von Hippel and Riggs (1997), Oliveira and von Hippel (2011) and van der Boor, Oliveira, and Veloso (2014) present examples of lead user innovation in banking, Lüthje and Herstatt (2004) report on lead user innovation in healthcare. It has been derived from empirical results by Carbonell et al. (2012) that the integration of lead users fosters the creation of new ideas and of services that enable competitive advantage. But, it was also found that the ideas of lead users might be too far ahead of the mass market, and that these should be evaluated and conceptualized with general customers and users (Carbonell et al., 2012).

The identification of lead users for service innovation is a challenge. While online ethnography and survey-based lead user identification is reported to be a successful means for lead user recruiting (Eisenberg, 2011; Belz & Baumbach, 2010; Bilgram & Brem, 2008) for product and service innovation, a study by Faullant et al. (2012) shows from practical experience that the identification of lead users for service innovation is challenging. Matthing et al. (2006) faced this issue and suggested the application of technology readiness as an aid to indicate lead user attributes, at least for technology-related service innovation.

For the integration of trusted customers, Alam (2006a) as well as Nicolajsen and Scupola (2011) argue that confidentiality issues can be overcome easier with trusted partners (Weterings & Boschma, 2009; Alam, 2006a) and the readiness to collaborate is higher (Nicolajsen & Scupola, 2011). Moreover, Alam (2002) and Carbonell et al. (2012) showed that the integration of close customers leads to a better speed to market and superior services, since relational closeness and trust leads to a better understanding and more fine-grained information. Still, for managers, knowing all these advantages and specifications, it remains a challenge to identify which innovative customers will be the most helpful in their current situation (Matthing et al., 2006).

1.2.3 Other external stakeholders

Beyond customers and users, research studies on stakeholder integration for service innovation also discuss other external stakeholders groups, such as suppliers, partner organizations, outside collaborators (such as non-users) or the public as relevant groups, but do not investigate them in depth (see e.g. Johne & Storey, 1998; Rubalcaba et al., 2012; Prahalad & Ramaswamy, 2004a). This is in spite of the fact that, according to Lee et al. (2012), these "other external stakeholders" create that extra inimitable value for the organization. Scholars further propose that the integration of external resources and knowledge might foster unique service innovations and more radical innovation (Ordanini & Parasuraman, 2010; Schleimer & Shulman, 2011; Lee et al., 2012).

The integration of suppliers and partners has the potential to identify improvements in order to remain competitive, to bring in wider expertise and to reduce costs and quality problems (Pittaway, Robertson, Munir, Denyer, & Neely, 2004). Tether and Tajar (2008) show in their study that supplier integration is prominent in cases of organisational and relational changes within supply chains or networks. Universities as a special type of external partners can be integrated, for instance to access basic knowledge and to improve problem solving capabilities (Perkmann, Neely, & Walsh, 2011).

Learning from product development and open innovation literature, it can be surmised that the combination of resources and exploitation of joint capabilities through supplier integration is already beneficial early in the innovation process (Gassmann, 2006; Wagner & Hoegl, 2006). In a production context, the discussed benefits of supplier integration are, amongst others, faster time-to-market of new products, quality, development costs and access to new resources. Measured negative effects are costs, development time and increased complexity. Wagner and Hoegl (2006) also found that supplier integration for product development tends to be applied in none-core technologies, products or components.

Overall, a key challenge of external stakeholder integration is that the management of these additional stakeholders in the service system potentially takes away resources from the management of internal stakeholders throughout the course of the innovation process. The integration of customers and other external stakeholders demands human resources, budget, time, and might even lead to strategic risks and consequences. This includes resource-intensive information processing, the need to articulate an innovation strategy together with suppliers, or short term negative impact on economic performance due to process innovations (Mention & Asikainen, 2012; Weber, 2008).

From empirical evidence, Gottfridsson (2012) adds that in addition to these different experiences, knowledge and cultures are adding challenging complexity to service innovation. Just as in customer integration, processes are required to extract value from the supplier or partner relationships (Gottfridsson, 2012).

1.3 Internal stakeholders

With different departments, disciplines and functions, already the organization itself represents a service system with different internal stakeholder groups. Internal stakeholders constitute actors in the service system who potentially have to be considered for integration (Carlborg et al. 2013; Kowalkowski et al., 2013). In particular the stakeholder groups "customer contact employees" and "experts from other units" are emphasised for service innovation as they possess explicit and tacit knowledge (Schilling & Werr, 2009). Accordingly, it is suggested that these internal knowledge contributors (Blazevic & Lievens, 2004; Gottfridsson, 2012), with their individual and collective knowledge should be integrated and facilitated in service innovation (Leiponen, 2005; Mattsson, 2010; Neyer et al., 2009).

Overall, employees are found to be the number one source of ideas (Schulteß, Wegener, Neus, & Satzger, 2010). But they are not only a source for ideas - employees in general are contributing to service innovation (Nicolajsen & Scupola, 2011) by taking the role of "scouts" or "connectors". With their networks inside and outside the company, employees are able to access knowledge sources and bring them into the organisation. They might as well function as connectors between different stakeholders for a project (Whelan, Parise, de Valk, & Aalbers, 2011). Neu and Brown (2005) reveal in their study on service innovation at product-dominated firms that such intra-firm collaboration helps to understand complex systems and serves as a driver for successful innovation.

The integration of employees plays a strong role during development and testing. During this stage, specialized skills from other departments might be needed. Other internal units and cross-functional teams can provide input that helps, amongst others, to identify and evaluate consequences of a service innovation project (Johne & Storey, 1998; Schleimer & Shulman, 2011¸ Smith & Fischbacher, 2005; Nicolajsen & Scupola, 2011). In the following paragraphs, the discussed groups in service innovation research are presented in more depth, starting with the core innovation team, followed by experts, senior management and customer contact employees.

1.3.1 Core innovation team

> *"An integrated development team captures the skills and capabilities of the employees, and the team should be comprised of individuals representing a diverse set of skills."* Edvardsson et al. (2013; p. 28)

The core innovation team is often discussed only implicitly in the analysed literature in service innovation. Johne and Storey (1998) suggest that in most cases, the core innovation team is newly assembled for a new service innovation project. The importance of the arrangement of this team is stressed by Schilling and Werr (2009), Leiponen (2005) as well as Blazevic and Lievens (2004): they find that the overall success of service innovation is dependent on the assembly of the core innovation team with employees from different functions, bringing along required and helpful knowledge and skills. The compilation of employees and their experiences enables exchange for joint problem solving (Blazevic & Lievens, 2004); the combination of different skills of the individuals in an innovation team leads to fresh insights (Edvardsson et al., 2013; Gottfridsson, 2012). The core innovation team, as the decision maker on integration, has the task to capture a diverse set of skills and capabilities on the one hand, and on the other hand to offer an organization-wide platform for internal stakeholder integration (Edvardsson et al., 2013; Kindström et al., 2013; Smith & Fischbacher, 2005; Schilling & Werr, 2009).

1.3.2 Experts and employees from other functions

The integration of internal stakeholders is motivated by the integration of specific functions or skills, as they can bring in "*different knowledge and competences to the innovation process which could facilitate creativity, learning and knowledge development for innovation*" (Schilling & Werr, 2009; p.32). The organization-wide integration, engagement and mobilization of internal stakeholders from different departments is promoted in service innovation. This is due to the fact that innovations directly affect the organisational structure, communication networks, working processes and the internal stakeholders' daily work (Bessant et al., 2010; Stevens & Dimitriadis, 2005).

1.3.3 Senior management

The integration of senior management positions is discussed as vital for the success of service innovation (Gupta, Raj, & Wilemon, 1985; Hegarty & Hoffman, 1990). Scholars put forward that senior management constantly engages in service innovation (de Brentani & Ragot, 1996; de Jong & Vermeulen, 2003; Smith & Fischbacher, 2005). In smaller companies, the owner or manager and employees strongly contribute to service innovation (Gottfridsson 2011; Nicolajsen & Scupola, 2011), especially during development and testing (Smith & Fischbacher, 2005), but also as a source for ideas (Gottfridsson, 2011). As service innovation in non-service organizations is often not a formalized process, it falls to the roles of senior management to assign resources and give weight to service innovation throughout the service innovation process. Moreover, it is specified that senior management should provide practical help to the innovation project (Johne & Storey, 1998; Smith & Fischbacher 2005; Ettlie & Rosenthal, 2011).

1.3.4 Customer contact employees

A special group of employees emphasised in service research is "customer contact employees"[33]. This stakeholder group is expected to share a deep understanding with the customers due to their frequent contact (Alam, 2006a; Smith & Fischbacher, 2005). The emphasis on customer contact employee integration has its roots in the context of service quality (Zeithaml, Bitner, & Gremler, 1996). Zeithaml et al. (1996) point out that customer contact employees need to be integrated in service innovation if services are to be delivered to a high standard. De Brentani (2001) describes the potential benefits for the integration of customer-contact employees: they can share customer needs and opportunities for innovation in the early stages of innovation, they can help define "*the appropriate level of service customization, user-friendliness, and complexity*" (de Brentani, 2001, p. 182) during concept development and during the launch and they can forward the benefits of a new offering to the customer.

Despite these proven benefits, present research shows only isolated cases of customer contact employee integration in the idea generation phase (Gustafsson, Ekdahl, & Edvardsson, 1999)[34]. Still, Alam (2006a) finds in his empirical study that customer contact employees, in their daily contact with customers, are developing ideas for service innovation as they interact with customers. It is shown that customer contact employees draw ideas from formal and informal meetings with customers, from open dialogues about their problems and needs. Different to this empirical evidence, results by Melton and Hartline (2010) and Sonesson (2007) suggest that the integration of customer contact employees is more likely to be seen in later stages of the innovation process, during development (Sonesson, 2007), testing or training, and foremost in the launch phase of a service innovation (Melton & Hartline, 2010; Sonesson, 2007).

An explanation for the scarce implementation of this stakeholder group in practice might be that it is challenging for managers to set aside time for customer contact employees to take part in the service innovation process (Schilling & Werr, 2009), especially in customer services. Moreover, scholars recommend that customer

---

33 Customer contact employees are also named "customer contact personnel" (Gremler, 2004; Johne & Storey, 1998; de Brentani, 1995), "front-line employees" (see e.g. Melton & Hartline, 2012, 2010; Holopainen, 2010; Bruins, Dolfsma, & Meijaard, 2003; Schilling & Werr, 2009) or "front-line staff" (Carlborg et al., 2013; Gottfridsson, 2011; 2010; Ostrom et al., 2010). The stakeholder group customer contact employees includes all functions with direct customer interaction, amongst others sales personnel, technicians or call centre agents.

34 Melton and Hartline (2010) would even state that customer contact employees are not integrated as a source of ideas.

contact employees should receive training and education to develop the skills needed to access customer knowledge, so that they are enabled to provide the organization with insights on their customers' needs and behaviour (De Brentani & Ragot, 1996; Lages & Piercy, 2012; Melton & Hartline, 2010).

1.4 Summary

The review of literature in service research shows a broad picture of benefits and challenges for stakeholder integration. For each of the stakeholder groups, potential benefits have been discovered. For some stakeholder groups, specific stages of integration are recommended as it is found that their integration in this relevant phase of service innovation will lead to special benefits. It is shown that different characteristics of integrated stakeholders such as "regular customers", "trusted customers" or "lead users" impact the outcome of stakeholder integration activities, just as the mode of integration does. Furthermore, for some stakeholder groups, there is no clear picture to be drawn on what the integration practice regarding stage and mode looks like or should look like. Especially for customers and customer contact employees, studies in different contexts reveal even contrary findings. Still, the literature review showed that benefits for the integration of stakeholders, there is also a struggle for resources: Stakeholder integration needs to balance the application of resources between different internal stakeholders as well as between internal and external stakeholders.

Within stakeholder integration, the access to sticky information and experiences has been discussed, for customer integration, but also for the integration of employees. Trust, communication and intense interaction with stakeholders have been mentioned as aspects of stakeholder integration that allow for access of sticky information. As Prahalad and Ramaswamy (2004) have suggested, an intense, direct dialogue all along the phases of a service innovation project is highly demanding in terms of resource and, as the different reviews of stakeholder integration practice show, not always beneficial or useful for paying back the effort. To get a more detailed picture of the modes for stakeholder integration that can be applied for the integration of the presented stakeholders, the next chapter will provide an overview on the different frameworks in service innovation literature. It will synthesise these frameworks to enable the empirical analysis of stakeholder integration.

2 Modes of stakeholder integration

For all presented types of stakeholders, internal and external, the choice of the "right mode of integration" was found to be a crucial factor for service innovation in the work by Perks and Riihela (2004). To find out about this "right level" of integration, an understanding of the potential modes for stakeholder integration has to be provided first. The following review presents customer and stakeholder integration frameworks that conceptualize the interaction of an organization with its stakeholders, varying in intensity, and emphasizing different roles of stakeholders as well as different activities.

For stakeholder integration, Russo-Spena and Mele (2012) present a model that stresses the process of innovation with others. Their "5 Co's in innovating" build upon insights in different innovation activities on online platforms and show how stakeholders like users, fans, experts and firms can *"co-innovate", "co-evaluate", "co-design", "co-test"* and *"co-launch"*[35] during all phases of service innovation. Another model by Gottfridsson (2012) proposes four different types of actors for knowledge transfer in the context of inter-organisational service development. These are *"information carriers", "information collectors", "information translators"* and *"supporting actors/facilitators"*[36].

The conceptualization of specifically customer integration has been elaborated more widely in research. Fang, Palmatier and Evans (2008) introduce the terms *"breadth"* and *"depth"* for customer integration. Here, "breadth" is reflecting how often customers are being integrated, whereas "depth" refers to the level of the integration, superficial or deep. Scholars such as Blazevic and Lievens (2007) specify this proposed continuum of depth. They distinguish customer integration respective to their active participation in the service innovation process. Customers can be integrated in three marked out modes: as passive users, active informers and bi-directional creators of solutions.

Similar to this is the model by Edvardsson, Gustafsson et al. (2010) that highlights the roles performed by customers. In their customer collaboration model, the customer can 1) take the role of a buyer, 2) be the subject of interest, 3) serve as a provider for information, 4) take the role of a co-developer or 5) be the developer.

---

35 See Annex C1

36 See Annex C2

In a similar vein with the latter, Alam (2002) presents four ascending levels of integration: the *passive acquisition of input* by the innovating organisation, *information and feedback* on specific issues, *extensive consultation* with users, and highest, *representation*, the user joining a development team. Piller, Ihl, Vossen, and Group (2011) show a tool-oriented concept in the same vein, in open innovation research. Their framework builds upon previous work by Dahan and Hauser (2002). They present three modes for customer integration: *"listen to"*, the usage of existing customer data, observations and third party reports; *"ask"*, the surveying and interviewing of customers and third, *"build"*, open innovation to actively design innovation together, with the customer in a social and creative process.

Another differentiation in service innovation literature is given by Edvardsson, Kristensson, Magnusson and Sundström (2012). Their framework of four types of customers emphasises the contexts of information gathering. 1) In the context of a service enactment, information can be gathered by the so called *"correspondent"*, a customer type that reports live from the actual situation of service experience, or 2) the *"reflective practitioner"* who reports outside the situation, reflecting on direct experiences. Out of context is 3) the informant customer - *"the tester"* - who reports from simulated or imagined usage situations, and 4) *"the dreamer"*, contributing with wild and imaginative ideas that are not connected to the actual service situation or present experiences[37]. The presented frameworks for categorizing customer integration according to their depth, are summarized in Table 2.

The review of attempts to categorize customer and stakeholder integration shows that the idea of categorizing customer integration according to their depth is widely accepted[38]. Yet, the presented frameworks and models differ in the number of categories and the modes of customer integration taken into account, as Table 2 shows. All frameworks include the modes where customers can be "passive subjects of interest", "information provider" or "co-developers for service innovation". The aspect of customers being active developers themselves is considered only by Edvardsson, Gustafsson et al. (2010) consider the mode "customer as a buyer" as the lowest degree of customer integration for service innovation[39].

---

37 See Annex C 3.

38 The lead article by Alam (2002) shows 518 trackable citations in the Goole Scholar citation count on Aug 6, 2015.

39 The mode of "customer as a buyer" is not taken up in the aligned model, since the information from sales data is, in the context of this thesis, considered as passive integration, whereas information from the interaction between buyer and customer contact employee which is getting forwarded through the employees will be categorized as stakeholder integration, in its' respective mode.

Table 2: Overview of frameworks for customer integration

<table>
<tr><td colspan="12">Ascending depth of customer integration, from low to high
low ←——————————————→ high</td></tr>
<tr><td colspan="12">Roles of customers according to the degree of knowledge coproduction
Blazevic and Lievens (2007)</td></tr>
<tr><td colspan="2"></td><td colspan="2">passive users</td><td colspan="2">active informers</td><td colspan="2"></td><td colspan="2">bi-directional creators</td><td colspan="2"></td></tr>
<tr><td colspan="12">Role of the customer in co-development for service innovation
Edvardsson, Gustafsson et al. (2010)</td></tr>
<tr><td colspan="2">buyer</td><td colspan="2">subject of interest</td><td colspan="2">provider for information</td><td colspan="2"></td><td colspan="2">co-developer</td><td colspan="2">the developer</td></tr>
<tr><td colspan="12">Ascending levels of customer integration in service innovation
Alam (2002)</td></tr>
<tr><td colspan="2"></td><td colspan="2">the passive acquisition of input by the organisation</td><td colspan="2">information and feedback on specific issues</td><td colspan="2">extensive consultation with users</td><td colspan="2">represen-tation, users joining a development team</td><td colspan="2"></td></tr>
<tr><td colspan="12">Modes of using and generating customer information
Piller et al. (2011)</td></tr>
<tr><td colspan="2"></td><td colspan="2">Listen into – usage of existing information</td><td colspan="2">Ask – input for customer orientation</td><td colspan="2"></td><td colspan="2">Build – open innovation/ collaboration with customers</td><td colspan="2">User as an innovator</td></tr>
<tr><td colspan="12">Roles of customers as sources for information in and out of context
Edvardsson et al. (2012)</td></tr>
<tr><td colspan="3">The correspondent</td><td colspan="3">The reflective practitioner</td><td colspan="3">The tester</td><td colspan="3">The dreamer</td></tr>
</table>

Building predominantly on Alam (2002) and Edvardsson, Gustafsson et al. (2010), the modes have been summarized and brought into an aligned model for customer integration, as shown in Figure 8. Here, the modes for customer integration are visualised as a continuum from low to high depth of customer integration, starting with "subject of interest", then "provider for information" and "co-developer", finally ending with "active developer".

Depth of integration from low to high:
(Carbonell et al., 2012)

low ← mode of customer integration → high

"subject of interest"	"provider of information"	"co-developer"	"active developer"
(Blazevic & Lievens, 2007; Alam, 2002; Edvardsson et al., 2010); Piller et al., 2011;	*(Alam 2002; Blazevic & Lievens, 2007; Piller et al., 2011; Edvardsson et al., 2010)*	*(Alam 2002; Blazevic & Lievens, 2007; Piller et al., 2011; Edvardsson et al., 2010)*	*(Edvardsson et al., 2010; Piller et al., 2011)*

Figure 8: Modes of customer integration - aligned model

The work by Russo-Spena and Mele (2012) and Gottfridsson (2012) follows another way of categorization, yet includes different types of internal and external stakeholders, creating frameworks going beyond customer integration. The different aspects of the presented customer and stakeholder integration models have been taken up to create an overall model for the analysis of stakeholder integration. Such a stakeholder integration model reflects the system view as described by Kowalkowski et al. (2013), who propose that it is the task of the organisation, in the centre of the value creation system, to align and manage stakeholders and other resources throughout the service innovation process. In order to analyse the modes of stakeholder integration in service innovation, the summarized customer integration model in Figure 8 needs to be transferred to an organisational management perspective for stakeholder integration. This demands for adaption of the depicted customer integration model, regarding its four modes.

1) As subjects of interest, stakeholders are integrated without knowing about their integration. As there is no active communication, the role of the stakeholder and the mode of integration is **"passive integration"**. In this mode, stakeholders might be observed, as in market analyses, ethnographic studies or test purchases.

2) When organisations integrate stakeholders as providers of information, the stakeholder is answering to an invitation, a request for feedback, given by the innovating organisation. This mode is called **"reactive integration"** from an organisational management perspective. Here, interviews or surveys are implemented for stakeholder integration.

3) When a stakeholder is integrated as a "co-developer" (Edvardsson, Gustafsson et al., 2010), the stakeholder takes an active role. This reflects the definition by

Gustafsson et al. (2012) seeing *"customer co-creation as a frequent, bidirectional, and face-to-face communication process that is used when attempting creative problem solving"* (Gustafsson et al., 2012, pp. 314-315) . This mode, called "representation" in Alam's (2002) customer integration model, is characterized by an active dialogue and the joint development of new offerings (Prahalad & Ramaswamy, 2004a). Here, the stakeholder is integrated as an equal partner for a discussion, to solve a problem jointly; this mode is characterised by mutual exchange. This mode for stakeholder integration is hence called **"mutual integration"**. A typical example for mutual integration would be a workshop for problem discussion and solving or an online discussion board with employees from the organisation and a stakeholder committee.

4) The fourth mode for stakeholder integration is the possibility that stakeholders take proactive initiative and approach the service innovation team with their impulses. Edvardsson, Gustafsson et al.'s (2010) framework calls this mode "the customer being the developer". In this mode, stakeholders are acting as "active developers"; they are developing service innovations more or less autonomously from the organisation and pro-actively approach the organisation with their idea or request. In this mode, the organisation is reacting to the initiative of the stakeholder, providing a channel for the reception and potential absorption of the created solution from the stakeholder. Accordingly, this mode of stakeholder integration is called **"proactive initiative."** From the perspective of an organisation, this mode could be enabled via an open platform where proactive stakeholders can come up with their desires and requests. Even with such platforms provided, true proactive stakeholder innovation can be difficult to actively anticipate or plan (Piller et al., 2011; Edvardsson, Gustafsson et al., 2010). Figure 9 shows the modes of stakeholder integration rising from low to highly active roles: passive integration, reactive integration, mutual integration and proactive initiative.

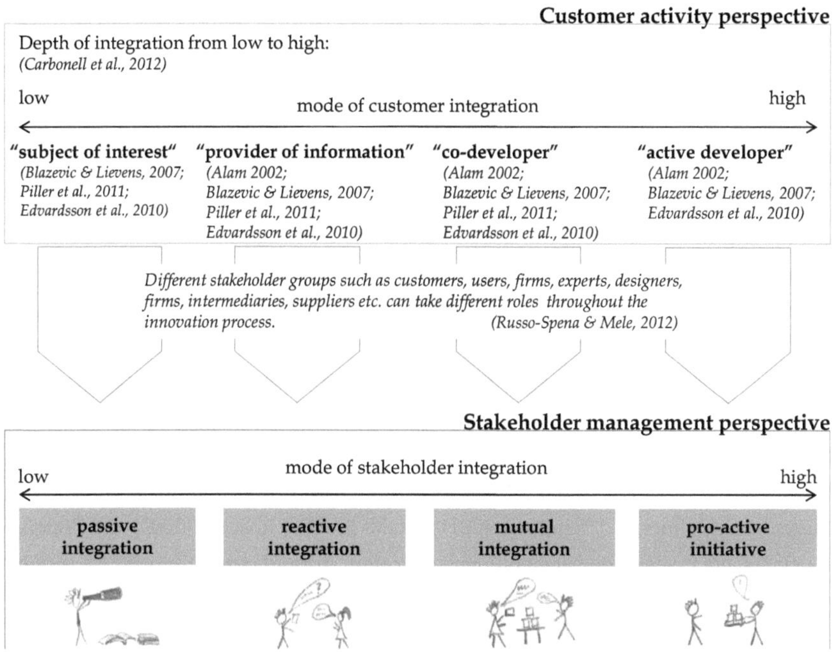

Figure 9: The derivation of the stakeholder integration model

All modes reflect the involvement of stakeholders in service innovation, as conceptualized by e.g. Alam (2002) or Blazevic and Lievens (2007). For this concept, all modes of stakeholder integration are taken into account even though, in a strict interpretation of the service-dominant logic, only the modes that include activity of the stakeholder (reactive and mutual integration and proactive stakeholder initiative) and joint processes would account the co-creation of service innovation (see e.g. Grönroos & Voima, 2012; Vargo & Lusch, 2015). Nevertheless, all modes can be interpreted as participation in service innovation (compare Lusch, 2006).

The relevance of differentiating these modes for stakeholder integration is supported by empirical findings in various studies, e.g., by Magnusson et al. (2003), Matthing et al. (2004) or Skiba and Herstatt (2012). They have shown in experimental settings that the integration of stakeholders, such as lead users and experts, is possible in the mode mutual integration and that it is beneficial for service innovation outcomes. Edvardsson et al. (2013) support this understanding. Their quantitative study suggests that it is not only important that information is collected from and with the customer, but also information is collected and how it is collected; whether tacit knowledge is integrated and made use of. Accordingly, it has been suggested that stakeholder integration for service innovation in different modes leads to different outcomes and effects. Mattsson (2010) argues that more open ended and natural settings for stakeholder integration will provide innovations beyond the incremental level.

It is postulated that direct interaction and communication may allow access to tacit knowledge of stakeholders, if the organization is able to apply skills and processes to capture the information and further process it (Gustafsson et al., 2012; Matthing et al., 2004; Böhmann et al., 2014). From these often experimental pieces of research it cannot be derived who is integrated in regular service innovation practice, where stakeholder integration cannot be regarded in isolation from other processes in the service system. The studies do not clearly indicate in which mode and in which stage of the innovation process the stakeholder integration occurs naturally. First studies by Schleimer and Schulman (2011), Smith and Fischbacher (2005) and Perks et al. (2012) have investigated stakeholder integration throughout the stages of a service innovation process, taking into account the systems view on service innovation. Still, these studies have been conducted in rather unique settings and do not explicitly analyse the mode of stakeholder integration.

3 Stakeholder integration practice as seen by outside intermediaries - an interview study

To gain a better understanding of stakeholder integration practice, a pre-study on stakeholder integration in service innovation with intermediaries gives an inference-free outside impression of organisational practice. This pre-study is carried out in order to learn more about the current state of practices for stakeholder integration in service innovation and to give guidance for the setting-up of the main study. Furthermore, it helps the researchers learn about how to access the data needed for the case studies to be conducted subsequently. This also includes language in use, identification of the right addressees the case organisations and the approval and finalisation of the used interview guidelines.

The motivation for conducting this study originates from a perceived lack of clarity in service innovation and stakeholder integration. As the previous chapter has outlined, empirical research has shown varying findings and ideas about the appropriate level of stakeholder integration, e.g. when it comes to customer contact employees. Also the attention given to the different stakeholder groups in literature varies and leaves open some questions about the integration of these groups for service innovation, e.g. in relation to experts from the organisation or the type of customers integrated.

Furthermore, it can be seen that specific industries such as banking (Alam 2006b; Oliveira & von Hippel, 2011; van der Boor et al., 2014; Smith & Fischbacher, 2005) or mobile communication services, transportation and health care have been well explored in quantitative and qualitative studies (Carlborg et al., 2013), whilst other industries have only been subject to single experimental studies. In the last five to ten years, since the data for the presented scholarly work on stakeholder integration was collected, the development and acceptance, especially of open innovation practices (Chesbrough & Brunswicker, 2014; Vanhaverbeke, Chesbrough, & West, 2014) and design thinking (Wetter-Edman, 2014, 2011; Meroni & Sangiorgi, 2011; Blomkvist, 2014) has matured. This has led to the assumption that the addressees for stakeholder integration and the applied modes of integration may have changed in the meantime. The methods and tools for interdisciplinary and open innovation practices are often introduced through intermediaries such as consultancies and innovation agencies. These experts in service innovation are expected to gain a broad overview of industries, practices and challenges for stakeholder integration from their projects and briefings, and are therefore utilized as a primary source of information about the current state of practice in stakeholder integration for service innovation.

Intermediaries themselves are, according to Bessant and Rush (1995) and Howells (2006), defined as organisations that provide intermediary services which are complimentary to an organisation's knowledge. Intermediaries such as consultants and innovation agencies act as enablers for the transfer of technology as translators of information and as change agents for innovation activities (Bessant & Rush, 1995, Howells, 2006; Rau, 2012). Additionally, it can be assumed that their employment leads to the formalization of innovation practices due to the creation of contracts for specific tasks, in specific phases of an innovation project. Accordingly, intermediaries for service innovation are viewed as bridge builders and providers of information for a broad variety of firms and industries. The interview study in this chapter seeks to explore the perceptions of these intermediaries' regarding the current state of internal and external stakeholder integration in service innovation. How do they experience in which stages of the process and in which modes, stakeholder integration is enabled. It aims to thereby answer the question "Is the mode of stakeholder integration, passive, reactive, mutual or proactive?"

3.1 Research approach - interview study

3.1.1 Data collection

The data collection builds upon service innovation intermediaries as its source of information, in order to gain insight into the contemporary practice of stakeholder integration in service innovation across various industries in Germany. As put forward, they incorporate practical expertise in the field and provide access to service innovation processes that are suitable for data collection. This suitability is expected to be a result of the formalisation that comes with the assignment of an intermediary; through the contracting of an intermediary, even unsystematic service innovation can be researched and evidence collected. Moreover, intermediaries in service innovation usually follow an explicit pattern of service innovation this enables them to compare and draw conclusions from different client projects they have conducted.

An interview study with a semi-structured interview guideline was chosen as a research approach to explore the practice of stakeholder integration, moderated or enabled by intermediaries. This more flexible approach allows improvisation and the exploration of relevant topics in natural conversations (Miles et al., 2013). According to Creswell's guidelines (2014), the purposeful selection of participants was accomplished through a systematic three-step approach (see Figure 10).

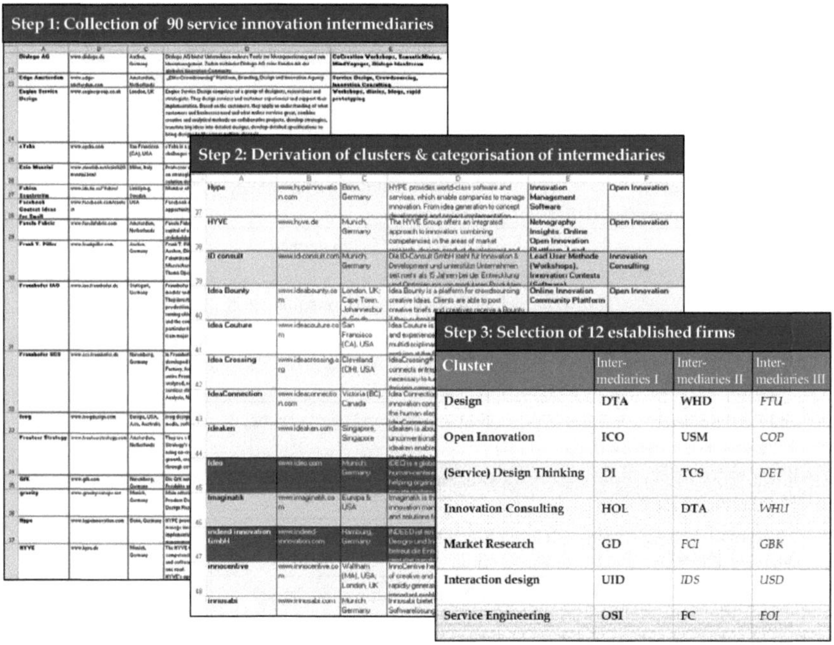

Figure 10: Three step approach for the selection of interviewees

These three steps were realised as follows: (1) after a broad web search for intermediaries (consultancies, agencies, freelancers) working in the field of service innovation, open innovation or service design to widen the scope, 90 intermediaries were identified. (2) Within this list of results, categories of intermediaries were inductively created, resulting in seven clusters which represent the background of intermediaries. These are "Design", "(Service) Design Thinking", "Innovation Consulting", "Interaction Design", "Market Research", "Open Innovation", and "Service Engineering"[40]. (3) From each of these seven categories, the most representative and well-established firms in central Europe were selected and their

[40] The full list of 90 intermediaries allocated to the seven clusters can be provided. Step three, the selection of firms from every category, is not depicted in detail to guarantee the anonymity of the interviewees.

CEO or business unit manager contacted. After approaching potential interviewees at 15 intermediaries, a sample of 12 interviewees could be finalised, as shown in Table 3.

Table 3: Overview of interview partners, intermediaries and their background

	Interviewee position and personal background	Intermediary[41]	Intermediary's sphere of activity
1	Business Manager Service Design, Service designer (WHD)	WHD, Design Agency	Design
2	Director Insights & User Experience, Designer (DTA1)	DTA, Design agency	Design
3	Founding Member, Design Thinking expert (DI)	DI, Design Thinking consultancy	(Service) Design Thinking
4	CEO, Service designer (TCS)	TCS, Service Design agency	(Service) Design Thinking
5	CEO, Business & IT (HOL)	HOL, Innovation Consultancy	Innovation Consulting
6	Director Business Design, Business (DTA2)	DTA, Design Agency	Innovation Consulting
7	Studio Director, Interaction designer (UID)	UID, Interaction Design agency	Interaction Design
8	CEO, Business & IT (GD)	GD, Market Research agency	Market Research
9	Head of Online Co-Creation, Business (ICO)	ICO, Open Innovation agency	Open Innovation
10	Founder, Engineering & Business (USM)	USM, Innovation consultancy	Open Innovation
11	Service Developer, Service Engineer (OSI)	OSI, Service Innovation institute	Service Engineering
12	Head of Service Group, Business & Servitization (FC)	FC, Service Innovation institute	Service Engineering

The 12 interviewees, selected for data collection are either the CEOs or the leaders of the service innovation unit from predominantly German intermediaries. Their backgrounds are in domains such as service design, service engineering, open innovation, user experience design, servitization, market research and general business development, as Table 3 shows in more detail. Interviews were held face-to-face, if possible, or on the telephone. They took an hour on average, with durations varying between 35 minutes and 1 hour 25 minutes. The majority of interviews lasted about an hour. The relevant questions from the interviews for this study were

41 For privacy reasons, the names of the interviewees and their organisations are anonymised.

"Whom do you integrate into the innovation projects, from within the company or external?", "Do you integrate users or other stakeholders that are not in the core project team into the service innovation process, and at which stages of the innovation process does this integration occur?".

3.1.2 Data analysis

All conducted interviews were audio-recorded and transcribed by a team of researchers. Additionally, information from the intermediaries' website and a written feedback sheet were utilised to strengthen the validity of the interview study and to enable a triangulation of the researchers' interpretations after coding. Transcripts were analysed by two independent researchers making use of MaxQDA content analysis software to help with the structuring and recombining of data, as proposed by Miles et al. (2013).

After reading all the interviews carefully for several times, coding was organized deductively according to categories taken from the literature review and research questions (Miles et al., 2013), following the guidelines given by Coffey and Atkinson (1996). After this initial coding to allow the structuring of data according to major themes such as "integrated stakeholders", "stage of the innovation process", "mode of integration", "reason for integration" "reason not to integrate", the codes were re-defined and inductively derived codes were added, to reflect aspects emerging from the explorative research approach, as suggested by Miles et al. (2013), Schreier (2012) and Andrade (2009). The 788 derived codesings were further processed in two Excel sheets for recombination and co-occurrence analysis. For each quote on stakeholder integration, the stakeholder group integrated, the method used, the mode of integration and the phase of the innovation process were extracted and analysed in depth.

3.2 Findings

To give a first, broad overview of the study's findings, it can be stated that the interviews with service innovation intermediaries show that the passive and reactive integration of stakeholders such as users and customer, experts and customer contact employees and the mutual integration of stakeholder groups such as employees, users and customers, customer contact employees, partners and experts, play an important role in service innovation (visualised in Figure 11). Pro-active integration, i.e. the autonomous development of solutions by stakeholders, was not measured in the present study and is therefore left blank in Figure 11. From data analysis, users and customers emerged as a strong stakeholder group, for the passive and reactive integration in the research phase. Employees from the organisation are the most strongly emphasised stakeholder group for mutual integration in service innovation, followed by the stakeholder group customers and users. Overall, the modes "passive and reactive integration"[42] and "mutual integration" were considered equally relevant by the interviewees.

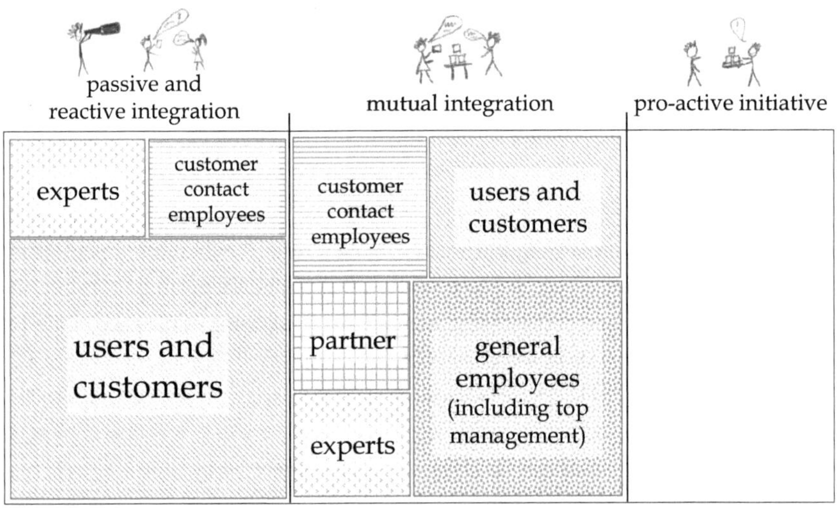

Figure 11: The identified stakeholder groups concerning their prevalence in the modes of integration

From the interview data, stakeholder integration was mapped according to the stages of the service innovation process[43] of their clients. Through this, it was identified that stakeholder integration occurs in all stages of the innovation process, with a much higher intensity in the early phases of the innovation process, as presented in Table 4.

42 As a clear distinction between the modes "passive integration" and "reactive integration" could not be derived from all interview data, these two modes were summarized in this pre-study. The need to specify the distinction between these two modes was a learning from this pre-study and taken into account for the data collection in the following empirical studies of this thesis.

43 The stages of the service innovation process were not pre-defined during the interviews. To access the underlying definitions of the interviewees, their view of the service innovation process was inductively synchronized ex post, reflecting the consensus of the interviewees. Interesting is the distinction between idea screening and idea generation. In literature, both stages are mostly understood as part of the innovation process stage "idea screening" (see e.g. Alam & Perry, 2002; Schulteß et al., 2010; Kindström & Kowalkowski, 2009).

Whilst stakeholder integration in the idea screening phase has a passive and reactive character, the idea generation phase emerges as the stage for the mutual integration of stakeholders. During development, only employees of the client could be derived, as mutual integration, whilst in prototyping and testing, stakeholder integration is implemented as reactive integration of customers and users.

Table 4: Integrated stakeholders along the innovation process

	Idea Screening	**Idea Generation**	**Develop-ment**	**Prototyping & Testing**	**Launch & Promotion**
Users / Customers	passive/ reactive integration	mutual integration		reactive integration	
Employees		mutual integration	mutual integration		
Customer contact employees	passive/ reactive integration	mutual integration		reactive integration	
Partner		mutual integration			
Experts	reactive integration	mutual integration			

3.2.1 Internal stakeholders

3.2.1.1 Employees from the organisation

Looking closer at the integrated stakeholders from inside the innovating organisation, it can be seen that they fall into three distinct groups. Integrated employees are 1) responsible representatives of the units that are affected by the service innovation, 2) interested volunteers from the service innovating department or the affected departments or 3) experts within a specific professional field that is needed in the project.

Regarding the mode of integration for these internal stakeholders, it can be derived from the data they are foremost integrated in the mode of mutual integration. This happens foremost in workshops, during the innovation process stages "idea generation" and "development". In a few given examples, employees were integrated reactively, in interviews.

Which internal stakeholders will be approached to take part in a service innovation project is jointly decided by the intermediary and the client unit[44]. The stated selection criteria for integrated employees are that someone is a) is affected by the topic, b) is an expert for the topic or c) has a specific role in the company, like a networking position. The integration of a person holding a networking position is of strategic reasoning to position the project in the organisation. In a few cases, employees can be integrated to be an active part in customer integration for the innovation project themselves: in other words, they take the role of an observer or interviewer for customer integration in the idea screening phase. This practice is implemented to transfer knowledge and to create an understanding of the tools and methods that are applied by the intermediary. Under these circumstances, internal stakeholder integration is implemented with the purpose to create a change of culture in the organisation from the organisations' side, or alternatively, from the intermediaries' side to foster the acceptance and ownership of developed solutions. The main reason for the integration of employees is the constant need to keep the client informed of the process and to avoid the not-invented-here syndrome. As one interviewee put it,

> *"you need the people from the company with you, because they will have to deliver the service afterwards. And if they are more involved in the process, they are more willing to accept a new service that they'll have to deliver, because it's their own baby. And they thought of the idea. The change management aspect is of course something very important."* (Interviewee WHD)

The data from the interviews shows that challenges for the integration of employees are the willingness to participate and the resource availability in the schedule for the innovation project. Interviewee HOL formulates this to the point: *"we cannot always*

44 This joint decision making and forming the project is itself an act of value co-creation. As this thesis is focussing on co-creation for service innovation, no further analysis of the value co-creation processes between the intermediary and its client, the innovating organisation, is carried out. Nevertheless, the value co-creation in the service system, including the organisation, the intermediary and external customers as the key stakeholder groups, is an interesting topic for a separate research study in the future.

get the people at the client that we want due to time and resource management" (HOL). Furthermore, it is stated explicitly and implicitly that the projects of innovation intermediaries cause extra work, not only for the unit that ordered the project, but even for the other internal stakeholders.

Table 5: Exemplifying quotes on the motivation to integrate specific employee groups

Integration of employees as interviewers and observers for the avoidance of the Not-invented-here syndrome	*"The so called 'Not-invented-here problem' can be solved by integrating the product manager from the first observations, at the users' kitchen table at home, in workshop. The observation turns into an idea that he/she takes home to his/her unit. 'I have basically developed this or found out this collaboratively'. This creates a totally different drive to press ahead with the concept in the organisation."* (UID)
Integration of professionals / expert employees for the solution of a problem	*"Our client is often part of the team somehow. In one case, the sales director who said 'We are doing this five week project with my customer, so he will think that we are cool and will buy the project.' But the people who are in the innovation team for building prototypes and work with that customer are experts from the organisation, put together through our team. We have to search and find those people with the right skills that are keen on participating. It is hard to find these experts and they have to be good at what they are doing."* (HOL)
Integration of network positions and operational employees.	*"We recommend [to integrate] professionals that are not on top management level. Only in that case they can set time free and are free from politics. [...] We even recommend networking positions like corporate communication or marketing, who bring a broader perspective. The final selection is at the project manager of the organisation."* (ICO)
Integration of opinion leaders	*"Yes, we do integrate employees from other units, as far as the client allows us to. The selection of [internal] stakeholders is not objective, but is oriented towards important opinion leaders in the organisation. With new topics, firms do not want to cause a sensation in the organisation, that's why the group of participants is limited on purpose."* (FC)

3.2.1.2 Customer contact employees

The data from this study show that customer contact employees, as a special internal stakeholder group, are integrated in a passive or reactive mode in the idea screening phase when being observed or interviewed and in the testing/prototyping phase to give feedback on what has been developed. It is only in two of the twelve intermediaries that customer contact employees were mentioned stakeholder group that is mutually integrated as a resource for idea generation.

3.2.1.3 Senior management

Besides the presented internal stakeholders, a high management position is always integrated in service innovation, mostly for the reason that the commitment of managers is seen as a crucial factor for the success of a project.

> *"We always want to have a decision maker [on board]. If he/she is not in the core team, there will be presentations to provide an impression about the status of the project."* (DI)

3.2.2 External stakeholders

External stakeholder groups which are integrated in the aforementioned service innovation processes are predominantly customers and users, or sometimes experts and partners.

3.2.2.1 Customers and users

The passive and reactive integration of customers and users through observations and interviews is described as a basic and necessary step of the service innovation process. This process is predominantly implemented in the early, fuzzy stages of the innovation project, the idea screening stage.

> *"What we see is that the user is of really high value in the beginning of the innovation project. Users are essential in this phase and will always be observed or interviewed and asked to write a diary and much more."* (DTA2)

> *"First of all we start with observations and interviews and so it's in a more traditional way to catch the insights. And, for example for a hospital we gave we gave diaries to the elderly to capture their needs."* (WHD)

For the mutual integration of customers and users in the idea generation phase, the selection of the "right users" emerges as a critical issue. Interviewee WHD stated that

> *"a co-design workshop only works well, if you have the right people around the table [...] the right people are crucial, very negative people can ruin the whole workshop."* (WHD)

This is why intermediaries stress that they carefully select only motivated customers of the targeted customer group for mutual integration. But beyond finding and selecting the "right users", the present data shows that time constraints, willingness to participate and motivation of identified users and customers is a further challenge for their integration in the mode of mutual integration:

> *"The motivation of people to participate in a time consuming process with no financial incentives can be tough. They might be committed, but they have to have time and invest in the project, so they might quit their participation. [...]For co-creation, people have to be motivated, they have to be ready and there at the specific moments when different methods are applied to get feedback from these people. That's critical - people commit themselves easily. But whenever they realize that this costs more time that estimated, it is only 70% that shows up at the appointments. All the more when they realize that this is an investment they make and there is no incentive or other reward."* (OSI)

> *"The customer has to be handled with utmost care since you are very grateful for his/her participation."* (TCS)

As some of the intermediaries specialize in open und user innovation topics, the mutual integration of customers and users emerged as a strong topic within the interviews. Nevertheless, it can be seen that mutual integration of customers and users for the joint development of ideas is not always the true aim of mutual integration. The evaluation of ideas and concepts and the understanding of customer needs is a second, more important layer behind the joint creation of new ideas, as the in-depth analysis of the interviews reveals. This is exemplified in the following quotes:

> *"It's about understanding other people's perspectives not about finding a solution from these people."* (DTA1)

> *"We have to work with these people, we have to bring them together with their customers to check if the idea is good or bad. That is really our big question, not to develop some other additional idea."* (HOL)

Customer integration in the mode of mutual integration for service innovation is perceived as a challenging task for a part of the interviewed intermediaries. Even though their working methods would include mutual integration of customers and users, their client organizations do not always allow for this to happen; they are restrictive in providing resources such as time and budget or are reported to be sceptic about the processes and practices. Interviewees FC and DTA2 express this issue as follows:

> *"We try to implement customer orientation with our clients. But there is a huge inhibiting threshold to customer integration. [...] Even if we communicate that we would like to develop new solutions with the customers rather than on the drawing board, we face quite some scepticism and lack of understanding."* (FC)

> *"We have tried to integrate the customer more, but we could only realize an insights phase. We talk to them [customers] and interview them and so on, but when the project goes on... What we do is user testing in the end. Prototyping, testing is always implemented in the end. Yet, we would wish for having the external stakeholder, the customer in the whole process."* (DTA2)

As the latter quotes show further, the integration of customers and users for testing is well established and practiced in the reactive mode, in the majority of intermediaries in this empirical interview study.

3.2.2.2 Experts

External experts are identified and selected by the intermediary, to be a reactive resource in the research phase. Experts are mutually integrated for idea generation in few idea generation cases, to stock up the agencies' resources. Partners are reportedly integrated only in one case, for co-creation in the idea generation phase. The following statements from the interviews depict this practice and its challenges:

> *"I find experts extremely difficult. They have pretty preconceived opinions and have problems to integrate in teams, from our experience. It happens rarely that people who are so convinced of themselves find their way into teams. Often, these experts do not want to play along or are afraid of their status when being contradicted."* (DI)

> *"Sometimes we have external experts on board. For sustainability at the office, we had someone from a sustainability consulting."* (UID)

> *"We talk to experts like architects, franchise experts, in the present case, that are specialized on the design of such environments. For different questions, we define experts and ask for their opinion."* (OSI)

3.3 Discussion and conclusions

This exploratory interview study with service innovation intermediaries shows that, within the analysed processes, the strongest external stakeholder group emerged as customers and users - integrated passively and reactively in the early fuzzy stages of the innovation process and in the mode of mutual integration for idea generation. The main internal stakeholders for service innovation are found to be employees from inside the organisation, product managers, networking functions and volunteers, complemented by high management positions.

The fact that, in the given setting, the integration of customers is strongest in the research phase, as passive and reactive informants, affirms earlier findings by Schulteß et al. (2010) who showed that customer integration tends to occur chiefly in the very beginning and at the end of the innovation process. In contrast to the findings of Melton and Hartline (2010), the results of this empirical study amongst service innovation intermediaries show that customer integration is put into practice rather in a reactive and passive mode than in the mode of direct mutual integration. It is only during idea generation that customers are integrated mutually, in bi-directional and face-to-face communication (Gustafsson et al., 2012). Consistent with the importance of the early innovation process stages in service innovation literature (Carbonell et al., 2009), the passive and reactive stakeholder integration of customers and users emerges as a key process, to gain access to customer and user needs before idea generation. The analysis of interviews indicates that mutual customer integration is restricted by factors such as resource allocation (as suggested in an empirical research by Mention and Asikainen (2012), Schilling and Werr (2009), and Weber (2008) and scepticism about the needs and benefits of customer integration practices.

The findings of this interview study suggest that external expertise from experts is seldom integrated. If successfully integrated, external experts are a resource of information, coming from the intermediaries' network, not from the client's network. This result might depend on the research setting where the innovation intermediaries might or might not be engaged in the innovating organisations' collaboration with experts, suppliers or other partners. Perks et al. (2012) and Gottfridsson (2012) give evidence that service organisations do integrate partners and suppliers in service innovation processes. Stewart and Hyysalo (2008) present findings about the bridge building function of innovation intermediaries. Whereas intermediaries for service innovation, the source of information in this study, were integrated here, the integration of stakeholders such as partners, suppliers or experts showed to be limited in the observed setting.

In the context of service innovation, the focus of intermediaries could be seen in the provision of knowledge and services (as assumed at intermediaries DI, FC, DTA and OI). This impression from data analysis is supported by details at the intermediaries WHD and OI, where the interviewees express that experts such as architects or sustainability consultants are integrated as a support and complement for the intermediaries' resources. An alternative possible explanation for the underrepresentation of external expert integration might be that managers are aware of the fact that mutual integration for services innovation is a tough process: it is costly and timely and the methods used in innovation workshops *"need to push you until your brain hurts"* as one interviewee (DTA1) expressed it. It may be that a service innovation project manager might retract from burdening a business relationship with new and challenging task that can have unsecured dynamic and outcome.

From inside the organisation, managers have been verified as definite stakeholders as presented in the work of Smith and Fischbacher (2005). To prevent not-invented-here reactions, to keep internal stakeholders informed and to gain access to internal experts, the integration of employees from different units is mutual in most stages of the service innovation process. The empirical data strongly confirms the perception that internal stakeholders are integrated as experts with necessary knowledge for the innovation project during development (Schilling & Werr, 2009; Smith & Fischbacher, 2005; Nicolajsen & Scupola, 2011), especially in the case of intermediary HOL.

In the context of not-invented-here syndrome (Katz & Allen, 1982) within the organisation, literature suggests that the units innovating the service and the units delivering the service should be aligned (Payne et al., 2007). In the present setting, the integration of, for instance, Marketing or customer contact employees is mentioned in single instances. The bridging of the not-invented-here syndrome between the external innovation intermediary and the innovating organisation is a repeatedly stressed challenge in the interviews.

Still, in a few cases, the integration of customer contact employees such as sales or service was mentioned. For customer contact employees, the analysed data shows an intermediate level of mutual integration in the idea generation phase and of reactive integration in the early research phase idea screening. Even though stated only in a small number of cases, this finding on one side confirms the descriptions by

Gustafsson et al. (1999) and on the other side contradicts Melton and Hartline's (2010) and Smith and Fischbacher's (2005) findings, which present research results in which customer contact personnel remain a reactive resource at the very end of the innovation process, during full launch and promotion only.

Even though a number of findings give the impression to be influenced by the set-up of the research study, there are a number of general implications derived. Customer integration is implemented in a passive and reactive mode since mutual integration is perceived to be more risky and resource demanding. When implemented as mutual integration, the aim of integration is to derive the hidden needs behind developed solutions by the customers, rather than the utilisation of the solutions themselves. Internal stakeholders are integrated mutually, not only for information and engagement in the innovation project, but also to learn about new innovation tools and methods. All in all, mutual integration in practice shows to be most prominent in the idea generation stage.

It remains a limitation of this study that intermediaries, as the object of research, cannot reflect upon all organizational stakeholder integration activities throughout the innovation process of the clients, since they might only participate in certain aspects of a clients' service innovation project. Furthermore, intermediaries themselves are an external stakeholder group integrated in service innovation projects; accordingly they cannot discuss the reasons why intermediaries as external stakeholders are getting integrated by their clients. Overall, the external stakeholder group "intermediaries" and their roles in service innovation processes shows to be unsatisfactorily discussed in service innovation research. Intermediaries, and other suppliers in service innovation, should be in focus of future studies in service innovation, profiting from existing scholarly research in i.e. technology management (see for example Bessant and Rush, 1995).

In the next step, the service innovation processes of those organisations which put stakeholder integration into practice shall be examined. Second, the study does not imply that all stakeholders are integrated in several stages of one project over time. More in-depth insights into the practice of stakeholder integration regarding stakeholder groups such as customer contact employees and partners, IT suppliers and further external groups are still needed. More qualitative research, for instance case study research, is required to explore stakeholder integration practices and provide insights into stakeholder integration strategies.

4 Summary and conclusion

The literature review and the interview study presented in Part IV gave a broad overview on stakeholder integration from an outside perspective. The knowledge regarding the different stakeholder groups from empirical research in service innovation presented the benefits, challenges and individual characteristics for the integration of different stakeholder groups. Aiming to shed light on which stakeholders are integrated in which mode, and in which stage of the innovation process, it has been shown that despite the theoretically and experimentally proven benefits of mutual stakeholder integration, especially with customers and users, the picture of stakeholder integration in practice remains difficult to pin down. Stakeholder integration is stressed in the early stages of service innovation, to gain access to customer needs and to understand their behaviour. The integration of management and responsible internal stakeholders is emphasised throughout the innovation process as crucial for the success of service innovation. In the context of service innovation, when supported through intermediaries, their integration is required to avoid the not-invented-here syndrome.

The evidence, derived mostly from service industries contexts indicates that stakeholder integration for service innovation is challenged by the availability of resources. Even though, for instance, customer contact employees are regarded as a valuable stakeholder group for service innovation, their integration seems to be scarce in the organisational practice of service providers. The availability of resources was found to be an overall critical factor for internal stakeholder integration, as shown in the interview study.

The review of literature showed that research studies on stakeholders in service innovation mostly analyse stakeholder integration in isolation from other stakeholders of the service system. Few recent studies approach stakeholder integration from a holistic service system perspective. The findings in the interview study indicate that external stakeholder integration is a process interdependent with internal stakeholder integration. Yet the research work cannot provide a clear picture all over the service innovation process as intermediaries are not necessary accompanying an innovation project from the fuzzy front end of innovation to the implementation of new services.

Part V

The management perspective on stakeholder integration in service innovation – a reactively engaged exploration of case studies

After a look on stakeholder integration in service innovation from an outside perspective, with the analysis of existing empirical research and an interview study with innovation intermediaries, the next step of this thesis takes up the need to explore the organisational practice of stakeholder integration as perceived by responsible innovation managers. This chapter will investigate how stakeholder integration in service innovation is implemented in practice. Two case studies are conducted: a first in-depth case study on a service innovation project for hybrid healthcare solution will explore service innovation as a process with interfaces to products, in a Germany-based international manufacturing company. The second, multiple, case study will re-apply the research design and enrich the findings from the first case study with insights on stakeholder integration in service innovation at IT and manufacturing companies. After a short introduction, this chapter will present both case study approaches in detail. Overall findings will be synthesised and conclusions for this part of the thesis will be drawn, in chapter 4.

The management perspective on stakeholder integration in service innovation - a reactively engaged exploration of case studies

How is stakeholder integration in service innovation seen from the management perspective, in the context of manufacturing and IT companies?

Healthcare solutions development in a manufacturing context - an in-depth case study	Service innovation in medium-sized organisations in manufacturing and IT - a multiple case study

Figure 12: Part V - a reactive exploration of case studies

1 Stakeholder integration in service innovation from a management perspective

Taking up the results from the literature review and the interview study, the next section of this thesis aims to gain a deeper understanding of stakeholder integration in service innovation in its naturally occurring context. The first part of this thesis with a literature review on stakeholder integration in service innovation and the interview study builds a foundation of knowledge on stakeholders in service innovation. A variety of potential possibilities and benefits from stakeholder integration have been brought up in this "look from outside" on stakeholder integration in service innovation. Yet, it is shown that there are only few empirical studies that consider and analyse service innovation from a service system view, including necessary internal and external stakeholder groups at once. Previous work by Smith and Fischbacher (2005), Perks et al. (2012) and Schleimer and Schulmann (2011) provides a number of first case studies on stakeholder integration in a service system understanding of multiple stakeholders, in service industries (e.g. insurance or financial services).

From these first studies, it can be understood that services, as provided to customers, are an amalgam of stakeholder interests, expressed within a series of relationships and bargaining processes, filtered through permanent or temporary coordinating structures. (Smith & Fischbacher, 2005). It is seen as the rather challenging job of a service innovation project manager to decide about the right resources and stakeholders from inside and outside the organization, and to manage the multiple interdependencies and stakeholder interests as Smith and Fischbacher (2005) put forward. Thereby, service innovation (as the joint formation of a value proposition) is expected to reflect even conflicting interests amongst resource integrating actors (Kowalkowski, Persson Ridell et al., 2012). As a consequence, the management of stakeholder integration is described as a balancing act for project management. Gottfridsson (2012) considers the need to balance between informality and creativity on one side and the need for structure and coordination on the other side. Perks and Riihela (2004) discuss the balance of resource allocation as the management of external stakeholder integration is taking away resources from internal functional stakeholders. Thereby, it is suggested that cognitive, social and behavioural skills to deal with the complexities of stakeholder integration are required in service innovation management (Smith & Fischbacher, 2005). This includes the competencies required for the acquisition and conversion of stakeholder knowledge as well as the practice of communicating the service innovation, its benefits and requirements amongst relevant stakeholders (Leiponen, 2012; Mention & Asikainen, 2012; Perks & Riihela, 2004). The findings show the need to understand the integration practice of different internal and external stakeholders in service innovation (Ettlie & Rosenthal, 2011; Rusanen et al., 2014) and the different assigned or taken roles of stakeholders in interdependent multi-dimensional systems (Tossavainen, 2013; Kindström et al., 2013), from a management perspective.

In the context of service innovation in service systems, special emphasis is put on the lack of an in-depth understanding of service innovation and stakeholder integration practices in the context of business services and other industries than core service industries (see e.g. Mele, 2009; Lempinen & Rajala, 2014; Carlborg et al., 2013). Service innovation in industries such as engineering, manufacturing or IT is receiving attention as subject of interest in recent research (see e.g. Mathieu 2001; Raddats & Kowalkowski, 2014; Kowalkowski, Kindström & Brehmer, 2011)[45]. In these domains service innovation often happens ad-hoc without a formal procedure in parallel to product innovation. Since service innovation in organisations in e.g. a manufacturing context coheres not only with other offered services, but at the same time has to be aligned with products (Carlborg et al., 2013), there is a strong demand for deep knowledge of customer processes and the innovation managements' interaction with sales personnel. In this context, the complexity in information handling and communication is emphasised (Gremyr, Löfberg, & Witell, 2010; Martin & Horne, 1993).

Still, in product-oriented organisations, the interfaces and networks for service innovation are expected to be a) more crucial since product and services are related to each other or are even parts of a combined product-service bundle, and b) more evident from the trackable interfaces. This allows the identification and collection of

---

[45] Beyond these examples, service innovation in product-oriented firms, especially in the context of manufacturing is highly discussed in recent research. Most prominent is probably the topic field of servitization (Baines & Lightfoot, 2014; Brax, 2005; Lightfoot & Gebauer, 2011), hybrid offerings (Ulaga & Reinartz, 2011; Velamuri, Bansemir, Neyer, & Möslein, 2013) or service infusion (Gebauer, Gustafsson, & Witell, 2011; Oliva & Kallenberg, 2003; Ostrom et al., 2010), describing the step-by-step shift from product sellers to solution providers in the manufacturing industry (Kowalkowski, Kindström, Alejandro, Brege, & Biggemann, 2012; Raddats & Kowalkowski, 2014). In the context of this thesis, service innovation in product-oriented firms is discussed without the integration of the strategically steered shift of the whole organisation towards becoming a services or service-bundle provider.

data on stakeholder integration in service innovation in an easier accessible and more structured way. Taking up these findings and propositions of research in the context of service innovation in service systems, this next part aims for a better understanding of stakeholder integration for service innovation. By taking a management perspective, current stakeholder integration practice is approached to create a real-life context understanding of integrated stakeholders. The study aims to depict the chosen modes and the reasoning behind the allocation of stakeholder integration throughout the stages of the service innovation process. As described, the context of organisations that are not purely service providers is advised as a field of research, since this setting offers a maximum of researchable interfaces in complex service system.

As explained in the presentation of the research design of this thesis' Part II, the exploration of a rather new research field, aiming to access deep insights about complex processes and interactions of stakeholders in service systems, is best supported by an open qualitative research approach such as case studies. They offer the possibility to grab the characteristics of real-life events and processes (Miles et al., 2013; Flick, 2014; Yin, 2014). Swanborn (2010) and Yin (2014) put forward that case study research should be implemented with a pilot study first, to be followed by several other multiple case studies. Such repetition of case analysis broadens the boundaries of the field and enables to test the descriptions and explanations of earlier cases. This is why the exploration of stakeholder integration, with the questions "in which mode and at which stage of the service innovation process is stakeholder integration realised in practice", is approached first by an in-depth case study in healthcare solutions development, and second, a multiple case study, to confirm, disconfirm, refine and to extend first findings (Eisenhardt, 1989).

2 Healthcare solutions development in a manufacturing context – an in-depth case study[46]

The review of research on stakeholder integration in service innovation has shown that service innovation is to be understood as a multi-dimensional process including a variety of internal and external stakeholders. It can also be extrapolated from theoretical and empirical work that the mode of stakeholder integration affects the outcome of stakeholder integration and will lead to different results and effects. This empirical research investigates and exemplifies stakeholder integration from an organisational management perspective on a micro level. To identify and understand, at which stage of the innovation process stakeholder integration is implemented, and in which mode, this study is set up to explore the practice of service innovation at a product-oriented engineering organisation.

2.1 Research approach – in-depth case study

As in-depth knowledge on service innovation practices is best to be achieved by an open approach (Swanborn, 2010), an explorative research design is recommended for the present research question. To gain a thorough understanding of innovation practice, a single case study with the analysis of one service innovation project has been chosen.

The case study approach allows researchers to discover the world as it is seen by the participants in the system (Swanborn, 2010). For the case selection, a service provider had to be found which showed the ability to interact intensively and the willingness to reveal even sensitive data. Offering the possibility to access an interesting case and building upon a high level of trust and interest in the research topic, the case of the firm ECH, a German provider of engineering and electronics solutions, has been approached through the network of the researcher. Whilst other companies struggled with the intensity and openness required by the case study approach, the selected organisational unit agreed to cooperate. They agreed to provide the necessary deep insights into service innovation processes, alongside access to longitudinal data from a soon-to-be implemented healthcare innovation

[46] An earlier version of this research study has been presented at Euram 2014 in Valencia, Spain (Jonas et al., 2014a). An adopted version of this article is published in the International Journal of Technology Management (Jonas & Roth, 2017). See Annex A for more information.

project, from the first idea to its current status. The selected case is a product-centric firm in a matrix organisation, with multi-dimensional interfaces. These prerequisites and the dynamic environment of IT service development make the selected case a rich and interesting case for observation. The project to be analysed in this case study is a service innovation for remote services to be offered as a product-service bundle.

2.1.1 Data collection

The case study is based on a variety of primary and secondary data. The collected primary data consists of a series of interviews, telephone conversations, formal and informal meetings. Secondary data was provided by interviewees, in form of internal and public presentations, documentation of the service innovation process map and an Excel table of stakeholders with detailing comments. Additionally, the notes of the interviewees made during the interview have been collected. Together with research protocols, they served as supportive material during the data analysis. This usage of a variety of sources and documents in addition to interviews is of importance to verify interviews, to confirm information and to find inferences, according to Creswell (2012) and Yin (2014).

Interviews are seen as the primary source of rich data for case studies (Yin, 2014; Eisenhardt & Graebner, 2007). In this case study, ten interviews and meetings with members of the organisation have been conducted. The interview durations were from 30 minutes up to more than two hours. All interviews followed a semi-structured interview guideline. The longer interview sessions were strongly characterized by dialogue elements, to enhance openness in answers and to gain access to narratives, in favour of a "question and answer" format of interviewing.

The manager of the service innovation project was given a strong role in data collection to better understand stakeholder integration practice, since the "*managers' beliefs are put into practice*" (Edvardsson et al., 2013; p.26). Edvardsson et al. (2013) suggest that the active enabler of and decision maker on stakeholder integration can provide information to generate a deep understanding of the studied phenomenon. A number of four interview meetings with the project manager allowed a step-by-step data collection and analysis. This sequential approach provided the possibility to address open questions ongoing, to gain in-depth knowledge and at the same time to secure the researchers' right understanding of processes, organisational settings and routines.

The data collection took place during summer 2013, simultaneously from three different angles, to capture, contrast and compare the views of personnel from the service innovation project, complemented by the views of related stakeholder groups of the firm (Gann & Salter, 2000). First, the manager of the remote service innovation project was interviewed in repeated sequences, as a central point of the matrix setting of the innovation project. The few weeks' time which passed between each of the encounters as well as parallel E-mail and telephone meetings allowed constant contact and feedback loops. Second, the team of researchers was able to gain access to different interview partners through parallel reputation sampling and snowballing, enriching the case with different or independent viewpoints and stories (Swanborn, 2010). Third, the internal innovation management unit of the company was approached as an internal intermediary to provide information about the standard procedures of innovation projects in the organisation. Table 6 provides an overview of the conducted interviews and protocolled meetings conducted for this case study.

Table 6: Data collection at ECH - overview on interviews and meetings protocolled

Interviews		
#	**Interviewee**	**Duration**
1 & 2	Product Manager New Services (PM)	1 hr 30min and 2 hrs;
3	Project Manager Healthcare (PMH)	1 hr 10 min
4	Head of Business Development (HBD)	33 min
5	Healthcare Manager (HM)	1 hr 10 min
6	Quality Manager (QM)	1 hr 20 min
Protocolled meetings		
7 & 8	Product Manager New Services (PM)	about 1 hr 30 min each (formal and informal)
9	Innovation Management (IM)	1 hr 30 min
10	Product Manager external unit (PME)	1 hr 15 min

2.1.2 Data analysis

The data analysis pursued an inductive analysis of interview transcripts, in a first step, as suggested by Miles et al. (2013). All protocols and further secondary data were put together and notes scanned. All interviews were audio-recorded and transcribed verbatim to facilitate the analysis. Data was read carefully several times and structured according to inductively derived, descriptive codes such as "integrated stakeholders", "stage of the innovation process", "mode of integration" and "reason why". This was enabled through a sequential data analysis as suggested by King and Horrocks (2010). In addition to these inductively developed codes, deductive codes were developed in a second round of analysis to allow researchers to benefit from the open exploratory research approach. This included e.g. the codes "informal integration" and "indirect integration" (Miles et al., 2013).

A detailed analysis of the empirical data was conducted for each of the key themes, after the coding was finalised. To gain a full overview on stakeholder integration, all identified stakeholders, the modes of integration and the stages for stakeholder integration were first considered as independent angles for analysis, and only after that they were these combined according to the co-occurrence of the codes "stakeholder group", "stage of the innovation process" and "mode of integration". This co-occurrence analysis, together with another content analysis of the grouped data, served as the basis for Table 8 and Table 9. To illustrate the findings and to make the underlying data material transparent, quotes from the sequential analysis have been selected in order to illustrate the findings. This overarching analysis of all the data allowed a holistic picture of stakeholder integration practices and led to the creation of fourteen representative instances for internal and external stakeholder integration.

To ensure the credibility of data analysis, respondent feedback was taken in (Guba & Lincoln, 1994); early versions of the research findings and a draft of the research report were validated by the project manager (PM). The triangulation of data sources, as well as the methodological triangulation for data collection and comparison such as official documents, interviews, the transcriptions and an additional written stakeholder integration overview, verifies and confirms propositions in the interviews (Creswell, 2012; Yin, 2014) and enhances the validity of the case study (King & Horrocks, 2010).

2.1.3 The case organisation and the case "remote services for healthcare solutions"

The case company, a German provider of engineering and electronics solutions, offers remote services for clinical appliances, e.g. X-rays and computer tomographs with approximately 50,000 employees worldwide. The service solutions offered in the context of the medical appliances consist of infrastructure, remote monitoring and remote maintenance and repair. The potential of the newly implemented remote service system, as well as the pressure derived from the progress of technology, served as triggers to create new value added services in the field of health care.

2.1.3.1 The service innovation process of the healthcare services unit

At the case organisation, through service innovation and the development of holistic solutions was gaining strategic importance for differentiation from competitors. Still, the service innovation process reflects the traditional product orientation of the organisation: it is managed by a highly standardized service engineering process. The stages of this service engineering process are shown in Figure 13.

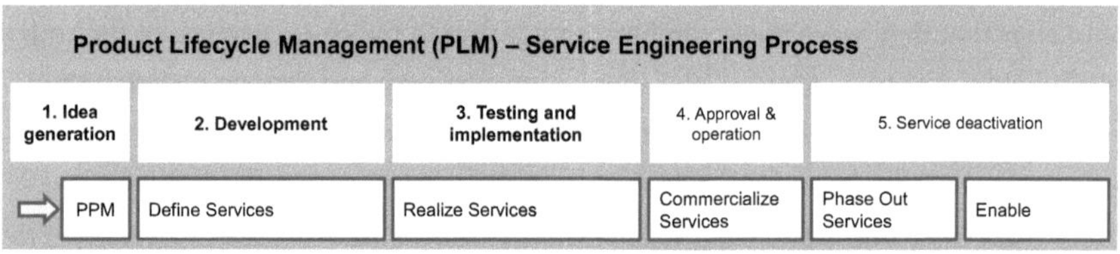

Figure 13: The service engineering process at the case company (adapted from case material)

This case study on a remote service innovation project primarily deals with the first three stages: (1) "PMM" - Product Portfolio Management, for finding new ideas (Idea generation), (2) "Define service" (development) and (3) "Realize services" (testing and implementation) (see Figure 13). At the time of the data collection for this case study, the observed service innovation project was just about to enter its implementation stage, at the end of the third phase ("realize services").

2.1.3.2 The team of the service innovation project

The case organisation is a matrix organisation working with matrix project management. After a project idea is created and has been elaborated up to a degree that meets specific requirements, the project manager for the case project is responsible for the establishment and management of a project team consisting of "all required functions". To accomplish this, and all the tasks along the upcoming service innovation process, the project manager receives consultancy from one business and one quality management partner. After an initiative for a service innovation has been defined and approved as a project, the core team is assembled as a matrix project team, from stage 2 of the innovation process onwards (see Figure 14).

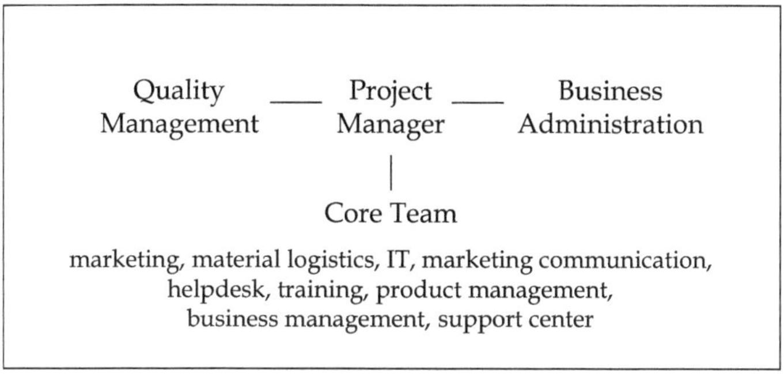

Figure 14: The matrix project team set-up from stage 2 onwards

The necessary resources to accomplish the innovation tasks of the project are derived from so called "use cases". They have been developed during the project initiation, in the idea generation phase (PM, QM). The resources from the respective units are allocated to the project team as described by the interviewee PM:

> *"The allocation of team members is issued by the team leader. You go there and say 'I have this and this task, could you please give me a contact person' and then you get 'someone'."* (PM)

The required team members are assigned to the project depending on resource availability, experience and work focus, from specialized departments (e.g. IT, product management, training and marketing), one after the other, as the project is built up.

2.1.3.3 Idea screening and idea generation outside the service engineering process

The initiative to start an idea generation panel for future innovation projects was established due to the need within the organisation to develop new services for the existing hard- and software infrastructure for remote services in healthcare. The project manager, who had joined the organisation not long before the research project began, needed to start an innovation process from the very beginning, with new ideas. In the established process of the organisation, new ideas are continuously developed through an internal suggestion scheme, through new patents and inventions or through new business ideas. But these practices could not provide satisfying input for the innovation task of the project manager at that particular moment. This is why an individual idea generation process was required (PM; QM). Whilst the stage gate process of the case organisation is clearly regulating tasks and stakeholders for every step of a service innovation project, the project manager found that there were no detailed guidelines for the phase of idea generation.

> *"The process description is so detailed, but ironically the ideation process is or was not depicted at all. [...] A black box."* (PM)

2.2 Findings

The data collection with the involved core project team and further service innovation responsible employees gave evidence on the service innovation process and the associated stakeholder integration. The narratives from the interviews for this case study provided evidence for manifold stakeholder integration practices. From the analysis of the reported stakeholder integration instances, the modes of stakeholder integration throughout the observed three stages of the service innovation process will now be presented in detail. First, to give a broad overview, the range of integrated stakeholders will be depicted, followed by a presentation of identified stakeholder integration instances along the stages of the innovation process.

2.2.1 Overview of integrated stakeholders

From the data analysis, eleven different types of integrated stakeholders from within and outside the organisation were identified (see Table 7): Internal colleagues, senior management, external colleagues, support functions, country representatives, customer contact employees and internal consultants are internal stakeholders of this service innovation project. External stakeholders identified are customers, pilot customers, suppliers and the private network of the project manager.

Table 7: Identified stakeholders in the innovation project

Internal Stakeholders	
Internal colleagues	functional departments with existing regular interfaces with the project manager
Senior management	steering board and project decision board members that are minimum two steps higher in the hierarchical structure than project manager
External colleagues	employees of the organisation working in other business fields
Support functions	specialized departments, e.g. legal, data protection, internal reporting and business units of hardware
Country representatives	direct correspondents in the countries, responsible for the local service delivery and implementation
Customer contact employees	service engineers in the local branches
Internal consulting	department for innovation and technology, research and consulting
External Stakeholders	
Customers and users	physicians, IT administration, medical technicians and hospital managers, working with the technical appliances in a clinic
Pilot customers	clients, hand-selected by the country organisations because of their good relationship with the case company
Suppliers	IT, legal and marketing agencies; specialists and additional resources assigned via the specialised units of the organisation
Private network	friends of the project manager

2.2.2 Incidents of stakeholder integration

The presented stakeholders were integrated throughout the observed stages "idea generation", "development" and "testing" (a part of the stage 3 "Testing and implementation" as shown in Figure 13). From the present data, a variety of stakeholder integration incidents[47] could be derived. Table 8 provides an overview of the identified instances for stakeholder integration, their mode and motivations, in sequential order along the three analysed innovation process stages.

[47] In Poole, van de Ven, Dooley, & Holmes (2000) an incident is defined as *"a major recurrent activity"* (Poole et al., 2000, p. 133). In the context of this case study, incidents are defined as coarse-grained and refer to typical repeated or special actions of stakeholder integration.

Table 8: Overview of instances for stakeholder integration throughout the service innovation projects' stages

	Stakeholder	Mode of integration	Stage	Reason why
1	Internal consulting	pro-active initiative and mutual: joint workshop preparation and implementation, consulting	idea generation	implementation and usage of internally developed tools for idea generation; motivation of internal colleagues to participate via participation of the "star guest" from internal consulting
2	Internal colleagues	mutual: workshops, ICTs, in three stages	idea generation	generate ideas, integrate them into innovation processes, joint decision making
3	Senior management	mutual: workshops, ICTs, in three stages	idea generation	generate ideas, integrate them into innovation processes, joint decision making
4	Country representatives	mutual: telephone conferences	idea generation	integration into processes
5	External colleagues	mutual: workshops, ICTs, in three stages	idea generation	access to expertise from other organizational units
6	Country representatives	reactive: question & answer and discussions	idea generation	arrangement of customer visits
7	Private network	reactive: question & answer; informal	idea generation	consulting and arrangement of customer visits
8	Customers & users	passive and reactive: personal visits, interviews, group discussions, observations	idea generation	"step into the customer's shoes": understand pain points; understand situation of usage and receive input from users
9	Suppliers	reactive and mutual: telephone calls, personal meetings	development	direct problem solving for work packages of the specialized departments
10	Selected customers	reactive: question & answer	development	feedback on service innovation activities
11	Support functions	reactive: question & answer	development	problem-solving and advice for specific requests, get interfaces on board
12	Country representatives	reactive: question & answer and discussions	testing	identification of suitable customers for piloting and according arrangement
13	Pilot customers	reactive: question & answer and discussions	testing	trial of new products in beta phase
14	Country representatives	reactive: sales meetings, informal conversations	ongoing	complaints, wishes and customer demands are collected and called up in person

From these empirically identified instances, it can be derived that internal stakeholders are integrated in the mode "mutual integration" in the idea generation phase and in the mode "reactive integration" during development and testing. Special attention has to be paid to the integration of senior management, showing the characteristics of mutual integration even during development. Reactive integration is realized with internal stakeholders during development and testing.

The most prominent external stakeholder group in this multiple case study is "customers". Selected customers are integrated reactively during idea generation and development. The reactive integration of pilot customers is observed during testing. Customers are integrated directly and indirectly and are all carefully pre-selected by the country representatives, with the exception of specific customers in the idea generation phase. Suppliers are a second external stakeholder group that integrated in a reactive way as well as in form of mutual integration during development. An overview on the modes of stakeholder integration on an aggregated level is provided in Table 9. Going into detail, the practices of mutual integration and reactive integration will be presented forth following.

Table 9: The modes of stakeholder integration along the stages of the innovation process

Idea generation	Development	Testing
Mutual integration with senior management	**Mutual and reactive** integration of senior management	
Mutual and reactive integration of relevant units from the organisation	**Reactive integration** of relevant units from the organisation	**Reactive integration** of relevant units from the organisation
Passive and reactive integration of customers	**Reactive integration** of customers **Mutual and reactive** integration of suppliers	**Reactive integration** of customers

2.2.3 Mutual integration of stakeholders

Mutual integration is realized with different members of the organisation. In particular, the idea generation workshops with close and external colleagues, management, and specialized functions are characterized by true mutual integration.

Mutual integration is further implemented in the development phase with the internal stakeholder group "senior management" for consulting.

2.2.3.1 Mutual integration of members of the organisation during idea generation

The first incidents of internal stakeholder integration (1-5), as shown in Table 8, are part of the joint idea generation initiative which took place as the first step of the service innovation project. To come up with new ideas for the given field of innovation and to create awareness of the initiative, the project manager started internal joint idea generation activities with members from the organisation. The integration of these stakeholders was realized in three outbound waves, supported by the internal consulting team: from a safe space with close and local colleagues of the project manager, outwards to close units and groups around the project team (e.g. marketing, product management and steering board) and then further to country representatives (see Figure 15).

The colleagues of the local health care service unit were the first to test the methods for idea generation in workshops, which were established especially for this purpose. The next round of mutual integration with units and groups around the project managers' team was implemented through utilizing and extending the established Jour Fixe meetings. Last, the joint idea generation with the country representatives was realized in telephone conferences.

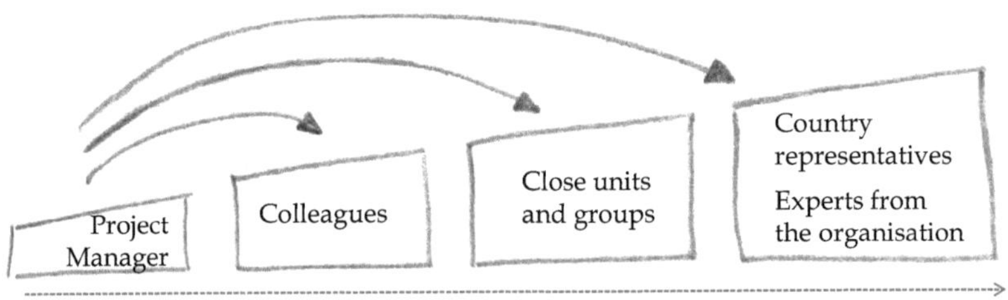

Figure 15: Mutual integration of organisational members in three outward waves for idea generation

In the second round the project manager aimed to integrate experts from other units of the organisation through word-of-mouth in different communities. This procedure was successful for the integration of two external experts, even though the approach was perceived as "a bit risky and naive" retrospectively. One invited expert reacted in an angry manner and "*showed this way that he was not suitable as a participant*" (PM).

The integration of organisational members was implemented in the form of workshops for joint idea generation, trend analyses and discussions, in personal interaction or via a telephone conference. The internal consulting unit provided the tools used, amongst others the business model canvas and an innovation scorecard. To evaluate the generated ideas and user stories, online collaboration tools like sharepoint and surveymonkey were implemented. This way, about 50 internal stakeholders were integrated for three times in a gradual, Delphi method style approach. Whilst the first rounds of joint idea generation workshops was perceived as successful by the project manager, the idea generation with the country representatives via telephone did not work well; nor did the evaluation and discussion of ideas through online collaboration tools lead to a sufficient amount of given feedback. The internal stakeholders integrated in all these mutual integration activities did participate voluntarily to support the service innovation project, taking their time off from other tasks:

> *"Here, you don't have any resource commitment. Their support is based on best effort or they are just nice with you and they support you. [...] in the analysis phase... you can ask, and if you are lucky, they will answer. But they can also say I'm not interested in that."* (QM)

To motivate the participants and to foster the curiosity of internal stakeholders, a "star guest" from the internal consulting department was invited. This "goodie" as well as an open innovation culture and the positive attitude of the internal stakeholders moderated the success of the initiative, according to the perception of the project manager.

2.2.3.2 Mutual integration of senior management during development

Next, the mode mutual integration was identified during the stage "development" with senior management, represented by the so called "steering board". The steering board is a group of three senior managers of the same hierarchy level, configured by the project manager, with the help of his supervisor and the quality manager. In this case, the steering board was composed of the process owner for healthcare services, the process owner for marketing and the process owner for material logistics.

> *"The steering board has to be composed by relevant people where the business will take place."* (QM)

> *"The members depend on the project – to have your bosses' boss seems just consequential, but is not defined somewhere. [...] I went to those people and asked them. But it can be predetermined sometimes, there is no rule for that."* (PM)

The steering board is perceived as an advisory group which supports and coaches the project manager, when approached by the project manager. The steering board is integrated throughout the service innovation process, before milestone meetings, but even in critical situations, in a reactive mode and in the mode of mutual integration. Their advice is utilized e.g. as a filter before important decision board meetings. Such steering board meeting are, amongst others, held as a dress rehearsal before milestone presentations where they give feedback and recommendations for improvements.

> *"But sometimes this is irritating because these misters have different tastes. And many things are a matter of taste... It is mostly about coaching."* (PM)

Further, the steering board, high managers, have their teams and networks behind them. They are willing to support the project manager with recommendations whom to ask for details, how to solve problems, when to connect the service innovation project with other projects and the like: *"...if you put that guy there, it's simple – he will take care."* (QM)

2.2.3.3 Mutual integration of suppliers during development

Suppliers are the only external stakeholder group integrated into the service innovation process in the mode of mutual integration. In general, the specialized departments of the core project team coordinate tasks with suppliers, according to organisational procurement rules. The project manager and his team do usually not interact with suppliers, and would integrate suppliers only reactively. Still, for the specific project in this case study, direct interaction with suppliers as mutual integration was reported as an exception. Misunderstandings with the marketing department and their supplier, a marketing communication agency, led to the need to solve acute problems. To develop possible solutions, workshops in the mode of mutual integration were initiated.

> *"Our marketing communication department is only a coordinator of suppliers, they don't do anything by themselves. So I thought I would save some time by working with an agency but right now, it looks like I have to invest more time. Maybe, but I still have hope that they will find the twist... but I need them."* (PM)

From this quote by the project manager, it can be understood that mutual integration of suppliers is happening, but it is neither foreseen in the service innovation process nor a desired interface for mutual integration.

2.2.4 Reactive integration of stakeholders

The data analysis shows that stakeholder integration does predominantly happen in a reactive way. Customer integration was found to be an organisational practice in a reactive mode, as well as the integration of different internal stakeholders. In the next paragraphs, the details for reactive stakeholder integration will be presented, detailing findings for internal stakeholders first, for customer integration afterwards.

2.2.4.1 Reactive integration of internal stakeholders

Internal stakeholders integrated in a reactive way are: internal consulting during idea generation, support functions during development, country representatives during idea generation and testing, and customer contact employees throughout the service innovation process. The stakeholder integration for these groups is presented just in this order, according to their strongest presence in the innovation process.

Reactive integration of internal consulting

Internal consulting was the first internal stakeholder group to be integrated in a reactive way. As already mentioned, they provided the tools for the internal idea generation sessions and accompanied the process of idea generation. The reactive integration started because of an internal word-of-mouth process: after the project manager had started a workshop using the business model canvas, the internal consulting team heard of the initiative and offered to support the project manager with internally developed tools. Internal consulting was only integrated due to this active approach of the consulting team, and the fact that no additional internal costs occurred[48]. As of today, the project manager would not integrate them again, since he received training in the tools and would not invest budget in their internal service. Overall, the support was evaluated positively by the project manager.

Reactive integration of support functions and global units

[48] The internal consulting service normally comes with internal billing, as interviewees PM and IM report. An exception was made for this project, presumably for internal marketing of the consulting service.

During service development, support functions such as different specialized departments of the organisation were approached by the core innovation team: Examples of support functions are legal advice, data protection, internal reporting, and related business units. They were activated as reactive stakeholders to solve specific questions, to create an understanding of the new service or to position the service offering in the product portfolio. The integration happens for the most part via internal communication (E-Mail/telephone conversations) and is characterized strongly by a mode of "getting business done."

Reactive integration of country representatives and customer contact employees

Since the project manager and the core innovation team have no contact with customers in their regular work processes, the reactive integration of country representatives and customer contact employees was seen as necessary to gain access to customers' perceptions of the offered remote services. In the idea generation phase, the local country representatives have been integrated to establish contact and recommend customers for the participation in the customer visits. For the majority of customer visits, the selection of customers and the arrangement of the appointments were accomplished by the respective country organisations.

Whilst the customer visits by the project manager were seen as an extraordinary approach to find out about the needs of the customer, the "usual approach" would have been the indirect reactive integration through the local service contact employees:

> *"The first way is to contact them [the customers] directly. That means we call them, sit down with them and analyse them. And the second thing is, we use what we have placed out there: regional units, the corresponding markets or countries responsible for their business. So these guys are the ones who have to tell us the end customer requirements. [..] That is wise because they have to translate more or less - and this is not the language - their requirements into a common language technically speaking."* (QM)

The collection of requirements and customer feedback is in the regular cases implemented through the technicians and the projects' service engineers as so called "customer advocates" during the installation of a new product, service delivery or in maintenance situations (HM, PMH). The customer contact employees and the local country representatives are the stakeholders who continuously collect and forward customer needs. Whereas customer information is mainly forwarded within the organisation, direct reactive integration of customer contact employees is not frequently practices. A typical incidence by which customer contact employees communicate and discuss the experiences and customer requirements with the service innovation managers are training sessions:

> "*mainly at the end of training, we are discussing with the service engineers about problems and ideas on how to improve things.*" (HM)

This representative incident (incident 10 in Table 8) describes the forwarding of experiences with customers for future service innovation from customer contact employees to the core innovation team. This is not a formalized process in the service innovation process, but a recommended informal practice in the case organisation. The project manager of our case study did not discuss this practice during interviews, but the quality manager and other health care managers reported on this practice.

The reactive integration of country representatives during the innovation process stage "testing" is yet determined by the service innovation process. Just as in the idea generation stage, the country representatives are approached to select customers for piloting and arrange the testing of the new service:

> "*When you do a pilot in the countries, you discuss with the country organisation and tell them 'look we have a new service and would like to evaluate it in your country. Are you willing to do so? Do you have customers we can select in your country which would be interested in participating in testing our new service' [...] They are then drilling down and involving the country business manager.*" (PMH)

2.2.4.2 Reactive integration of external stakeholders

The integration of externals stakeholders in a reactive mode was a topic emerging as a strong issue during the case study. To establish contact with customers in the German market, the private network was integrated in a reactive way during idea generation. Customer integration in a reactive mode was observed during all the three stages of the innovation process observed in this case study. The instances for reactive customer integration will be described and presented according to the order of the innovation process.

Reactive integration of the private network

As described above, the customer visits in the selected countries have been enabled by country representatives as connectors to suitable customers. For the German market, this pattern of customer selection through the country representatives was, unconventionally, replaced by the integration of users identified through the private network of the project manager:

> *"I called some friends of mine who studied medicine and established contact myself – because I did not want to go through such a long process or because I wanted to avoid the filter of our sales organisation that provides happy customers only. The same ones as usual..."* (PM)

To gain access to customers and users that are not close and content with the service provider, the project manager chose an unofficial method of customer integration. The private network of the project manager was used as a subsidiary for the country organisations and enabled visits to customers and users who were not pre-selected by the responsible organisational unit.

2.2.4.3 Reactive integration of customers

Coming to the realization of reactive stakeholder integration with customers, the findings show formal and informal implementation throughout the observed service innovation process stages. In different intensities, project management, customer contact employees and specialized departments interact by customers to find out about their problems, needs and routines. This is accomplished i.e. with the customer visits within the so called "stepping into the customers' shoes" programme in the idea generation phase. Here, customers and users were reactively integrated to a certain degree of active personal engagement and for the evaluation of ideas, amongst others.

Reactive integration of customers during idea generation

The programme "stepping into the customers' shoes" ran parallel to the presented internal idea generation activities to get to know the customers, to understand their routines and to receive feedback on generated ideas. For this reactive integration of customers, the project manager selected six countries for personal visits, according to the criteria "piloting partner", "strongest revenue", and "general openness to new things". A team of the project manager and the local country representatives conducted interviews and group discussions with customers and users such as physicians, medical technicians, hospital managers and IT administrators.

Additionally they conducted observations of "a live in the day" at clinics in Germany, Switzerland, Sweden, USA, Canada and Japan. Project manager PM describes this experience:

> *"The greatest example was at a clinic where I sat together with the CFO, the head of medical equipment and the head of radiology at a table. I had interviewed them individually before and after that had a group interview with a group result. That means, they came to an agreement how they evaluate this and that idea."* (PM)

In the project team, such reactively collected customer feedback is perceived as the starting point of innovation that distinguishes service from product innovation:

> *"Here we are just dealing with customers. So we are just dealing with people. [We ask them] 'What do you want? What do you need? How do you use it? What is easy? What is not easy? What are your needs?' So, it's a little bit different... and this defines how we start the service development process."* (QM)

In retrospect, the visits of the customer are evaluated as fruitful activities - except the visit with Japanese customers. Due to culture and hierarchy barriers, meaningful exchange on usage and habits could not take place during the customer visits in Japan. Overall, the personal visits of this variety of customers and users are perceived as an extraordinary practice within the organisation. Notwithstanding its success and its lighthouse character, the activity was only possible due to chance to combine budgets of two parallel projects. Otherwise it would not have been possible to realise the customer visits in this way and in this mode. The formal service innovation process includes only a small budget to "*perform certain customer surveys or to visit some customers and understand their workflow*" (QM). To access this budget, the service innovation project manager has to apply for it in the first project presentation with the senior management. This shows that direct reactive customer integration is not only costly and resource intensive in execution, but also includes an application process of high effort upfront.

Reactive integration of customers during development

Also during development, reactive customer integration is realized by individual employees through an informal process of customer contact. Customer contact employees in their own regions consult selected customers to obtain feedback during the development, in direct conversations, as an informal ad-hoc procedures (HBD, PMH):

"'Look, soon we would offer you such a service, would you be interested in it?' - We need feedback from them, definitely yes."(PMH)

Nevertheless, this practice of reactive customer integration during development is is reported upon differently; according to the project manager, there is no customer interaction in the development phase (PME, PM, IC). Interviewees from central units of the organisation state that it is part of the organisational culture to only go out and test a new service offering after it has already been developed into a highly standardized product, proven to be profitable (PME).

Reactive integration of customers during testing

For the testing of new services, the integration of pilot customers is implemented as a task of the country organisations during testing (stage testing and implementation) according to the guidelines of the service innovation process. The customer integration for piloting is indirect:

"The customer is involved and approached, but not directly through us." (PMH).

Since the formal integration of customers in a reactive mode was not explicitly discussed at the testing phase, it is suggested that this is a rather unproblematic standard procedure of the organisation.

In conclusion, it has to be added that the organisational practice of customer integration is discussed critically in the organisation. It was found that the internal consulting team criticise the practice of reactive customer integration can only give short term input for service innovation. The customers' feedback relies on the current product portfolio only. Factors that inhibit the integration of customers as external stakeholders in the mode of mutual integration are mentioned: a culture and mind-set to present only perfect products to the outside world and the fear to face imbalanced or difficult relationships with the customer.

2.2.5 The organisational perspective on "internal" and "external"

Assessing and analysing the practice of stakeholder integration predominantly from a central perspective of the organisation, it was often difficult to decide whether a stakeholder groups in the narratives collected in the case study were to be categorized as internal stakeholders or as members of the core team. Specialized departments such as Marketing and IT are formally assigned members of the core team as shown in Figure 16, and yet have been referred to as internal stakeholders. It could be revealed that the internal perspective on stakeholders regards everyone in a different quality management and reporting system as an external stakeholder within the organisation.

Following the internal perspective that core team members are internal stakeholders of an innovation project, the number of stakeholders to be managed and integrated from a central project and stakeholder manager is increased. Consequently, the task of the project manager in this matrix team and organisation could be compared to constant stakeholder management with a variety of stakeholders. The resources, and the benefits and challenges, of stakeholder integration have to be balanced, as the interviewee HBD summarizes:

> *"If you involve too many people, you can stop yourself. If you are always thinking about the best solution, with the integration of too many people, innovation can stop or be limited. Therefore it is important to have [...] one responsible guy who leads the project in a way balancing the involvement of stakeholders. So it is always a mixture of quality and speed."* (HBD)

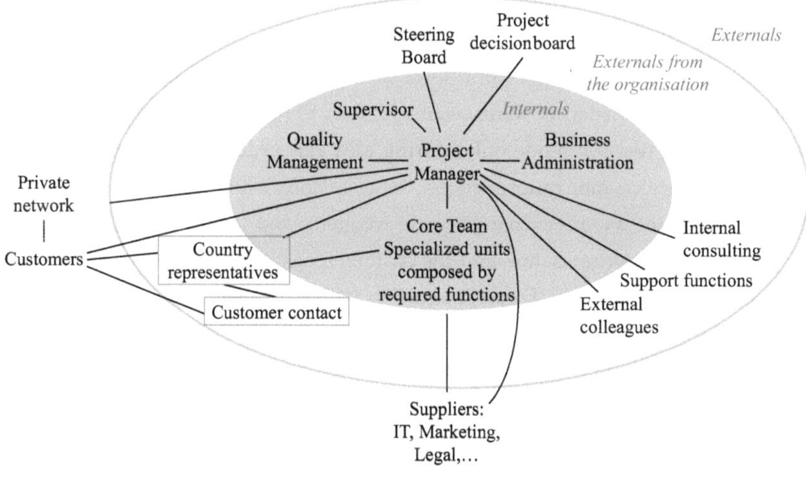

Figure 16: Overview of stakeholder integration from the organisational boundary perspective

2.3 Discussion and conclusions

Looking at stakeholder integration in service innovation as a micro level process, this research study analysed the different modes of stakeholder integration during idea generation, development and testing of a service innovation project. As shown by the previous research by Perks et al. (2012) and Smith and Fischbacher (2002), this case study also presents a broad range of internal and external stakeholders which are being integrated for service innovation.

The findings reveal that senior management plays a vital part in the innovation process, for example, for mutual idea generation. This validates initial findings by Ginzburg, Higgins and Lichtenstein (2007). Though, in the past, the importance of management integration has been emphasized in the development stage (de Brentani & Ragot, 1996; Perks & Riihela, 2004; Smith & Fischbacher, 2002). For the observed project, the higher intensity of mutual integration with senior management during the development phase proved beneficial, since it created new interfaces for problem solving and helped to establish a wider internal network. In addition to this networking and the legitimation function, which were also discussed in an earlier study by Smith and Fischbacher (2005), it is found that senior management plays an active role in idea generation and knowledge contribution. Such contribution of senior management has previously been associated with innovation practices in SMEs, e.g. in a study by Gottfridsson (2011), and might be transferable to the context of large organizations, too.

Customer integration, a central topic of the service-dominant logic (Normann & Ramirez, 1993; Prahalad & Ramaswamy, 2004a; Vargo & Lusch, 2004), is in this case realized in a reactive mode only, during idea generation and testing, according to the formal service innovation process, or even informally during development. Mutual integration as an exchange with frequent and ongoing communication streams between the organisation and the customer, as partners, was not observed in the setting of this case study. Direct interaction with customers and users could only be seen during interviews in the idea generation phase. Still, there is a consensus that reactive methods can only skim the surface of customer needs, and do not provide access to latent needs. Edvardsson et al. (2013), Matthing et al. (2006) and Gustafsson et al. (2012) discuss, that reactive integration does not allow access to tacit knowledge of the customers. Such direct access to customers and the application of methods for mutual customer integration are found to be prevented by the structures and the culture of the organisation.

Observing the findings of the case at hand through the lens of value co-creation in service systems, it became evident that customer integration is facilitated by a bridge-building third party; only by integrating a third party such as country representatives or private networks, could access to customers be provided. This has a bearing on the selection of customers for reactive integration. In this case, only close and content customers were integrated since their selection filtered through third parties, the local subsidiaries.

Even though customer integration in this case was put into practice as direct interaction between project management and the customer during idea generation, the collection of information at the customer's site during development and testing was implemented by customer contact employees. They gathered information, translated it into the corporate language and subsequently forwarded it via the hierarchical structures of the organisation. For this indirect customer integration, it remains unclear how well-functioning and rich the transfer of customer feedback, wishes and observable needs from the customer contact employees to the service innovation project management is.

The customer contact employees, as an internal stakeholder group, are according to the empirical findings not integrated before the "training" stage. This practice is in line with findings by Melton and Hartline (2012) and Smith and Fischbacher (2005). Perks and Riihela (2004) have showed that positive interfunctional behaviour in the later stages of the innovation process can be fostered through reactive integration in the form of e.g. short notes sent from the beginning of the project.

Overall, this case study highlights the multi-dimensionality of service innovation in respect to stakeholder integration. The empirical study created transparency, indicating that not only the integration of customers and suppliers as external stakeholders requires the allocation of resources, such as time and budget. The same resources are needed for internal stakeholder integration as well and have to be balanced in multiple dimensions, as first discussed by Gann and Salter (2000). It is even shown from the data in the present case, that the integration of stakeholders creates interdependencies between stakeholders from the central unit, between central and local units and between the customers, the country organisations and the core innovation team.

As a single case study, the findings of this empirical research cannot be generalised per se. Still, other large and established organizations with a matrix organization including parallel product and service development could possibly benefit from and make use of the findings from this case study. In this empirical work, an organizational view of service innovation was chosen. The context for this case study did allow for the analysis of the first three stages of service innovation. The implementation and commercialization stages of the project are not covered in this case study and should be subject to consecutive research.

Furthermore, the study is built upon a limited number of data sources. Even though milestone presentations and various other secondary data were utilized to secure the reliability of propositions, a longitudinal approach or more data sources could possibly have advanced this study. As the stakeholder integration modes "proactive initiative" and "passive integration" were not strongly evidenced in this study, more data sources could reveal whether the identified modes are limited by data collection or if they are a feature of the case. Future research could provide insight whether this is a common phenomenon in large, established organizations. To fully reflect the concept of mutual value co-creation from the service-dominant logic perspective, the scope of the research approach could be expanded by additionally taking into account the view of the integrated stakeholders.

3 Service innovation in medium-sized organisations in manufacturing and IT - a multiple case study[49]

To deepen the insights of the previously presented single case study, this second multiple case aims to reflect and enrich the insights from the first study in related industries. As the findings from the first case deal with IT services in healthcare appliance engineering, the second multiple case study chooses IT solution providers and manufacturers of engineering products in Germany-based medium-sized organisations as its research field. The cross-case analysis applied in this multiple case study aims to verify and enrich the findings of the first case and seeks to identify patterns that allow for a better generalizability of findings (Eisenhardt, 1989; Creswell, 2012). Thus, this study re-applies the research question from the first in-depth case study and asks two questions: a) "Which actors from inside and outside the organization are being integrated throughout the stages of the service innovation process?" and b) "In which mode is this integration happening in the different stages in organisations within IT and manufacturing?".

3.1 Research approach - multiple case study

To address these research issues, a qualitative explorative approach is chosen. Qualitative research in this rather new field of research allows to explore in-depth insights on real world experiences (Miles et al., 2013). This empirical study builds upon the first insights from the presented in-depth case study for IT service innovation in engineering as well as the services industry related case studies by Perks et al. (2012) and Perks and Riihela (2004). A multiple case study approach is chosen as allows to verify earlier findings and to develop in-depth knowledge on a wider variety of cases. The case selection is based on the need to gather insights on stakeholder integration practices for service innovation in manufacturing and IT, both knowledge intensive services (de Jong & Vermeulen, 2003). Since medium-sized and family-owned businesses constitute about two thirds of business volume in Germany (IfM Bonn, 2014), only companies from this segment were approached. This resulted in a sample of four organisations with a manufacturing industry background and two organisations with a background in software development as presented in Table 10.

49 An earlier version of this research study has been presented at the Reser 2014 conference in Helsinki, Finland (Jonas et al., 2014b) and is currently under review in a service research journal.

The level of analysis is "service innovation projects", with product or innovation managers as a primary source for information on service innovation practices. The perspective of project management is considered to be suitable to tackle the present research question since people in these roles decide about stakeholders to be integrated as well as the mode and timing of integration, as demonstrated by Stevens and Dimitriadis (2005).

Table 10: Overview and background information on selected cases

Name	Type of enterprise	Industry Background	Number of employees	Annual turnaround in €
ESC	family owned business	Manufacturing	2900	~ 400 mio.
BSN	family owned business	Manufacturing	460	~ 64 mio.
RFS	family owned business	Manufacturing	1300	~ 140-160 mio.
EMS	family owned business	Manufacturing	1360	~ 120 mio.
LSC	cooperative society	IT, Software	6000	~ 800 mio.
OSP	family owned business	IT, Software	130	~ 10 mio.

3.1.1 Data collection

Accordingly, the data collection for this multiple case study is first and foremost based on interviews with service responsible managers, completed by document-based data collection. Each case consists of two interviews with product and innovation managers. Other data sources such as internal presentations, student theses or sales material were collected and used for verification and comparison during data analysis. Using these different materials in addition to the main source of information - interviews - helps to verify and confirm interview propositions, according to Creswell (2012) and Yin (2014).

Twelve interviews were conducted in the time between July 2013 and June 2014 (see Table 11). A team of four trained researchers was involved in the conduction of interviews according to a semi-structured interview guideline. Interviews included the application of the critical incident technique to gain access to narratives and vivid examples from the near past of the interviewees' experience with service innovation (Gremler, 2004; Flanagan, 1954). According to Chell (2012), this method is useful with in-depth and multi-site investigations to capture the thought processes involved as well as the frames of reference of the studied phenomena.

Critical incidents were defined as a typical or recent service innovation project, to exemplify stakeholder integration practices. This way, reflections on common routines and extraordinary behaviours could be recorded, alongside insights into operating procedures and general attitudes (Flanagan, 1954). All interviews were conducted face-to-face at the interviewees' office and lasted about one hour in average.

The interviews were held on an open style, to allow natural conversations, alike the previous case study. In the majority of interview situations, the interviewees spontaneously referred to explanatory or supporting documents (e.g. marketing material such as brochures or website information, a quality management guideline or innovation process visualisations). The interviewers invited them to provide material and secured anonymity, in those cases where additional data was not provided by itself (Miles et al., 2013; Gibbert & Ruigrok, 2010).

Table 11: Interviews for each case study

Company	#	Interviewee	Duration
ESC	1	Manager Service Engineering (ESC-MSE)	1 hr 15 min
	2	Product Manager 1+2 (ESC-PM1, ESC-PM2)	1 hr 37 min
BSN	3	Sales Manager (BSN-SM)	47 min
	4	Product Manager (BSN-PM)	1 hr 3 min
RFS	5	Innovation Manager (RFS-IM)	1 hr 29 min
	6	Product Manager (RFS-PM)	1 hr 20 min
EMS	7	Manager Sales & Service (EMS-MSS)	55 min
	8	Head of Sales & Service (EMS-HSS)	1 hr 11 min
LSC	9	Manager Product Management & Service (LSC-MPS)	44 min
	10	Product Manager (LSC-PM)	43 min
OSP	11	CEO (OSP-CE)	40 min
	12	Product Manager (OSP-PM)	57 min

3.1.2 Data analysis

All interviews were audio-recorded, transcribed and categorized with the help of qualitative data analysis software MaxQDA, as suggested by Miles et al. (2013). Thereby coding was conducted, building upon the experiences of the data analysis of the previous single case-study to allow for comparison. The codes were derived deductively according to analytic categories as proposed by literature, that is, "mode of integration", "integrated stakeholders" (internal and external), and "stage of the innovation process". Codes such as "indirect integration" and "informal integration", which emerged from the previous single case study, were adapted. To allow for open exploration, inductive codes were developed after the first round of analysis (Coffey & Atkinson, 1996; Smith & Fischbacher, 2005). Following the guidelines by Yin (2014) and Stake (2006), each case was first analysed individually and then summarized in individual case reports to identify patterns within cases. Only after that, a comparative cross-case analysis and discussion was conducted, as advocated by Eisenhardt (1989). Key quotations are used in the description of findings as they add to transparency and depth of understanding (Patton, 2007).

3.1.3 The cases of the multiple case study

For an overview of the cases in this research study, the case companies' background and information about the role of service innovation in the respective case companies are provided in Table 12. The overview thereby indicates which service innovation projects have been referred to in the interviews.

Table 12: Services and service innovation – background information for the studied cases

ESC	BSN	RFS
Industry		
Engineering & Production of Electronics	Engineering & Production of Metalware	Engineering & Production of Metalware
Reported project(s)		
New solution for a customer process, new warehousing solution.	Software-based individual calculations and consulting.	New coating solution for a specific customer request.
Position of services		
ESC offers operational services such as individualized engineering, calculations, simulations and warehousing. Supplementing services are currently in development. Services are accounted rarely and reflect only 1% of sales.	Offered services are consulting, offered free of charge, upon customer request. Product-related services like specific calculations are supporting long-term relationships with customers. Engineers in the sales team are responsible for services.	Services provided are consulting, engineering for customised products, mostly initiated as customer pull, often free of charge. Training and repair are offered as operational services on own products, providing solutions for the customer.

ESC	BSN	RFS
Position of service innovation		
The company has a referent for services, driving service accountability and innovation in the respective organizational product units. A service engineering process is in use.	Rather informal and unsystematic processes guide service innovation, initiated by sales or customers. Resources for service innovation are few.	Services are developed alongside products in the respective product divisions. There is no systematic service innovation process, but a step-by-step project management guideline, for the fulfilment of quality management requirements.

EMS	LSC	OSP
Industry		
Production & Service in machine building	Software	Software
Reported project(s)		
Internal IT service; Online platform for the provision of customer information.	Customer online cockpit, software adaptions, development of consulting services.	Online sales platform for product presentation, office management software development.
Position of service		
Maintenance and repair reflect about 50% of the company's business. EMS offers even maintenance and security checks for third party machinery and equipment.	Next to the development of software, infrastructure and counselling services account more than a third of the organizations offerings. Still, the organizational culture is product-centric.	Individualization and adaptions of software are the main services. Consulting, helpdesk, legal consulting and software development are amongst service offerings.
Position of service innovation		
There is no clear service innovation process. Service development is steered by the responsible sales and service unit.	Service innovation is led by product management units, supported by a central innovation management. Innovation management initiates service projects independently, in parallel. Even though there are various regular meetings, there is no clear service innovation process or guideline.	Service innovation is a senior management topic, coordinated by product and software development.

3.2 Findings

The empirical data of this multiple case study provides evidence about stakeholder integration from a wide variety of stakeholder integration instances. It reveals that the internal stakeholders integrated in service innovation in manufacturing and IT organisations are senior management, support functions and other units, local offices, sales and customer contact employees such as technicians, consultants or production. The external stakeholders integrated in the examined cases are foremost customers. Additional external stakeholders are suppliers and external service providers, universities and competitors.

3.2.1 Stages and modes of integration

Concerning the mode of stakeholder integration, the case study analysis reveals that stakeholder integration happens in a reactive mode in the majority of cases. The mode of mutual integration is shown for the integration of internal units, especially partner units, in the very beginning of the innovation process and during development. Customers play an important part as passively and reactively integrated resources: they are integrated during idea screening, idea generation and idea evaluation. Further, customers and sales representatives are integrated for the testing of new services. These findings are summarized in Table 13 and will be depicted in detail in the following section.

Table 13: Aggregated modes of stakeholder integration in the different stages

<table>
<tr><th>Idea screening
& idea generation</th><th>Evaluation</th><th>Development</th><th>Testing</th></tr>
<tr><td>Mutual integration
- of members/other units of the organisation</td><td rowspan="3">Reactive integration
- of customers and users, informal
- internal support units and experts
- sales
- senior management</td><td>Mutual integration
- of members/other units of the organisation</td><td rowspan="3">Reactive integration
- of customers and pilot customers
- internal experts
- sales representatives</td></tr>
<tr><td>Reactive integration
- of customers and users; direct and indirect
- consultants
- sales and service employees with customer contact</td><td rowspan="2">Reactive integration
- suppliers/service providers
- internal units and support units
- local units
- senior management</td></tr>
<tr><td>Passive integration
- of competitors; direct and indirect</td></tr>
</table>

3.2.1.1 Stakeholder integration in idea screening and idea generation

The early stages of the innovation process show the highest levels of stakeholder integration: internal units and colleagues are mutually integrated for idea screening and generation. The majority of this occurs in workshops, in which internal work groups brainstorm to align input such as customer feedback and strategic guidelines to improve business by joint idea generation. Internal units are integrated foremost to pool knowledge about market developments, customer input and technical know-how. The example of the case company RFS is extraordinary in this context. They organise a yearly retreat for mutually engaged innovating across the organisational divisions to align expertise across disciplines and units:

> *"It's already something like a tradition to sit together in a hotel on a weekend or somewhere else, once a year, to brainstorm and throw ideas together. This way, we identify new breeding grounds for innovation that gets more and more interesting by its concretization."* (RFS-PM)

Though, in the majority of stakeholder integration instances, the integration in this stage happens predominantly in the mode of reactive integration. The most prominent stakeholder group for reactive and passive integration in idea screening is "customers and users." In formal and informal processes, customers are observed, interviewed and asked for feedback in informal conversations. Customers are given an important role in triggering the initiation of new services or consultancy activities: the interviewees report that customers, when approached, take the initiative in suggesting solutions to their problems, as e.g. interviewee EMS-HSS describes it.

> *"It's a lot from the customer. We have an enormous amount of machines in maintenance, a lot of customer contact. So our customer comes and says 'there is that service person that does these smaller motors here. That's a simpler quality test than the ones you do. Couldn't you do the service for these motors as well?' This is one of the projects that we are looking at, currently."* (EMS-HSS)

Customer integration and the integration of internal sales and customer contact employees during the stage of idea generation go often go hand in hand in the cases examined. Interviewee LSC–PM stresses how colleagues in service and consulting become aware of customer needs and forward them to the product managers:

> *"Service is important since they talk to customers, on everyday basis. They see where problems and potential for improvement lies. [...] We also have consultants in the field who administer projects at the clients' location and spend several days with them. They really get a feeling for what is needed and bring that back."* (LSC-PM)

The active approaching of customers to find out about needs and behaviours is prominent in the cases that deal with service innovation in IT-LSC, EMS and OSP. Regarding the cases in manufacturing, the customer integration has a stronger emphasis on detecting and recording customer needs when already engaged in interaction with the customer, because of another project or a sales process. These are the occasions when customer contact employees ask their customers about their needs and observe their behaviour. In this context, it was not distinguishable from the data which kind of personnel from the customer organisation was approached.

The integration of sales and other internal units is characterized by the mode of reactive integration, being rather a provision of feedback and answers to questions than a method of solving problems and joint brainstorming. Reasons for integration are, above all, to gain access to their knowledge about customers and the market. Further, project managers aim to build up a stake in service innovation projects early on or to integrate the expertise of other units to create unique innovations.

To give employees at all organizational units and levels the possibility to engage in product and service innovations, in three of the case companies, RFS, EMS and LSC, all employees are encouraged to pool their ideas for idea and future trend screening. This happens online at LSC, via e-mail at RFS and through a post box at EMS. What all three cases have in common is that they gave the impression of a strong culture of innovation.

A third point in the fuzzy front-end of innovation is the passive integration of competitors or "the market". The screening and observation of competitors' offerings was reported as common practice amongst all case companies. This passive integration is undertaken by the product managers themselves and additionally by innovation management working in parallel at LSC and ESC.

3.2.1.2 Stakeholder integration for idea evaluation

After a concept for a service innovation project has been established, internal stakeholders, customer contact employees and customers are integrated reactively. The evaluation of innovation initiatives is primarily accomplished after receiving a first assessment, feedback and opinions from internal stakeholders who are then asked for their "go" so that the idea can become a project. In the majority of cases, these internal stakeholders are senior management, internal units with a link to the idea, for instance Marketing, IT or Sales. This reactive integration for idea evaluation can be formal; in weekly or monthly board meetings, or informal.

In one case, at company BSN, sales representatives are not employees, but external agents. They are integrated reactively in the idea generation phase as well.

> *"You talk about these things with the sales agents and they say 'this and that would be important, too'. It's interplay between the development team and sales."* (BSN-SM).

Either directly or through sales representatives, customers are integrated in a reactive mode in order to obtain feedback. This happens in many cases in a rather informal way, building upon trusted relationships.

Parallel to these informal conversations, case company LSC has an established customer board that meets twice a year and is informed and reactively integrated into new ideas and ongoing development projects. Even ESC reported integrating customers in special sessions:

> *"We tried it for the customer online cockpit for the first time. We asked two, three larger customers to our table, separately. We presented the basic structure and asked them questions about it. It's not the usual way,that was the first time."* (ECS - MSS)

Another instance of reactive customer integration is reported at case company RFS who invite customers for an "open house day" to present the latest developments and create the opportunity for open exchange and feedback.

3.2.1.3 Stakeholder integration during development

During development, internal stakeholders are the predominant stakeholder group. The project managers integrate IT resources, experts and product related units into the innovation process in order to define the future service in depth and to solve problems as they occur. Senior management and boards as well as local units are reactively integrated so that they can stay informed about progress and maintain a stake in the project. Interviewee ESC-MSE summarizes the need for the early integration of internal units as follows:

> *"All units should be participating from the beginning of the project, this is important. Because, if a department is not informed, but needs to participate in some sort of production process… and they realize we cannot do it that way – then we are in trouble. From the beginning you need to have everyone on board who is affected by the project."* (ESC- MSE)

In this stage of the service innovation process, external service providers are integrated in a reactive mode in order to fill resource gaps. These might be human resources, like engineering or programming resources or equipment that is required. The suppliers for services might be engineering offices, software agencies and rarely, innovation management consultants. In three cases, universities and students were integrated reactively to support the organization with specific equipment, tools, time and know-how.

3.2.1.4 Stakeholder integration for the testing of services

Throughout all the observed cases, stakeholder integration for the testing of new services is enabled in a reactive way. It can be seen from the data that internal experts and sales representatives are the first stakeholders to be integrated in the stage "testing" for feedback and adjustments of the service innovation as well as for strategic reasons.

In the cases focussing on software development, the integration of pilot customers was evidenced. They are integrated in several formal and informal feedback loops, through surveys and usability tests on one hand and direct conversations on the other. This is different to practice in the manufacturing context cases where services are offered as an individual service first, to gather feedback from the direct interaction with and experiences of the customer.

Test runs with customers are reported in IT development projects and even in manufacturing: the innovation manager of case company RFS reported a test run with internal pilot users for an internal service, for a period of two years. In the cases of software development, reactive customer integration in testing can be conducted by product management, but also by the IT developers, sometimes even in parallel.

3.2.2 Further insights from the exploratory study

Benefiting from the exploratory set-up of this multiple case study, further insights about stakeholder integration could be obtained. It was found that (1) the management and balancing of internal and external stakeholder integration for service innovation is the task of the product manager, alongside his/her prior product management job. For internal stakeholder management, it has been concluded that (2) informal stakeholder integration and the (3) continuous integration of senior management are relevant subjects for stakeholder integration in service innovation. For external stakeholders the practice of (4) indirect integration was identified. Last but not least, it was revealed that (5) some case organisations are pursuing customer integration at the same time as they are getting integrated as suppliers for the innovation projects of their clients.

(1) Data revealed that in five of the six researched case companies, **service innovation is managed by product managers**, alongside their regular duties. Only at EMS there is a so called Sales, Service and Maintenance team that is in charge of service innovation. Accordingly, product managers report that their service innovation projects are competing for resources with their everyday business. Even in those organisations with an innovation management responsible for supporting service innovation activities, **managing and balancing internal and external stakeholder integration** is the task of the product manager.

(2) Next to formal and project management processes, a number of **informal and parallel processes** are observed, related to **the integration of internal stakeholders** like senior management, but also customer contact employees, other

units or rarely customers. These processes include for instance a question for feedback about ongoing testing activities, informal meetings with customer contact employees or a lunch meeting with the senior management to request the support for ideas.

(3) Regarding the **integration of internal stakeholders in all stages**, the empirical data shows that there are regular milestones meetings, where project managers report their service innovation project progress to a board of other units and / or **senior management**, even in those cases where there is no articulated service innovation process or strategy. The character of integration of senior management and internal units here is foremost reactive, but can develop into discussion and problem solving meetings that evolve into the degree of mutual integration, intended or not.

(4) A phenomenon emerging from the data analysis regarding the integration of external stakeholders is that the **integration of customers** in the very beginning and in the very end of the innovation process **is indirect** and mainly implemented by sales personnel. Project managers generate knowledge and triggers for service innovation from the interactions between sales and service personnel and the customers.

> *"We first diagnose what does the market need, what input do we get from our local offices, from our employees or even directly from the customer. That is, we do not have the direct contact here in our headquarters. Most of the times it runs via our sales employees out there. From that we derive our requirements for innovation, prioritize them and develop our two to three big projects per year."* (EMS- MSS)

In a majority of cases it was also found that the integration of customers for testing new services is not put into action by the service innovation project manager, but by a third party. In the example of ESC and BSN testing it is realized through sales representatives.

> *"We had our first inspection and approval from the technician. Then we, no, our people responsible for the services asked our best customers to participate in a three month trial."* (ESC-MSE)

Even at LSC and OSP this testing with customers is carried out by software developers, who forward their feedback to the service innovation project manager.

(5) Finally, the analysis of the present empirical data showed that manufacturers like RFS, ESC and BSN and also the software developer OSP **are being integrated from their customers**. The more know-how is demanded, the more mutually engaged and mutually trusted is the mode of collaboration. This can trigger service innovation or the ad-hoc development of a new service responding to an individual customer demand:

> *"The majority, 80-90%, of what we developed and even our current innovation topics are based on suggestions or wishes from the customer. What the customer says decides - we develop it this way and maybe a tick more to that. This is why our development is so strongly linked to the teams that deal with customers every day, who know about their needs and pains."* (OSP-CE)

3.3 Discussion and conclusions

This study was designed to give better insight into the stakeholder integration practices of service providing organisations with an IT or software background and to validate and enrich the findings from the previous in-depth case study. Through an exploratory research approach, the authors aimed to deepen the understanding of which stakeholders are integrated, in which mode and which of the stages of the service innovation process. The multiple case study shows that "mutual integration", the highest degree of stakeholder integration, is realized with the members of the organisation only, with an emphasis on the early process stages. In the presented cases in manufacturing and IT, employees are seen as one of the key sources for idea generation. They are integrated throughout the innovation process because of their knowledge about processes and customer needs, because of their expertise and technical know-how and also because of the need to maintain a stake in the service innovation project (strategic and political considerations).

This empirical research study shows that the idea generation with internal stakeholders is strongly dependent on the integration of customer contact employees as the major source of information about customer needs, problems and behaviours. Still, customer contact employees, just like customers themselves, are integrated in a reactive mode, with few exceptions. Scholars like Edvardsson et al. (2013), Matthing et al. (2006) and Gustafsson et al. (2012) have stated that reactive stakeholder integration might only skim the surface of customer needs in the context of service organisations. The access to tacit knowledge and latent needs is a central topic in service research (Edvardsson et al., 2013; Gustafsson et al., 2012). It is suggested that this tacit knowledge can presumably only be accessed in bidirectional communication processes (Gustafsson et al., 2012) and is difficult to process and translate into the organisation (Mention & Asikainen, 2012). In the present context of IT and manufacturing organisations, only trusted customers are integrated, foremost in a reactive mode. This practice is considered to reflect the importance of good and undisturbed relationships with the customers for future business.

This multiple case study also revealed that customer integration is in many cases not implemented by the decision making service innovation project manager, but by customer contact employees who forward information. This confirms findings from the previous single case study and another case study in service industries by Smith and Fischbacher (2005). Both pieces of research provide evidence that the needs and interests of stakeholders are channelled through other stakeholders. Given these practices, it is identified that customer contact employees should be consciously given the role of "translators of information" (Gottfridsson 2012) and be integrated intensively to "*make the voice of the customer heard*" in the organisation (Smith & Fischbacher 2005, p. 1042). The in-depth knowledge of customer processes and a high level of detail, derived from an immersion in the customer context, are found to be beneficial factors for service innovation in service organisations (Melton & Hartline, 2010; Gustafsson et al., 2012) and should be considered as a motivation for direct, yet more resource intensive, customer integration even in other industries.

The management of internal and external stakeholders for service innovation is, especially in the manufacturing cases ESC, BSN and EMS, a task that comes next to the project managers' core business. This indicates that the integration of external stakeholders is competing for resources with the integration and management of internal stakeholders, as research by Perks and Riihela (2004) has shown also for service organisations. The findings of this study contribute to current research showing that in IT and manufacturing organisations, the service innovation project itself is, additionally, conflicting with everyday product business.

Understanding service innovation as a multi-dimensional process, depending on and affecting internal and external stakeholders bi-directionally (Schleimer & Shulman, 2011), it is crucial for the management of service innovation projects - to know about the roles, modes and timing of stakeholder integration. This empirical study in business-to-business services in manufacturing and software development shows that stakeholder integration is rarely implemented in the mode of mutual integration. From a service-dominant logic viewpoint, the co-development of future value propositions, especially with customers, is a key issue. Mutual integration could be identified with internal stakeholders for idea generation only.

Confirming the findings of previous studies, the analysed cases in IT and manufacturing show that trusted customers are integrated reactively, in the very early and in the late stages of service innovation. This integration is, in some of the cases, realized as indirect integration through customer contact employees. This brings up the question whether such indirect stakeholder integration practice can provide the decision making managers with deep insights into customer needs and behaviour. As Matthing et al. (2006) state, this might only "skim the surface" of potential insights - but in the industrial context of this multiple case study, long-term customer relationships are omnipresent and affect the chosen modes of integration for customers integration.

This explorative research study gave evidence that the process "integration of stakeholders for service innovation" and the process "getting integrated as a stakeholder for other innovation projects" can happen at the same time. Future work could further examine this phenomenon and make the interplay of stakeholder integration in overlapping service systems more explicit.

Finally, the study brings up that stakeholder integration is interdependent with other processes in the organisation itself. The formal and informal integration of stakeholders can have effects on other stakeholders, on the resource allocation in other projects of the organisation as well as on the future relationship with the stakeholder. Here, more research is needed to deepen our understanding of these interdependencies and side-effects of stakeholder integration.

4 Synthesis of findings and conclusions

Building upon the findings from the single case study at company ECH and the multiple case study with six case companies, the summary of this part of the thesis will provide a synthesis of findings, showing which stakeholders are being integrated in service innovation, at which stage of the service innovation process, in which mode and for which reasons.

4.1 Identified stakeholders in service innovation

Answering to the research question of who is integrated in service innovation at product-oriented organisations in manufacturing or IT, it is shown that a variety of internal and external stakeholders are integrated: Internal colleagues, senior management, external colleagues, support functions and customer contact employees were identified as internal stakeholders in both empirical studies. Both studies refer to the external stakeholder groups "customers", "pilot customers" and "suppliers". In the case of ECH, an internal consultancy and country representatives were integrated, as well as the private network of the project manager. In this case, not only customers, but also users were integrated in a reactive mode. The multiple case study revealed additionally that also universities and competitors are integrated in service innovation (see Table 14 for a summary of identified stakeholders).

Table 14: Summary of stakeholders in service innovation identified in Part V

Case study ECH	**Multiple case study**
Internal stakeholders: Internal colleagues, senior management, external colleagues, support functions, customer contact employees. *External stakeholders*: customers, pilot customers, suppliers.	
+ internal consultancy + country representatives + private network	+ universities + competitors

4.2 Modes of stakeholder integration

As demonstrated in the two case studies, stakeholder integration is foremost implemented in the mode of reactive integration. Mutual integration is practiced only with internal stakeholders such as management and selected employees, in the idea generation stage. Customer and user integration are depicted in a reactive mode in the fuzzy frontend of service innovation (idea screening and idea generation) and during testing. Summarizing over all cases, the stages evaluation and development are characterised by the mode "reactive integration". Internal and external stakeholders are integrated mainly to receive feedback and to solve problems.

Table 15: Synthesis of stakeholder integration and its mode in the stages of the innovation process

	Idea screening & idea generation	**Evaluation**	**Development**	**Testing**
Internal stakeholders	**Mutual integration** - of members/ other units of the organisation **Reactive integration** - consultants - sales and service employees with customer contact	**Reactive integration** - internal support units and experts - sales - senior management	**Mutual integration** - of members/ other units of the organisation **Reactive integration** - internal units and support units - local units - senior management	**Reactive integration** - internal experts - sales representatives
External stakeholders	**Reactive integration** - of customers and users; direct and indirect **Passive integration** - of competitors; direct and indirect	**Reactive integration** - of customers and users, informal	**Reactive integration** - suppliers/ service providers	**Reactive integration** - of customers and pilot customers

In addition to the description of stakeholder integration and its modes, some exceptional instances for stakeholder integration could be identified. A first example comes from case ESC, a firm for electronic goods engineering. Here, an attempt to integrate customers in a formal mutual innovation workshop failed. After this negative experience, customer integration in this company is implemented only in the mode of informal reactive integration.

A second example is case RFS, a company in metalwork engineering. In this company, mutual integration is practiced as an institutionalized event in joint innovation workshops with other units, at a minimum of once a year. The mutually engaged idea generation between units who are working separately in different markets and disciplines in their regular routines is perceived as a benefit for the organisation. The results of this mutual integration practice are superior solutions which cannot be imitated by competitors due to the combination of unique resources, enabled by the innovation culture of a family-owned firm.

In the case of EHC, the single case study on healthcare solutions development, the indirect integration of stakeholders was observed in instances where customer contact employees and pilot customers were integrated reactively through the local subsidiary organisations. Also in this case, it was evidenced that customer integration is implemented in informal processes, independent from the given guidelines for service innovation processes; this emphasizes the interdependencies of stakeholder integration as well as its complexity.

4.3 The reasons for stakeholder integration

Regarding the reasons for stakeholder integration it can be summarised that they change with the stages of the service innovation process. Only three of the motivations are valid for all stages of the service innovation process, as depicted in Figure 17. Reasons for stakeholder integration can be that the organisations' guidelines for service innovation give prescriptions about stages and modes of stakeholder integration. Guidelines that have been referred to in the case studies include: the explicit innovation process (such as the stage gate process at case EHC), the directions given in quality management (e.g. in case RFS), specific milestones of an innovation project or even implicit rules of behaviour in an organisation. Another reason for stakeholder integration, as indicated in the last paragraph, is the need to build connections with required stakeholders that cannot be accessed easily otherwise. This is why stakeholder integration in the case of company EHC is implemented also through indirect integration.

For idea screening and idea generation, the motives for customer integration are to gain access to their needs and to create an understanding of their processes and routines, in a natural context. Moreover, the access to knowledge of different stakeholders, and motivation to create new ideas are reasons for stakeholder integration. For internal stakeholder integration, the importance to create awareness about the service innovation project is emphasised.

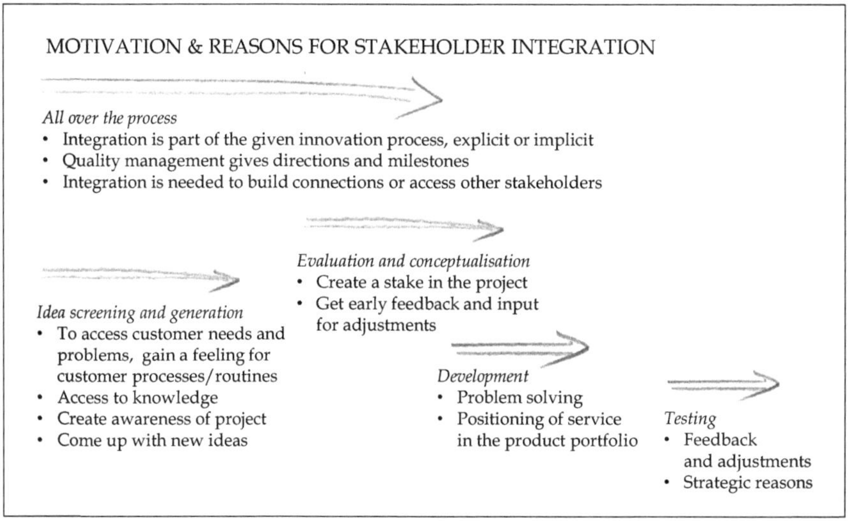

Figure 17: The motivations and reasons for stakeholder integration from Part V

During evaluation and conceptualisation, stakeholder integration is motivated by the goal to get stakeholders involved with the project, so that they will hold a stake in the service innovation in the future. Further, stakeholder integration aims to obtain early feedback and input for early adjustments of the service concept in this stage. In the next stage, development, the solution of problems is the main reason for stakeholder integration, in particular for the integration of internal colleagues. Another practical reason for stakeholder integration is the positioning of the service in the overall product portfolio of the firm. Here, stakeholders have to be aligned at interfaces with products and stakeholders need to be informed about the new service. In testing, the service innovation needs to be evaluated by customer contact employees such as sales representatives and pilot customers. Stakeholder integration in this context is certainly motivated by the need for crucial feedback, but also implemented for strategic reasons.

4.4 Conclusions

The two presented studies, an in-depth case study in a large matrix organisation and a multiple case study with medium-sized enterprises, deal with stakeholder integration for service innovation in the setting of manufacturing and IT. The findings show that a variety of internal and external stakeholders are integrated in service innovation, mostly in the mode of reactive integration. Mutual integration for the joint creation of value propositions (Alam, 2002; Prahalad & Ramaswamy, 2004a; Edvardsson, Tronvoll, & Gruber, 2010; Kowalkowski, Persson Ridell et al., 2012), is foremost implemented with internal stakeholders, for idea generation. The studies also reveal that customers and customer contact employees are integrated indirectly, through third parties who forward relevant information in the organisation.

The findings from both studies put forward that service innovation is a struggle for resources. The case of ECH evidenced that the resources for stakeholder integration in a service innovation project are limited. This has an effect on the applied modes for stakeholder integration and implies that the management of internal and external stakeholder integration demands thoughtful balancing. In addition, the multiple case study showed that service innovation is conducted next to the regular product related business and has to compete for resources, in the setting of IT and manufacturing cases. The exploration of interdependencies resulting from the interrelatedness of stakeholder integration with other processes in the organisation, but even with processes outside the organisation, evolve as a relevant topic for future research.

The integration of internal stakeholders, including employees from other units and senior management, is highlighted throughout the service innovation process. Senior management and employees from relevant internal units are integrated reactively throughout the service innovation process, to create a stake in the project and to include "affected stakeholders" at an early stage. Moreover, the present research studies both confirm that mutual integration is implemented for the creation of unique solutions with internal stakeholders.

Shedding light on the indirect integration and interrelated stakeholder integration processes in service innovation, both studies emphasise the multi-dimensionality and complexity of stakeholder integration. The formal and informal integration of stakeholders can have effects on other stakeholders, on the resource allocation in different projects of the organisation as well as on the future relationship with the stakeholder. More research is needed to deepen our understanding of these interdependencies. Here, future research could analyse the effects in service systems in more detail and depth. To reflect the co-creative nature of the applied service-dominant logic perspective on service innovation, it is advised to investigate the dynamics of service innovation not only from the organisational viewpoint, but also from the perspective of the integrated stakeholders.

Part VI
The service systems view on stakeholder integration – a mutually engaged case study on internal stakeholder integration

Exploring stakeholder integration practice from a management perspective, Part IV and V have created a picture of stakeholder integration in service innovation that

- implements stakeholders integration foremost in a reactive mode,
- strengthens the role of senior management as a stakeholder group for service innovation,
- includes indirect and informal stakeholder integration, creating interdependencies in the service system and
- clarifies how service innovation and stakeholder integration is standing in competition with the daily work of the innovation management team.

One more important finding from Part V is that mutual integration is implemented with internal stakeholders, e.g. expert employees from other departments, to create unique offerings in interdisciplinary innovation workshops. Mutual integration was found to have side effects, such as the establishment of new connections in the organisation (case ECH) or the request of a customer to purchase the jointly developed innovation (cases OSP and LSC). The following case study takes up these findings and aims to explore which factors influence mutual stakeholder integration and what effect does mutual integration have. The study is looking at mutual stakeholder integration, implemented as an interdisciplinary innovation workshop with internal stakeholders, from the multiple individual perspectives of the integrated stakeholders. This reflects the service system view of the theoretical foundation service-dominant logic and its characteristic multidimensionality.

A service systems view on stakeholder integration
- a mutually engaged case study on internal stakeholder integration

Taking the perspective of stakeholders, what factors have influence on mutual stakeholder intergation, and what effects does it have?

In-depth case study: Exploring the affecting factors and the effects of mutual stakeholder integration in a technical research institute

Figure 18: Visualization of Part VI - mutually engaged case study on internal stakeholder integration

1 Exploring the affecting factors and effects of mutual stakeholder integration[50]

The findings of Part V and VI show, amongst others, that mutual integration with interdisciplinary stakeholders from inside the organisation plays a strong role in service innovation. The integration of different disciplines creates the possibility to develop unique offerings, as evidence from the cases ECH and RFS shows. Not only the mutual integration of internal stakeholders such as colleagues with specific expertise, but also the mutual integration of senior management evolved as an issue for service innovation in case ECH: Here, senior management was integrated for idea generation. This resulted in a wider range of ideas, greater awareness of the project and the creation of new connections within the organisation. Also the literature review in Part IV of this thesis showed that scholars put high emphasis on customer integration in the mode of "mutual integration". Research in service innovation and open innovation suggests that mutual integration of stakeholders is needed to gain access to tacit knowledge, such as the experiences of internal stakeholders (Leiponen, 2005; Neyer et al., 2009; Gottfridsson, 2012; Schilling & Werr, 2009; Mattson, 2010; Narver et al., 2004). The integration of potentially affected stakeholders is advised to create a stake in the project and to potentially increase the successful development and implementation of service innovation (Edvardsson et al., 2013; Love & Roper, 2009; Story, O'Malley, Hart, & Saker, 2008), which is by its nature a multi-dimensional process (Kindström et al., 2013; Kowalkowski et al., 2013; Carlborg et al., 2013).

Mutual integration, defined as the joint development of solutions in bi-directional exchange (Gustafsson et al., 2012; Prahalad & Ramaswamy, 2004a), can be enabled through value creation platforms, such as innovation workshops[51]. They enable direct dialogical and collaborative processes between the service system actors (Grönroos & Gummerus, 2014) and are characterised by their interdisciplinary collaboration and by a dynamic environment (Kowalkowski et al., 2013). This way, innovations workshops reflect the dynamics of stakeholder integration in service

[50] Parts of this study have been presented in an earlier version at the EurOMA 2015 conference in Neuchatel, Switzerland (Jonas et al., 2015; see Annex A).

[51] Grönroos and Gummerus (2014) call these workshops "co-creation workshops". This expression has been replaced in by "innovation workshop" for semantic reasons, to avoid confusion with "value co-creation" in this context.

innovation on a micro level. Having in mind the findings about how stakeholder integration is interdepending within service systems and how side-effects of mutual stakeholder integration can occur, a need to better understand mutual stakeholder integration practice from a systems perspective can be derived (Carlborg et al., 2013; Perks et al., 2012). The investigation of an innovation workshop allows to explore the interdependencies of mutual stakeholder integration on a micro level and has the potential to create a better understanding of stakeholder integration practice. This is why the case study in this Part VI of the thesis seeks to explore on a micro level:

> *"What factors affect the integration of internal stakeholders in the mode of mutual integration"* and *"What are the effects of mutual integration for service innovation with internal stakeholders such as expert employees and senior management?"*

The study applies the theoretic lens of the service-dominant logic, viewing stakeholder integration in service innovation as embedded in service systems. It includes the notion of value co-creation in triads or larger value constellations, as described more in depth in Part II, chapter 1.2.

2 Research approach - in-depth case study

To explore the multidimensionality in service innovation in the mode of mutual integration and to understand the dynamics of interdisciplinary work, this study takes a qualitative explorative research approach. To examine the influencing factors and effects of stakeholder integration on a micro level, a case study approach is chosen.

The research method "in-depth case study" allows to explore the dynamics of stakeholder integration embedded in service systems and to create a deep understanding of stakeholder integration processes, from multiple perspectives. To conduct a case study, access to background information, interview partners and the possibility to accompany a stakeholder integration process are required. The case of an interdisciplinary innovation project at a German research institute was chosen as a research subject since it provides the possibility to access such a process within the context of a complex service system. This selected setting allowed participant observations and a close exchange between the group of researchers and the case organisation. The case study approach makes it possible to take multiple perspectives and to include the individual viewpoints and perceptions of all workshop participants (Swanborn, 2010) to explore the affecting factors and the effects associated with mutual stakeholder integration. The conscious application of an engaged scholarship approach in the form of "basic science with stakeholder advice"[52], as presented in chapter 3 of Part II, supports the interactive character of the case study, as it enhances closeness to the research subject. This makes it possible to assess the relationship and networks aspects of the studied case in their natural context and is expected to facilitate the contextualisation of the service system, the theoretical basis of this research study.

Van de Ven (2007) and Swanborn (2010) suggest that information about the background and structure of organisations should be provided early in engaged scholarship, to allow a better understanding of the setting and the circumstances of the researched case. Hence, the context of the case study will be presented next, in advance to the presentation of data collection and data analysis.

2.1 The case organization and the case "interdisciplinary innovation workshop"

This in-depth case study to explore influence factors for and effects of mutual stakeholder integration was realised at a research institute, as a complex service system, with about 800 employees at several locations in Germany. The background for the case study is that, within the past two decades, operations were going well and had led to massive growth in the need for personnel and physical work spaces. Due to this growth, the organization established more bureaucracy and finally perceived itself to have developed something like a silo mentality and inflexibility. After a change in management a couple of years ago, the restoration of agility and cross-disciplinary for more collaboration and openness became part of a strategic program. To bridge the separations between silos and different locations as well as to establish a more open corporate innovation culture, a strategic step-by-step program for more openness was developed. The present study, an interdisciplinary two-day innovation workshop, is embedded in this program and was initiated by the top management of the organisation.

The project analysed for this case study is an internal innovation initiative across several units, which had the goal to find a solution for a technical challenge. An interdisciplinary innovation workshop was initiated to generate possible solutions

52 Compare Figure 5 in Part II of this thesis

that would transfer a concept into a market solution. A team of innovation managers of the case organization was put in charge of the project, supported by a team of three researchers.

A key role in the preparation of the workshop was given to the selection and invitation of internal stakeholders. The identification of employees from interdisciplinary units of the organisation was organised through a bi-fold strategy. On one hand, suitable internal stakeholders were directly selected from the network of the innovation managers and managers in charge of the technical problem. Additional snowballing was implemented to find suitable workshop participants[53].

This approach led to a group of eleven participants from different engineering disciplines from nine different work groups in the organisation. The two day workshop was held in October 2013. The workshop took place in an external location and was structured as follows: After an introduction of the strategic background for the project and the technical challenge to be solved, the workshop of two days included an introduction of the participants, a brainstorming session, team building, team work and presentation of first results, a social evening event, intense elaboration of solutions, prototyping, transfer of solutions into business models, presentation of overall results, wrap-up and finally, a discussion of next steps. After the presentation of the team achievements, a winning team was selected and announced. This team was rewarded with a budget for further development of their solution path.

2.2 Data collection

To find out about the factors that affect mutual stakeholder integration and the effects of such stakeholder integration, the data collection for this case study is based on a variety of primary data. These are, for the most part, interviews and a number of participatory observations of project team meetings and the participatory observation of the innovation workshop, complemented by a follow-up discussion group with the workshop participants. This methodological triangulation, together with the data triangulation to interview a broad number of participants, is a measure to strengthen the quality of data (Flick, 2014). To gain access to the participants' perception and reflections of the workshop and to find out about influencing factors and effects coming along with the issue of stakeholder integration, interviews with all directly involved workshop participants and the workshop managers were held in a period of

53 Snowballing is inspired by chain referral sampling - the process of asking direct contact persons for a recommendation of people in their network who possess specific characteristics (see e.g. Goodman, 1961, Biernacki and Waldorf, 2004 or Noy, 2008).

two months after the interdisciplinary innovation workshop. This time frame was chosen to gain access to fresh memories on one hand and to allow the reflection on the event on the other hand. Only one interview with the group manager MST, the "owner of the problem to be solved", was conducted in advance to the workshop, to gain an understanding of expectations and perceived uncertainties to facilitate later reflection of the gained experiences.

Figure 19: Impressions from the workshop (left) and the group discussion (right)

All in all, fifteen interviews were realized face-to-face at the premises of the interviewees according to a semi-structured interview guideline with generally open questions. The interviews included questions such as *"How comes that you participated in the workshop?"*, *"What expectations and ideas for the workshop did you bring along?"*, *"How do you evaluate the workshop in hindsight?"*, *"What are the prerequisites for the implementation of such a co-creation workshop?"* and *"What effects does such an initiative have on the organisation?"* This interview guideline also included open questions about collaboration across the boundaries of organisational units and across the boundaries of work units. The interviews lasted from 24 minutes to 1 hour and 30 minutes, with an average duration of 51 minutes. An overview of all interviews is presented in Table 16.

The interviews were implemented by a team of trained researchers according to the guidelines given by Casell and Symon (2012). Due to the relational closeness of the interviewer to the organisation, special emphasis was put on the anonymity of interviews and the explicit separation of data collection and analysis processes from the workshop organisation and the management team.

Table 16: Interviewees of the in-depth case study[54]

Interviewee	Duration
Strategy and Innovation Manager (SIM)	1 hr 30min
Team Manager MT 1 (TM-MT1)	47 min
Senior Engineer CND (SE-CND)	47 min
Senior Engineer ROT (SE-ROT)	32 min
Senior Engineer MES (SE – MES)	1hr 28min
Group Manager MAV (GM-MAV)	44 min
Team Manager FUK (TM-FUK)	25 min
Innovation and Project Manager (IPM)	1 hr 16 min
Professor - Research & Consultancy (PRC)	24 min
Engineer UEC (E-UEC)	1 hr 8 min
Team Manager MT 2 (TM-MT2)	28 min
Engineer ROT (E-ROT)	38 min
Group Manager MST (GM-MST)	ex ante 57 min ex post 29 min
Senior Engineer FUK (SE-FUK)	24 min

In addition, details from a number of participatory observations of meetings for the preparation, the discussion and reflection of the joint innovation initiative are included in the data utilised for this case study. The protocols and notes from meetings and discussions are integrated as a second pillar of data. As displayed in Table 17, the participatory observations include a) four business meetings of the team of innovation managers from the case organisation and the team of researchers, b) the two day innovation workshop itself and c) a group discussion[55] with the workshop

[54] For confidentiality issues, the names and positions of the interviewees of this study are anonymised. As Flick (2014) suggests, this measure is taken to guarantee that "*colleagues cannot identify participants from information about the study*" (Flick, 2014; p. 59.)

[55] The group discussion was organized on May 28th 2014. After a tight presentation of findings that allowed full transparency into findings of the interviews, participants started to discuss with each other, on their own initiative. Only a minimum of moderation steered the dynamic discussion amongst the interviewees.

participants. The last named group discussion[56] took place to check data validity (as suggested by Swanborn, 2010 and Hartley, 2004) and served as feedback for the perception of findings by the researcher. The format of the group discussion was chosen to allow reflection in the group that participated in the workshop, additionally to facilitate feedback on the presentation of research findings. The more open format of a group discussion was preferred to a focus group to reflect the interactive set-up of the workshop. Overall, the data collection took place between July 2013 and May 2014.

Table 17: Participatory observation of meetings

Participatory observation of meetings		
Date	**Participants**	**Content**
2013-07-10	Meeting with SIM and PRC	preparation of activities; first draft of workshop proposal
2013-07-30	Meeting with CEO, SIM, IPM, PRC and project owner (group manager MST)	introduction of plans, joint discussion, next steps and task allocation
2013-10-24 & 2013-10-25	Innovation workshop with all interviewees plus another researcher	1,5 day workshop to solve a given technical challenge through interdisciplinary group work
2014-03-05	Meeting with SIM, CEO and PRC	presentation of lessons learned, discussion and next steps
2014-04-23	Meeting with SIM, IPM and PRC	review of activities since workshop and preparation of the presentation to the group
2014-05-28	Group discussion with SIM, SE-FUK, E-ROT, GM-MAV, SE-MES, SE-ROT and an intern of SE-MES	Review presentation, invitation to all members; discussion of format and activities

2.3 Data analysis

For data analysis, all interviews were audio-recorded and transcribed as soon as possible, to foster reflection about collected data at an early stage (Miles et al., 2013). The data analysis, utilizing the computer-assisted qualitative data analysis software

[56] Group discussions are, just as focus groups, the discussion of stimulus material in a group of up to twelve people. A dynamic discussion is stimulated and fosters the expression of single opinions and a group opinion (Flick, 2014).

MAXQDA for data structuring, applied an open, inductive data analysis approach (Miles et al., 2013; Eisenhardt & Graebner, 2007), similar to open coding as in grounded theory (Gremler, 2004; Suddaby, 2006). In the first step, themes and initial codes for the codebook were developed by reading the interviews. In the second step, all interviews were coded according to the developed codebook. Only few alterations were made during the coding process to fit the data more precisely. This process resulted in 585 codings, in codebook categories such as "workshop review", "influence factors" (with subcategories), "effects of interdisciplinary innovation activity" (with sub-categories), "organisation and culture", "project/innovation management" and "collaboration in general"[57].

After this first structuring of data, patterns, similarities and differences in the collected data were analysed and re-grouped according to the pattern matching logic (Yin, 2014). The triangulation of the data sources, observations, interviews and the discussion group is thereby used to enhance the validity of the case study. This "network of information" helps to give meaning to language (Creswell, 2012; King and Horrocks, 2010). As suggested by Swanborn (2010), the derived findings are presented in structured tables, summarizing the data and yet providing transparency and a feeling for the data through the usage of quotations (Patton, 2007).

[57] Following the guidelines for data analysis by Creswell (2012) and Miles et al. (2013), codes are seen as "*labels that assign meaning to the descriptive or inferential information compiled during a study.*" (Miles et al., 2013; p. 71). This implies that data pieces might be relevant to different sets of meaning, allowing overlaps in codes, Further, it implies that a first cycle of analysis is already applied while coding (Schreier, 2012) and codes may be re-defined as well as new codes from the data derived from the data inductively may be added (Miles et al., 2013; Andrade, 2009). This is different from the school of Mayring (2010) who proposes a step by step abstraction of data material that must not produce any overlaps in codings.

3 Findings

The dynamics of mutual stakeholder integration in an interdisciplinary innovation workshop could be explored in-depth through the analysis of a rich data set and the combination of the multiple data sources. The exploration of mutual stakeholder integration in this case study revealed a number of factors that affect stakeholder integration, and in parallel it revealed a number of effects of such stakeholder integration. The findings from this case study are presented in two main sequences - first, the affecting factors that influence the innovation workshop will be presented and second, the effects of the respective stakeholder integration will be detailed in the following paragraphs.

3.1 Factors affecting stakeholder integration

For stakeholder integration in the mode of mutual integration, seven influencing factors are identified. These are 1) time and timing, 2) previous experiences, 3) individual motivation, 4) invitation/the right people, 5) commitment of management, 6) organisational culture and 7) structure and modalities. Figure 20 shows an overview of the influencing factors. It emerged from the data that the factors can be grouped accordingly: factors that are on a participant level (1-3), factors that are to be seen in the sphere and design task of the project manager, the integrator, (4-5) and factors that are guided by the service system (6-7).

3.1.1 Factors on the individual participant level

On the individual level of the participants, time and timing emerge as a key influencing factor. This means that the stakeholders can **set time free** from their regular work, and that the timing of the workshop fits into their schedule, as there are no clashes with other fixed calendar entries. The participant has to be able and willing to allocate time, next to getting their regular work done. In addition, the manager of the participant has to agree that the employee can put aside time for the innovation workshop.

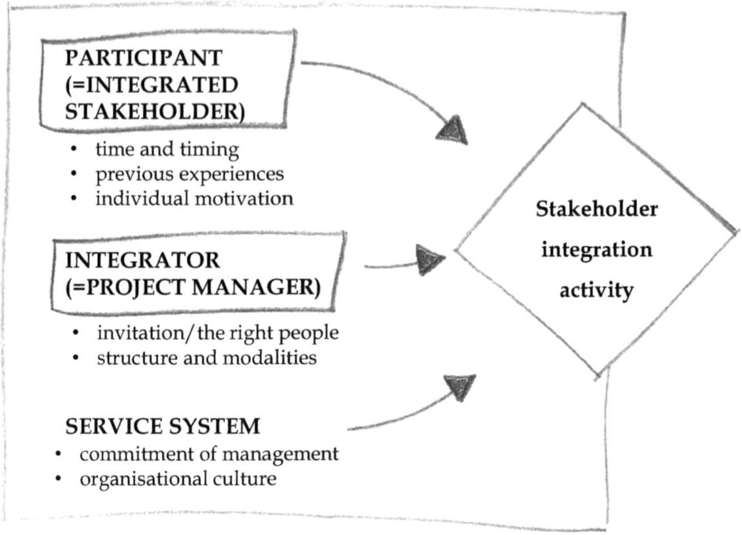

Figure 20: Factors that affect stakeholder integration in the mode of mutual integration

A second influence factor that emerged from the inductive data analysis is **the participants' previous experience** with any type of similar workshops, for instance creativity and innovation workshops and other cross-disciplinary activities in the organisation. Whilst for instance interviewees TM-MT1 and TM-MT2 had experienced stimulating innovation workshops before, interviewee SE-CND reported on rather boring experiences; interviewee GM-MST referred to negative experiences from trying to conduct a creativity workshop himself in his team. These experiences shaped the expectations and attitude towards the participation at the investigated innovation workshop.

Potentially intertwined with the influence factor "previous experience", is the **individual motivation** to participate in the innovation workshop. The interviewees reported that their motivations for joining the workshop were "because it would be fun to solve an engineering problem", "to get out of everyday life and meet other people" and because they would "get to know innovation methods". Those workshop participants, being engineers by background, but holding a team leader position, stressed that they participate because of the factor "fun to solve a problem".

Moreover, the majority of interviewees shared the motivation "getting out of the treadmill and see something else" or "see other people".

Table 18: Exemplary quotes for the influence factors on the individual participant level

time and timing	*"Time is really the most important factor. I see myself how many ideas are getting lost because daily business is always urgent. To get into a problem and analyse technical and economic feasibility all this post-processing work demands a lot of time. And this is the time you don't take, or you don't have, depending on your perspective. This is why I liked to be allowed to think freely for the time of the workshop. Of course, the time was missing somewhere else, but I did set it free happily."* (TM-MT1) *"The original candidate to participate could not make it at that day. So he asked if he could send someone else instead, which was fine. I was really interested in the topic. [...] You need the support from your supervisor, yes. And for me, it was a bit spontaneous and created some pressure for preparing the conference travels in the days after the workshop."* (SE-ROT)
previous experiences	*"This thing with creativity techniques... I tried to conduct a workshop myself after some training where we heard that we should use paper and that people should possible walk around in a room etc. There was a lot of resistance. I tried it in my group, but they thought it was silly or something. They are rather sceptical with new things and did not stand up to walk around."* (GM-MST) *"I participated in a series of workshops where there was space to play technically. There were expert tables to find solutions for specific problems. When it was about a sports device we went to the gym to exercise and solved problems right there. [...] I liked it a lot and would be happy to implement that for future creativity workshops."* (TM-MT1) *"Yes, I have participated in innovation workshops where somebody came with a past with pins, a flipchart and some brainstorming etc. Of course there is a wide variety, but most of the times experience was not that exciting."* (SE-CND)
individual motivation	*"I am quite open for things like that and looked forward to the workshop. Also, because it was communicated that the management wants us to learn new methods. And, by coincidence we were looking for new methods in our unit to generate ideas a bit more systematically. That's why I thought that I can make use of it since the topic was on the table already."* (TM-MT2) *"I really did look forward to it! I felt honoured because I knew this was something new. It is some kind of pioneering work – that simple made me curious."* (SE-MES) *"Maybe a change of scene, the creation of a situation to be creative and develop innovations further. I know it from other workshops and enjoyed it a lot. Not sitting in the office or a meeting room, but change of scene, a different atmosphere, some moderation. The mixture of a new task and the freedom to solve the task. That was I looked forward to."* (TM-MT1)

3.1.2 Factors at the integrator level

Interview statements and observations showed that the eleven workshop participants were highly motivated to attend the innovation workshop.

Nevertheless, some of the participants showed concerns that the right **combination of people** to participate in such a workshop is crucial for its overall success. In the interviewees' view, motivated and open minded people have to be invited to facilitate an engaged and friendly atmosphere as well as open exchange. In this context, the right strategy to invite people, to make people curious and to make the event somewhat special have been mentioned as further aspects that are designed by the integrator and under his/her control.

Table 19: Exemplary quotes for the influence factors on the integrators and project level

invitation & the right people	*"My only concern was that it depends on what people are coming together. If that doesn't fit, it cannot work out in my opinion. […] they were all people that were interested, had fun and took the time, not reading emails at the end of the day. That's a threat around here."* (SE-FUK) *"I think that this is funny: I heard that the combination of people was 'coincidence,' so, rather purposefully selected people from different units, engaged, open, communicative, younger. Younger people to avoid old ways of thinking. That means you leave out experience, but I understood that there should explicitly be young, fresh air at the workshop."* (TM-MT1)
supporting structure and modalities	*"I don't think you can say ‚co-creation is cool, let's do it ourselves!'. It has to be well prepared and moderated of someone who has done it before to generate good results. I don't think I could do it with five people. […] To have a room a bit off, to be in a closed setting is helpful, too."* (SE-FUK) *"People have to come open and on their own will…. That is contradicting with the idea that is has to be initiated from the top – because otherwise people won't come. But it must not be that it will be decided 'you go there because the big man said so'. It has to be possible to work on the problems freely. But then again you can't participate at a time where you are facing a though deadline [in your regular project] and face a lot of unsolved problem there."* (GM-MAV)

The next influencing factor emerging from the case study data relates to the **structure and modalities** that come along with the innovation workshop. According to the workshop participants, the design of the workshop has to be well thought through and has to enable an open atmosphere. The preparation and the creation of the right setting, moderation and a suitable agenda, are further factors that can and have to be designed well, as the interviewees express. The quotes in Table 19 show that the design and setting even is intertwined with the selection of the right stakeholders to be integrated; it is put forward by the interviewees that only an open invitation strategy and voluntary participation allow for a good and safe working environment.

3.1.3 Factors at the system level

On a service system level, the identified influencing factors are **commitment of management** and open organisational culture at middle and senior level. This is a factor which is implicitly and explicitly perceived to have a strong influence on the conduction of the mutual stakeholder integration workshop. As already mentioned for the individual factor "time and timing", the interviewees report that their direct supervisor or team manager has to agree with the participation in the workshop since it potentially affects the scheduling of other meetings and projects. Moreover, the middle and senior management have to support the interdisciplinary work. The participants of the workshop reflected about the silo mentality between the different departments which is built upon a struggle for budgets, impeding interdisciplinary projects. In the present case, the support of management is ensured trough the personal and financial engagement of the CEO. Some representative statements depicting these reflections are presented in Table 20.

The lack of interdisciplinary work across the different units is a subject of discussion in various contexts in the case. Interdisciplinary thinking was one of the main reasons for the initiation of the innovation workshop. This issue is not only reflected on by the CEO and project management; also the interviewed participants discuss the lack of interdisciplinary work in the organisation as one of the factors that formed the starting point for a mutual innovation initiative. In the perception of the interviewees, an interdisciplinary culture is lacking in the organisation. To enable mutual stakeholder integration, they refer to an **open communication style** and **a culture of curiosity** in the organisation that enables mutual stakeholder integration. Within the boundaries of the organisation, it is reported that the workshop participants did feel free to fail and to take some risks without performance pressure. According to the interviews, this influencing factor is perceived as a positive aspect that allowed for free thinking and working during the workshop, as illustrated in the quotes in Table 20.

Table 20: Exemplary quotes for the influence factors on the system level

commitment and support of management	*"Our bosses have to be behind it. I am still doubtful about this how to convince them. It is feasible, basically. And we have seen how new ideas can develop if people from other disciplines come in. They are free and less restricted to a discipline."*(SE-ROT) *"Internally, we have a long way to go until something like it [open innovation workshops] can happen unlike the senior management initiates it proactively."* (SE-CND) *"The CEO did come by and showed that he was truly interested. He wanted to know what our results were – that was nice."* (SE-FUK) *"That the CEO recognizes something like this and supports it. This was the case here. Some managers in our unit might see something like this as a burden. If they don't live this, it will be though, you will run against a wall. The two days had to be taken off time from other things and we didn't lose budget, so it was ok. But whenever this will not be the case, the signals will be more negative."* (TM-MT2)
open communication culture	*"I didn't feel it was linked to some kind of ‚obligation of results'."* (SE-ROT) *"The topic has to come more often, from senior management. Our CEO presented it at some event recently… reactions were not overall positive! How does that fit into our current structure?! – it is interesting and exciting to bring some movement here. But to get to the point to think about opening up a solution of a problem I cannot solve… it's about giving away control."* (SE-CND) *"We do have a culture to be very open and not to mince matters here. Input from outside is very meaningful. But I would reduce openness to trusted partners."* (TM-MT2)

3.2 Effects of mutual stakeholder integration

After this introduction of the influencing factors for the mutual stakeholder integration, now the derived effects of the mutual stakeholder integration "innovation workshop" will be presented. The effects of mutual integration in form of an innovation workshop cannot be split into distinct categories for the affecting factors for the mutual integration of interdisciplinary employees.

The identified effects relate to more than one level as they have an impact on the individual level, but also one the sub-system of the participants, their regular work unit, or on wider parts of the organisation. Amongst these are expected effects such as networking and short term motivation. The analysis of the observations and the reflections of all the participants in the interviews also showed that the initiative provoked the start of a thought process. This includes the reflections on the overall innovativeness and innovation culture of the organisation, a demand for information and transparency about the future plans that follow after the prototype workshop, as well as ideas and expectations about the repetition and adaption of interdisciplinary innovation initiatives. The nine identified effects are presented sequentially in the following paragraphs, with exemplary quotes from the selected interview data presented in Table 21.

1) Looking back at the workshop, all participants and management felt that the mutual integration resulted in the creation of **a really new concept.** This was enabled by the free thinking and the joint brainstorming of people from different backgrounds. 2) Next, all interviewees, including the initiator of the innovation workshop, gained **short term motivation** for their regular work from the innovation workshop. The playful team work, the interesting and challenging topic and the jointly developed results from the workshop were perceived as positive and fun. In line with these aspects, it was also reported that the participants enjoyed getting out of their everyday life. This reflects their earlier presented expectations, as presented in the influence factor motivation.

3) Another effect of mutual integration met the expectations of the workshop participants is **networking and getting to know new people**. Whilst about half of the workshop participants knew each other, other participants were new contacts. This situation was intended by the project management team, which had approached and selected the workshop participants. In this context it was mentioned how difficult networking in the organisation with its different locations is. The workshop enabled some exchange between former colleagues who enjoyed catching up on their work and other things during the coffee and lunch breaks, informally.

In the analysis of influencing factors, it emerged that there were three participants who explicitly stated that they joined the workshop since they were motivated to learn new tools. 4) Surprisingly, there were three other participants who reported that they took the workshop as an inspiration and **implemented some tools in their work units** right afterwards, as an effect of the workshop. These participants reported about their **plans to implement mutual stakeholder integration into their current or upcoming projects** for the mutual integration of internal stakeholders; one interviewee even started planning an innovation workshop with close customers for a new project.

5) An effect of the innovation workshop that emerged from the interview data is the fact that it **generated additional work** in form of a follow-up project for a group of participants that won some budget to continue with their idea. For the manager "owning the problem", this effect was positive, since the challenge received official project status after the workshop. For the further development of the solution after

the innovation workshop, technical parts and software could now be financed from the assigned budget. Thereby, the time to work on the further development of the idea was perceived as critical by other workshop participants. Whereas for instance participant SE-MES reported to be enthusiastic about continuing to work with the solution of the problem, participant SE-ROT explained that he had not expected that there would be work resulting from the participation in the innovation workshop and that he does not have any resources available to proceed with such an additional project within the next month.

6) Regarding the results of the innovation workshop, another effect that emerged from the data is that the integrated employees wanted to know what happened with the project in the next step. The participants **asked for an open communication of the activities that follow after the workshop**. This was not only clarified during the interviews, but a repeated issue even in the group discussion and meetings in between the formal meetings. Not only information about the progress of the work on the solutions, also information about the continued plans for repetition of similar mutual stakeholder integration activities was requested from senior management. From the exchange with the interview participants, it was shown that the workshop had a thought provoking effect on the integrated stakeholders.

7) It also shows that the integrated stakeholders, the participants in the innovation workshop, expressed that they were interested in the mentioned strategy towards more open innovation. Moreover, some participants stated that they started **thinking about the innovation culture** of the organisation, including the given space for creativity. The respective respondents used well known examples as 3M or Google for comparison to reflect upon the need to set some space free for employees to invest in innovation topics. As the interviewed participants explained, this was not an isolated process, but a thought process they took with them to their work units to discuss with close colleagues in the coffee corner.

8) These reflections, solitary or in the group with colleagues, led to some **ideas and suggestions of how to proceed with the strategy to create a more open innovation culture** and to initiate more projects across units. Without being asked, some suggestions for the adaptions of the innovation workshop format came up during the interviews; including for instance changes in the scheduling, a combination of individual and team work and the strategy to identify suitable workshop participants.

9) From the details of the named effects and from the meetings with the CEO and innovation management of the organisation, it evolved that the positive or negative **perception of the workshop results on the individual and the management level was leading to a go/kill decision** for the repetition or institutionalisation of the mutual integration practice. Depending on how the participants perceived the workshop itself and the developed results, they would report about their reflections to their close colleagues. Depending on the perception of the CEO, future attempts to conduct similar workshops would either be supported or be closed before they even started.

Table 21: The effects of mutual stakeholder integration activity – overview with illustrative quotations

What effects does mutual stakeholder integration activity have?	
1 **New concepts**	*"You come up with ideas, concepts that you would probably not achieve otherwise."* (SE-ROT) *"I considered the most interesting that people from different units with different backgrounds came together. We do brainstorming and discussions in our group, but the ideas are similar because we all share the same background. If you are together with different people and various experiences, new ideas will come. That's what I think."* (TM-FUK)
2 **Short-term motivation**	*"It was about ten hours net that the guys had to solve the problem. From the formula on paper and in their heads to that demonstrator, in such as short period of time. I found this unbelievable!"* (IPM) *"Yes, we all gained from getting to know people, to know how others do their thinking and see that there are other people that can see beyond their nose. Otherwise you don't really get this."* (E-UEC)
3 **New internal connections, networking**	*"It was nice to meet my former colleague. I talked to him more often in a former project, but he is now located at another site so we didn't talk for a long time. You find new interfaces while talking, that's nice. […] I think it is interesting to meet people from another discipline, too. You get these contacts only from projects or from trainings."* (SE-FUK) *"I did get to know these people, I liked that. So I guess whenever I will have a problem into that direction or have an idea that something could be solved like this and that, then I knew whom to ask from that unit. Because, I would not write an email to a group manager or fill in some form. I would just ask 'Hey, do you know someone who is dealing with this topic?'"* (E-ROT)

4 **Transfer of workshop tools and ideas into work-life**	*"So in the beginning when everyone talked to everyone – I did like that. I already applied it in a group résumé we did here. You take away some of these games."* (E-ROT) *"The method was really interesting, for my perception it worked really well. I am currently leading a project where we will start using a similar approach with support of the innovation management. It's about idea generation and we want to do something similar. Let's see how it works! We have to try, play with it and see how it works and if we like it."* (TM-FUK)
5 **Further work on solutions; legitimisation of the project**	*"The project has a new focus now: I have applied a student worker on some trials now. […] Other colleagues from other units are allowed to work on the topic that would never have thought about it before. […] I have contact to people that I can talk to and share my thoughts with now. – Overall, there is a much higher awareness, which is good."* (GM-MST) *"For example the software licenses – our colleagues needed the licence for their project so we had to leave the tool when someone else needed it. Now we have the legitimization to use it and to do the according work."* (SE-FUK)
6 **Demand for information, transparency and repetition with adaptions**	*"I would like to know, in a few months' time, what happened with the results. I think something like a status email would be interesting. If there is something, like a prototype, a little video or something, so you get an idea. I think that would be nice. It's not like they have to do it, but it would be a good gesture."* (E-ROT) *"Yes, I would be interested, but I didn't ask the project manager actively, and he didn't contact me either. I guess that would be something to do when clearing the desk at the end of the year, to ask 'what's your status? What did you do with it?'"* (SE-CND)
7 **Reflection on innovation strategy and culture**	*"You could see the innovation workshop as a signal that people are not innovative enough. That was an impulse I had. The problem in our team for example is not that we are not innovative, but that we have too much to do overall."* (SE-CND) *"There has to be free room for people to be creative. If I imagine a day at work, I have to go to meetings, get things done,… creativity simply gets repressed during everyday life."* (E-UEC) *"He said that you do research on innovation in other organisations, too. I would like to learn about how others deal with innovation. So I am interested in the results, what are differences, how do they function differently? I have been in this organization since university – I am sure there are other approaches."* (E-UEC)
8 **Ideas and expectations for future practices**	*"Monday after the meeting, we did discuss a lot about how to do this, to advertise innovation topics internally, to apply for. Like, 'hey this topic is interesting, I would take a day time for that!' So that you have to apply to participate, for example."* (SE-FUK) *"I would want this to be more sustainable and long-term. Not only 1-2 days and then we forget about it. But to have groups built at the workshop that meet over the run of a year and to have a final event. For sustainability. This setting was too playful for me."* (E-UEC)
9 **Evaluation decides about adaption and repetition**	*"What I need are practical examples. I have to see that I get something out if I try this for two, three times. If we do not get results, it takes too much time. We need examples where we see: We generated new ideas, it was a success."* (TM-FUK)

3.3 Effects of mutual stakeholder integration from a service systems view

The further analysis of these effects from a service system understanding shows that the effects of mutual stakeholder integration are all (apart from short-motivation) having effects that concern the individual and its subsystem and/or the service system. Figure 21 visualises the different effects of the innovation workshop and the system levels they affect - individual, sub-system or general service system. This visualises that a mutual stakeholder integration cannot be implemented in isolation - the integrated participants interact with their subsystems and affect them by reporting about their experiences or by implementing workshop tools in their work units; the reactions of all integrated and involved stakeholders spread in a service system and have an influence going beyond the service systems of the individual participants.

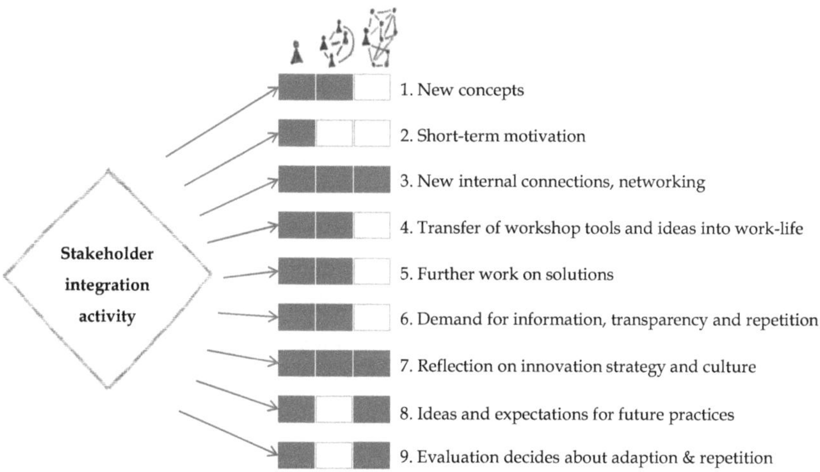

Figure 21: The effects of mutual stakeholder integration on individual, sub-system and service system level

When reflecting about the innovation culture, discussing ideas and expectations for the future practices in the organisation, the participants approach their colleagues in their sub-system and integrate them into their thoughts. But even senior management is asked for a reaction when employees formulate a variety of questions after their mutually engaged participation in the workshop. Important for organisational practice is the evaluation of the mutual stakeholder integration initiative - the perceptions of the individual participants, of the project manager as a resource integrator and middle and senior management determine whether future stakeholder integration practices, like in this case, will be possible and supported in the future.

4 Discussion

The present study investigates the affecting factors and effects of internal stakeholder integration for service innovation in the mode of mutual integration. Following an engaged scholarship approach, it was possible to analyse the case of an innovation workshop for solving a given innovation task in the organisation.

On a micro level, the empirical data confirms earlier research that the integration of different skills and expertise can lead to superior solutions (Edvardsson et al., 2013). This study verifies the development of new ideas through the mutual integration (Janssen et al., 2013) of internal stakeholder. Also, the interviews of the case study showed that even participants in mutual integration consider the choice of the right people for stakeholder integration in service innovation as necessary. Authors like Stevens and Dimitriadis (2005), Alam (2011) or Perks and Riihela (2004) stress the skills, knowledge and competences of the stakeholders to be integrated. In the present context the open communication, motivation and voluntary participation were named as important factors, confirming earlier findings. Yet the consideration of the individual motivation and backgrounds of the integrated stakeholders is stressed as part of stakeholder integration management which has to embrace cultural and environmental challenges. It has to balance resources, to decide about timings and to communicate with stakeholders in the right way to establish or to maintain their engagement with the respective project (Gottfridsson, 2012; Kindström et al., 2013; Payne et al., 2007; Perks et al., 2012; Perks & Riihela, 2004; Smith & Fischbacher, 2005; Stevens & Dimitriadis, 2005). Bearing in mind that the selection of stakeholders for integration was found to be a challenge in the interview study in Part III as well as in the in-depth case study of Part IV, this adds further emphasis on the usage of existing network connections and the explicit and implicit criteria used to find the "right people" for service innovation.

This case study strengthens the need to manage complexities and to recognize the need for behavioural skills in the organisation to deal with interdependencies and multi-faceted processes as proposed by Smith and Fischbacher (2005). Gottfridsson and Stålhammar (2014) suggest that service innovation requires the combination of actors with different types of knowledge, as in this mutual stakeholder workshop. They also stress that the processes for the interaction and cooperation between all integrated stakeholders has to be designed and communicated. As put forward by Gottfridsson et al. (2012) and Freeman (1982), communication plays a vital role for stakeholder integration. This case of a innovation workshop clarified that the integration of stakeholders demands communication to keep the integrated stakeholders up to date with the progress of the service innovation project. Moreover the mutual integration in this innovation workshop brought up questions about the organisational innovation strategy and culture that have to be caught and managed.

In addition, Carlborg et al. (2013) and Smith and Fischbacher (2005) put forward that the selection and management of stakeholders in service systems is a relevant topic in service innovation. This micro level process study provides a vivid example for the "real-life challenge" of stakeholder integration in practice. In the present case, the dynamics of stakeholder integration are shown. For instance, it was not anticipated by the initiators of the innovation workshop that the need to report on innovation strategies and alternative structures would emerge as strongly.

Whilst some side-effects represent rather critical issues, the implementation on of workshop tools and interdisciplinary work emerging from the participation was perceived as very positive by the innovation managers. The interview study with service innovation intermediaries in this thesis already indicated that the integration of employees is, in some cases, a possibility to teach new working methods for service innovation. In this case, it is shown that internal stakeholders are on the one hand motivated to participate in innovation activities to learn about new methods, and on the other hand that employees just naturally adopt the workshop tools and implement them in their work unit.

Another issue discussed in the literature review as well as in the interview study in Part IV and in the multiple case study of Part V (chapter 3), is the competition for resources for stakeholder integration. The empirical data supports earlier which gives evidence that setting free time as a resource is a key challenge for stakeholder integration (Schilling & Werr, 2009; Mention & Asikainen, 2012). The present findings confirm that time allocation is an obstacle for stakeholder integration and add that the participation in the innovation workshop requires even more additional time resources for the further development of the technical solutions after the workshop. The case study makes it clear that the struggle for the resource time does not only relate to time needed for the stakeholder integration workshop itself, but that it potentially also creates "homework" as a takeaway and that it has to fit in the schedule with other projects of the participants.

The major contribution from the case study analysis is that it exemplifies the multi-dimensionality of service innovation in service systems (Lusch, 2006; Vargo et al., 2008; Maglio et al., 2009). The derived effects of mutual stakeholder integration "networking", "application of tools" and "ideas and expectations for future practices" give evidence that stakeholder integration in service systems happens in value constellations (Kowalkowski, Persson Ridell et al., 2012; Kowalkowski et al., 2013; Vargo & Lusch, 2014) that reach beyond the stakeholder integration activity. In this case, the effects of mutual stakeholder integration go beyond the boundaries of the innovation workshop and affect wider parts of the service system, such as the work units of the workshop participants. Figure 22 visualises the service systems that are affected by and having effects on the stakeholder integration activity "innovation workshop". The innovation workshop in the centre is interrelated with the service systems of the workshop participants and the management team; all sub-systems are embedded in the overall service system "organisation".

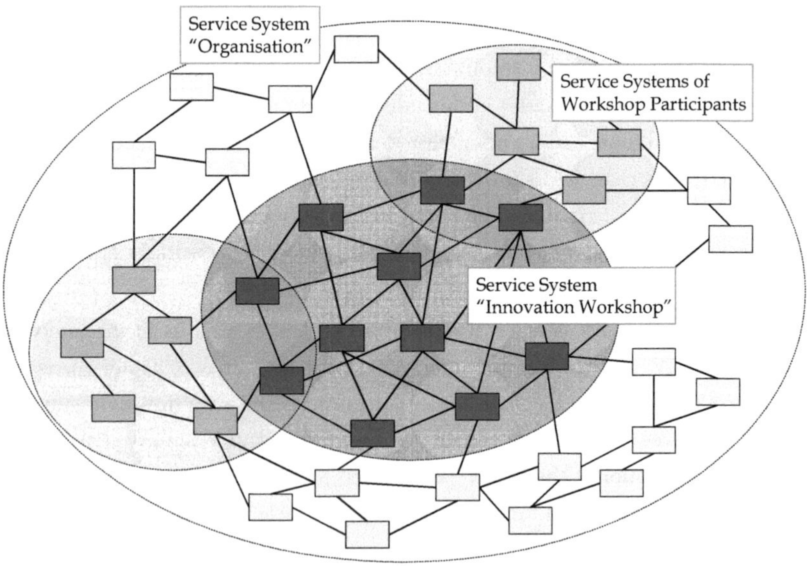

Figure 22: Embeddedness of the service innovation workshop in its' surrounding service systems

Whilst the multidimensionality of service innovation has been discussed in various scholarly papers in the past decade (Agarwal & Selen, 2011; Kindström et al., 2013; Schleimer & Shulman, 2011; den Hertog, 2010), service innovation has not explicitly been clarified. The micro level data of the case study indicates that the value creation for service innovation in service systems as depicted above does not have to result in "mutual exchange" of value (Vargo et al., 2008, p.145), in the meaning of bi-directional value transfer between the integrator and the integrated party. Instances from the observed case study show that the value creation in service systems does not necessarily build on reciprocal value exchange between the integrator and the participant. Return value for the participants' contribution to service innovation can also originate from other stakeholders. An example is given by interviewee E-ROT, who took a workshop tool to his unit and applied it for his team work. He gained return value from the participation in the innovation workshop in a different setting, with other system actors and with a time delay. Other interviewees, such as TM-MT1 and E-UEC reported that they gained value from networking amongst each other.

These are only examples for value co-creation that is enabled through or between the participants, not between the resource integrator and the integrated participant. This additional notion of multidimensionality extends the current understanding of interdependencies and mutual value creation between integrated stakeholders in service systems, as discussed by Janssen et al. (2013), Russo-Spena and Mele (2012), Vargo et al. (2010) or Blazevic and Lievens (2004), just to name a few.

5 Summary and conclusions

This case study aimed to explore the dynamics of internal stakeholder integration in the mode of mutual integration. Precisely it sought to answer the questions "What are the factors that influence stakeholder integration for service innovation?" and "What effects does stakeholder integration in the form of an internal innovation workshop have?" The study confirmed that previous findings derived in service organisations are applicable and valid for engineering services of a technical research institute. These findings are that a) mutual integration results in new, superior solutions, b) time is a critical resource for the participation in mutual innovation, and c) the support of middle and senior management is perceived as a crucial factor.

The in-depth case study, following the engaged scholarship approach with close interaction and observations, revealed that stakeholder integration in the mode of mutual integration comes with side-effects which have to be managed in the organisation. They demand competences, such as communication and transparency from the organisation.

As a main contribution, the case study exemplifies the multi-dimensionality of service innovation in organisational practice: The effects of stakeholder integration of this innovation workshop do not only affect the stakeholders that directly participated in the workshop, but also the sub-systems of the participants (their regular work units) and parts of the overall service system (the organisation). The effects can be direct, as in the context of resource allocation, or indirect, as through the discussions about the organisations' innovation strategy and the adaption or repetition of similar formats. Furthermore, it suggests that the value co-creation for joint service innovation is not only reciprocal (or mutual) and instant value exchange. Value may be gained from the participation in other contexts than the innovation workshop or through the interaction with the other integrated stakeholders.

To sum up, this case study contributes to knowledge on actor participation in service systems by providing concrete influencing factors and effects of mutual stakeholder integration. It puts forward that the integration of internal network actors for mutually engaged innovations is interrelated with on three levels – the integrating party, the integrated stakeholder and the system itself. The awareness of the depicted influence factors and effects can be seen as a step on the pathway towards a better understanding of how to manage the complexity of innovation in service systems and of how to design the structures that are required to facilitate mutual integration for innovation across disciplines.

Part VII

Summary of findings and implications

The final part of this thesis provides a summary of findings (chapter 1) and derives a model for stakeholder integration in service innovation as a process where stakeholder integration activities, the service system, the integrator and the participant are interrelated, influenced by and influencing each other (chapter 2). In chapter three, the implications for management and the implications for service research will be discussed. This is followed by an outlook, deriving future research directions, and a final conclusion. A personal final note will close this doctoral dissertation.

1 Summary of findings

Service innovation has been discussed intensively as a multi-dimensional process, highly dependent on the integration of internal and external stakeholders (Edvardsson et al., 2013; Kindström et al., 2013). Theory suggests that all affected stakeholders, including internal and external stakeholders, should be integrated in service innovation (Edvardsson et al., 2013), in order to capture the stakeholders' knowledge, skills and experiences for the joint creation of a service innovation. To explore stakeholder integration practice in service systems, consisting of both internal and external stakeholders (Tossavainen, 2013; Kindström et al., 2013), this thesis applied a three step approach.

The first step, "a look from outside" (Part IV), synthesises findings from scholarly work in service innovation research. This screening of literature in service innovation showed that the integration of stakeholders is generally considered to be highly beneficial for service innovation; customer integration in particular leads to solutions that more directly meet the needs of the customer with faster innovation circles. Empirical research has also found that stakeholder integration comes with some challenges, such as resource allocation, including the willingness and ability of stakeholders to participate in the process. It has also been derived from the review of literature that some stakeholder groups, such as customer contact employees (who are directly responsible for value co-creation with the customer and its satisfaction (Grönroos 1982; Parasuraman, Zeithaml, & Berry, 1988) are not integrated as much as it could be expected. The interview study with intermediaries in Part IV added to this, by emphasising the integration of management and employees from the firm, even for service innovation projects focussing on customer integration. The study showed that even though stakeholder integration aims to integrate the tacit knowledge and experiences of the integrated stakeholders, integration practice is foremost implemented in a passive or reactive mode, and not as mutual integration as literature would suggest.

The second step of this thesis applied a combined single and multiple case study approach to access the phenomenon "stakeholder integration in service systems" (Part V). An organisational management perspective was taken to explore which stakeholders are integrated in which mode in the different stages of the innovation process. The findings of the first in-depth study of an IT service innovation project, confirm that the majority of stakeholders is integrated in a reactive way. Mutual integration evolved to be relevant foremost for the integration of internal stakeholders in the idea generation stage. This investigation has been replicated to validate and enrich the findings in a second, multiple case study with German medium-sized organisations in the IT and manufacturing business. The analysis of empirical data from both case studies show that mutual integration inside the organisation, as a means to create superior solutions with interdisciplinary internal stakeholders, is practiced and valued since it promotes the creation of unique offerings to build competitive advantage.

The case studies of Part V also exemplify how stakeholder integration is not always a direct process, but can include indirect integration as well, for instance for the integration of customer contact employees. The interdependencies of stakeholder integration are evidenced by the practice of integrating third parties as bridge builders to access stakeholders such as customers or internal experts. Both case studies found out that the integration of senior management throughout the service innovation process is seen as important or even critical from a management perspective. Moreover, the explorative approach confirmed that service innovation competes for resource allocation with IT and/or product related business. The allocation of time for service innovation next to the regular daily business is a challenge for innovation management, as well as the balance of resource allocation between internal and external stakeholder integration.

In a third step, mutual integration of internal stakeholders was explored in a case study on an interdisciplinary innovation workshop (Part VI). The findings from this interactively engaged case study indicate that mutual stakeholder integration in form of an innovation workshop is interrelated in multiple service systems: the service systems of the participants, the service system of the integrator, the service system jointly formed by the integrator and all participants and the service system all of these systems are embedded in (in case of internal stakeholder integration, this is most likely the organisation). Empirical data evidences that mutual stakeholder integration has unexpected side-effects which demand active management and communication strategies for the individual, the sub-system and the service system level. The service system lens also helped to reveal that value creation in the context of joint service innovation with internal stakeholders does not have to be reciprocal between the integrator and the integrated party. Value co-creation does not even have to be limited to the workshop boundaries: return value may even be sourced in other settings, and with a time delay that makes the return value flow difficult to track. In a nutshell, the cumulated findings of this thesis are summarized in Figure 23.

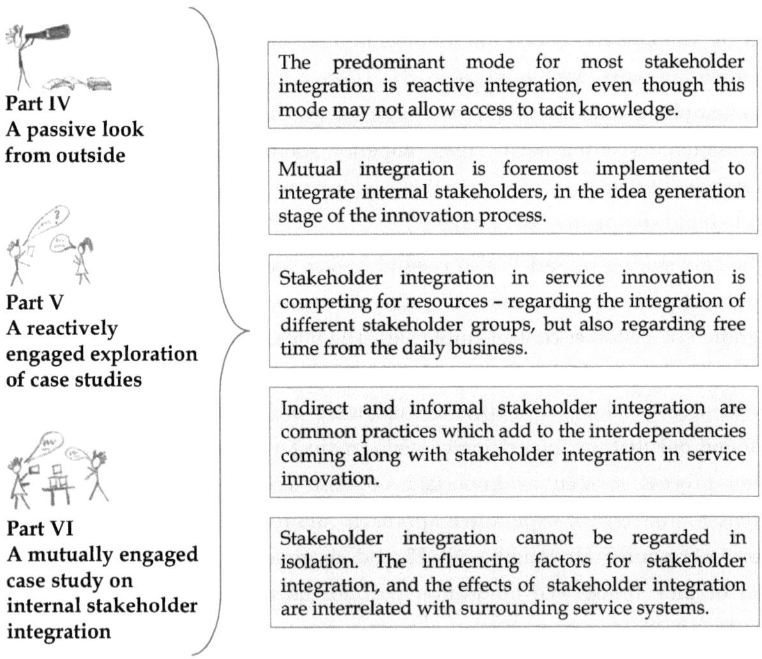

Figure 23: The key findings from the research in this thesis in a nutshell

Table 22 presents these findings on a more fine-grained level and gives reference to the parts of the thesis that they originate from.

Table 22: Overview on the derived results from the parts of this thesis

Summarized Findings	Part IV – State of the art	Part IV – Intermediary perspective	Part V – In-depth case study healthcare	Part V – Multiple case study with MSE	Part VI – Case study, mutual stakeholder integration
The integration of external stakeholders is implemented in a reactive integration mode in the majority of cases.			■	■	
Mutual integration of internal stakeholders is practiced to develop unique offerings for competitive advantage.	■		■	■	■
Customer contact employees as a source of information about customer needs are integrated reactively (or indirectly).			■	■	
The reactive and mutual integration of senior management is crucial/beneficial.	■	■	■	■	■
Stakeholder integration is a struggle for resource allocation, balancing between external and internal stakeholder integration.	■	■	■	■	
Working on service innovation projects competes for resources with the regular work of project managers.		■		■	■
The integration of stakeholders is implemented partly as indirect integration, creating interdependencies in the organisation.			■	■	
Informal stakeholder integration is implemented alongside formal integration, in the mode of reactive integration.			■	■	
Mutual stakeholder integration has effects on the participants, but also on their sub-systems and the overall service system.					■
Stakeholder integration and getting integrated as a stakeholder are simultaneous intertwined processes.				■	
Service innovation is not always reciprocal value co-creation between an integrating party and a stakeholder, but even multi-sided value creation that can create value streams out of the service system.					■

2 Towards a stakeholder integration model

From the analysed cases of this thesis, a number of influence factors and effects regarding stakeholder integration emerged. In Part IV and V, the multi-dimensionality of service innovation, as put forward by Kindström et al. (2013), den Hertog (2010), Agarwal and Selen (2011) or Schleimer and Schulman (2011), was evidenced and contextualised. Especially in the case studies in Part V, it was exemplified that stakeholder integration creates interdependencies because of internal intermediary function establishes contacts to access new stakeholders, or because of indirect integration, e.g. for the reactive integration of customers through customer contact employees such as sales personnel or country representatives in case ECH.

Part VI takes an organisational management perspective and explains that stakeholder integration is shaped by a number of factors (see Figure 24). (1) Existing relationships and network connections influence which stakeholders can be approached for integration. (2) The participation and commitment from management legitimizes the service innovation project and enables the integration of (new) stakeholders. (3) The availability of resources determines which stakeholders can be integrated. Stakeholder integration has to fit with other activities of the integrated stakeholders. At the same time, the stakeholders' schedules are determining which case-specific persons can be integrated for the service innovation. (4) Specific to the project manager his or her motivation and work approach influence the mode of integration. Amongst others, the previous experiences and training of the project manager, but also (5) "the way how things are done" (Vargo et al., 2015) as defined by organizational culture and institutions influence which stakeholders are integrated at which stage of the innovation process, and in which mode this integration is implemented.

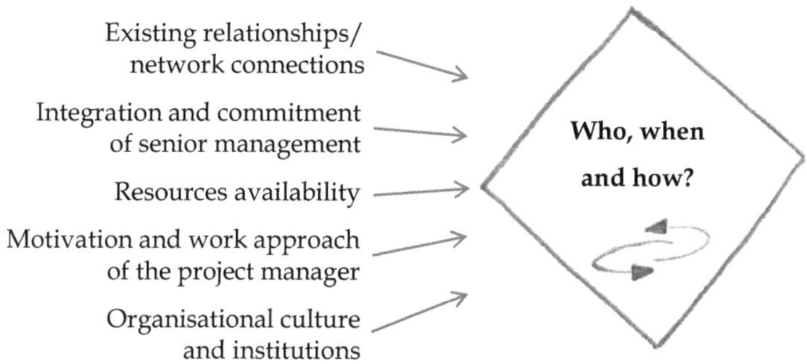

Figure 24: Determinants of stakeholder integration, derived from Part IV

Part V investigated the affecting factors as well as the effects of stakeholder integration. The example of mutual stakeholder integration in an interdisciplinary innovation workshop derives influencing factors and effects from a systems view. These factors and effects have been presented in detail in Part V of this thesis and show that there are affecting factors on three levels, the individual level of the participants, the integrator (project management) and the system level. The effects of stakeholder integration in the mode of mutual integration cannot be assigned to these separate levels: most of the observed effects of stakeholder integration relate to several levels of the three derived levels, the individual and its sub-system or even wider parts of the service system.

Looking at the empirical data through a service system lens, it can be evidence that stakeholder integration is affected by factors on the three levels "integrator", "participant" and "service system" and in return having effect on these levels. To visualise these dynamics, a model of the correlated stakeholder integration in service systems is derived. Figure 25 shows stakeholder integration model, synthesising the empirical findings. It summarizes the affecting factors and effects that have been revealed from the case study research and visualises the mutual interrelatedness of service system, integrator, participant and the stakeholder integration activity.

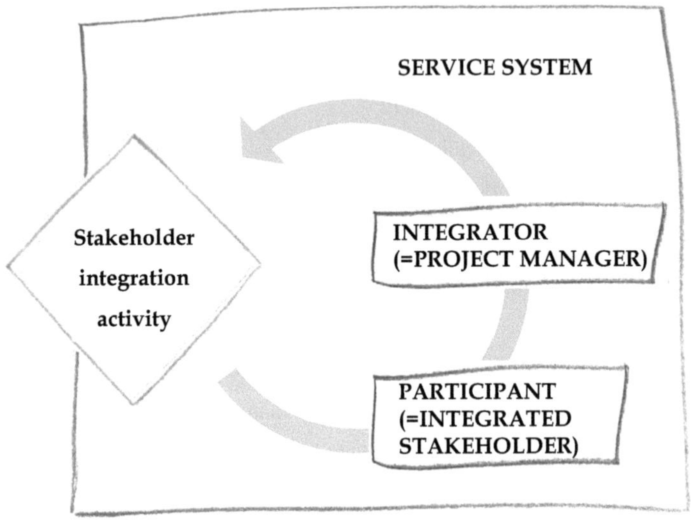

	Affecting factors	Effects
INTEGRATOR (=PROJECT MANAGER)	• Motivation and work approach • Access to stakeholders, existing connections • Invitation / assembly of the right people • Commitment of Management	• New concepts • Short-term motivation • New internal connections, networking • Transfer of workshop tools and ideas into work-life • Further work on solutions; legitimisation of the project • Demand for information, transparency and repetition with adaptions • Reflection on innovation strategy and culture • Ideas and expectations for future practices • Evaluation decides about repetition
PARTICIPANT (=INTEGRATED STAKEHOLDER)	• Time and timing • Previous experiences • Motivation	
SERVICE SYSTEM	• Organisational structure and culture • Structure and modalities	

Figure 25: Stakeholder integration - a correlated process

3 Implications

The analysis of stakeholder integration in service innovation, with a service-dominant theory perspective, revealed implications for management and service research, as an addition to the presented research findings. Implications for management from this case-based research relate to 1) the interdependencies coming along with indirect stakeholder integration, 2) the role of customer contact employees who forward relevant information, 3) the challenges of resource allocation for service innovation, 4) the dynamics of stakeholder integration due to their embeddedness in service systems, and continuous extended stakeholder mapping. A last managerial takeaway is the recommendation of integration modes for specific stakeholder groups. The Implications for service research address the more explicit portraying of value co-creation through multiple actors in service systems and the multi-sided value flows in service systems.

3.1 Implications for management

By investigating the practices and dynamics of internal and external stakeholder integration in IT and manufacturing companies a number of implications for management can be derived. The case studies of this thesis have shown how stakeholder integration is implemented as passive reactive and mutual integration. Thereby, it was made transparent how stakeholder integration, as a multi-dimensional activity, creates interdependencies between stakeholders. The interactions of integrated stakeholders as well as the integration of indirect stakeholders create complex information and value flows that may even reach out of the managed core service system of a service innovation. Accordingly, managers are recommended to pursue an active stakeholder management with the awareness of complexity and interdependencies of stakeholder integration as well as the recognition of the effects that these may create on the service systems they are embedded in.

3.1.1 Interdependencies through indirect stakeholder integration

This thesis illustrates that most important for service innovation in service systems is the integration of indirect and informal stakeholders. Evidenced especially in the single case study of EHC, the interaction between central (headquarters) and local units (subsidiaries) for the indirect integration of customers and users adds to dynamics in stakeholder management. Interdependencies in multi-sided processes arise, e.g. in situations where customer integration or the integration of new internal stakeholders are arranged through a third party. Examples are instances where the local units were needed to establish the contact to customers for reactive integration, where the marketing department integrates an advertising agency and where the IT department integrates an unknown supplier for a specific technical problem. Managers need to be aware of the added complexity that comes along with indirect integration. In such set-ups, the alignment or balance of multi-stakeholder processes and the interests of the integrated parties is necessary to avoid misunderstandings and conflicts.

3.1.2 Forwarding information and knowledge - the role of customer contact employees

Indirect integration has become transparent especially for the reactive integration of customers through the stakeholder group "customer contact employees". Here, two aspects of indirect stakeholder integration are relevant for the management of stakeholder integration: a) customer contact employees forward information from their customer contacts or the requests for reactive customer integration, and b) customer contact personnel is integrated in a reactive way.

Customer integration in practice is, in the majority of the observed instances, not implemented by the decision making service innovation project manager, but by customer-contact-employees that forward information. This implies, as expressed in the case of the company EHC, that the information from the customers is processed through customer contact employees and translated into the language of the organisation. This confirms findings from a case study in service industries by Smith and Fischbacher (2005), which gave first evidence that the needs and interests of stakeholders are channelled through other stakeholders. Given these practices, the customer contact employees who forward information from the interaction with customers ought to consciously be given the role of "translators of information" (Gottfridsson, 2012) and be integrated intensively to "*make the voice of the customer heard*" (Smith & Fischbacher, 2005, p. 1042) in the organisation.

From the data analysis of the case studies in Part V, it has been observed that the mode "mutual integration" is realized with the members of the organisation only, with an emphasis on the early phases of service innovation. One of the key sources for idea generation are employees from related organisational units, alongside senior management who get integrated throughout the innovation process because of their knowledge about processes, their expertise and technical know-how. They are also integrated to maintain a stake in the project or for strategic and political considerations. This is in contrast with the finding that customer-contact employees are integrated only reactively, with few exceptions, even though this stakeholder group is regarded as a useful and necessary provider of information about customer needs, problems and behaviours. The integration of customer contact employees in a reactive mode may prevent the access to sticky knowledge (Edvardsson et al., 2013; Gustafsson et al., 2012) that can presumably only be accessed via bidirectional communication processes (Gustafsson et al., 2012).

Customer contact personnel is seen as a key resource for service innovation as these stakeholders gain knowledge from their day-to-day experiences with customers, have the potential to translate their knowledge into the organisation (compare Mention & Asikainen, 2012) and contribute to innovation in valuable ways. In a similar manner to customers, customer contact employees are "experts in their experiences" and may possess tacit knowledge that can be accessed through mutual integration. Scholars like Edvardsson et al. (2013), Matthing et al. (2006) and Gustafsson et al. (2012) have discussed that reactive stakeholder integration might only skim the surface of customer needs in the context of service organisations.

Customer contact employees are found to be beneficial factors for service innovation in service organisations as they contribute with their in-depth knowledge of customer processes and provide high levels of detail as a result of being embedded in the context of customers (Gustafsson et al., 2012; Melton & Hartline, 2010). Accordingly, the empirical findings of the present case studies once again motivate managers to re-consider the integration of customer contact employees, and also customers, especially in the early stages of the innovation process, and to aim for direct, yet more resource intensive, integration of customers.

In those organisational settings where there is only a limited possibility for direct integration of customers, the indirect integration via exchange with customer contact employees, as discussed above, might be a possibility to fill this gap. All in all, direct mutual integration of customer contact personnel in innovation processes entails the chance to facilitate access to customer needs, in permeable organisational structures.

Thereby, the establishing of infrastructures for a dialogue between customer contact employees and the managers for service innovation is stressed by Prahalad and Ramaswamy (2004). Such infrastructures are expected to design information streams, but also to include the qualification of customer contact employees since they may lack resources such as time or an office space with access to computers to provide their feedbacks, depending on their industry and its setting.

3.1.3 Resource allocation for service innovation

The literature review has outlined that, from a management perspective, stakeholder integration is a struggle for resources such as human resources, time and money, especially for external stakeholders such as customers and users (e.g. by Perks and Riihela, 2004). The data analyses of the case studies in this thesis add to this that stakeholder integration for service innovation also competes for resources with the project managers' every-day business (building upon findings by Kindström and Kowalkowski, 2014). The cases ESC, BSN and EMS show that service innovation is, especially in the manufacturing context, a task that comes next or parallel to the project managers' core business in product sales and development. In these organisations, service innovation more or less "runs on the side" of product business. Even when gaining project status, after surviving the fuzzy frontend of innovation, service innovation has to "fight" for resources from the core business activities. This situation is different when it comes to services that prepare for product sales, such as calculations or applicability testing of engineers. These often freely offered services are perceived as a means of acquisition and are given priority.

From the participating stakeholders' perspective, setting time free for integrating activities has been shown to be a challenge (Part VI). It is not only about fitting into the schedule of the integrated stakeholder, but also about setting time free from other ongoing projects and the achievement of accountable project days per year. To find suitable models that help to support stakeholder integration activities and the respective resource allocation is a management task that should be supported through strategic guidelines of the overall organisation. A number of interviewees in the case study in Part VI (on affecting factors and effects of mutual integration of internal stakeholders) were stimulated to pro-actively reflect on the "Time off to Innovate" models known from 3M or Google. They found that measures were to be taken to support innovation activities next to the daily business. This would have to be adapted to the organisational set-up of the company culture.

3.1.4 Embeddedness in service systems - dynamic effects

The case study in Part VI looked at mutual integration of internal stakeholders and thereby highlighted the interconnectedness of stakeholder integration with the overall organisation. A relevant topic for managing stakeholders is to anticipate and react to dynamics that may come along with stakeholder integration, in terms of both planned as well as unexpected side effects. In the case study for interdisciplinary innovation, as an example, it was anticipated that internal stakeholders would have to account for the two days they spent in the workshop. Accordingly, a project for accounting the workshop was set up so that the participation in the workshop would not show up as "unused and unpaid time" in the end of the year. Even though requests to participate in the workshop were channelled by the supervisors of the participating stakeholders, this was still an issue for discussion as regular project work had to be interrupted.

It was an intended goal of the workshop initiative that participants would further discuss the workshop activity and spread the word about the initiative in their respective organisation. As part of a strategic initiative, the adaption of a more open work culture and the diffusion of the information that such activities are supported in the organisation were an aim for organisation team. Whereas this seemed to work out, it was not anticipated that the overall innovation strategy of the organisation would be discussed in groups with employees of the innovation workshop boundaries, or that a request for the quarterly repetition of such activities for every employee would emerge.

Also in the case of ECH (a case study on healthcare solution development in Part V), the embeddedness of service innovation in systems was evidenced. Senior management was integrated throughout the service innovation process, in the mode of mutual integration and reactive integration. This enabled the establishment of new links across the boundaries of the service innovation project's natural setting. Being integrated as contributors, not only as reviewers of the project, the board of senior managers was able and willing to support the service innovation team and create connections to additional stakeholders e.g. as resources of knowledge or support for challenging issues.

The cited instances are only selected examples representing the relevance of the surrounding service system for stakeholder integration in service innovation. Being aware of the fact that the different stakeholders are embedded in their original service systems (e.g. their units or other sub-systems in the organisation) can help to understand how service innovation activities should be set-up in an optimal way. The other way around, the awareness of different service sub-systems and their permeability can explain how intended and unintended effects of stakeholder integration emerge in an organisation. Therefore this thesis argues for stakeholder management as the organisation and leadership of stakeholder integration activities that is an aligned process over time and integrates aspects of accountability and performance, especially for internal stakeholders.

3.1.5 An extended approach for stakeholder mapping

To create an overview of the relevant stakeholders to be managed for service innovation, the mapping and analysis of stakeholders can be a helpful practice (Agarwal & Selen, 2009). Interviewee ESC-MSE in case ESC just naturally followed her own needs and intuition and created a stakeholder map for a service innovation project. The mapping (collection and placement) of stakeholders is an easy exercise, commonly used in Service Design. Building upon the findings from the empirical research in this study, it can be derived that stakeholder mapping, in order to have them visualised on one page, is a helpful practice. The inclusion of the mode of integration, as well as indirect and informal stakeholder integration can add to create a comprehensive overview. Stakeholder maps display the stakeholders integrated in the service innovation project and can thereby help to interpret and understand the stakeholder integration in a service system (Segelström, 2013). This way, the mapping of the stakeholders for service innovation can support the innovation management team to create a consensus about stakeholder integration, to define the required modes of integration, to early inform stakeholders about future integration plans and the needed allocation of resources (compare Stickdorn and Schneider, 2010, p. 150). Figure 26 shows an example of a stakeholder map that includes the modes of integration for the different internal and external stakeholders that are integrated by the innovation team in the centre: passive integration (dotted line), reactive integration (two arrows for forward and backward information flows) and mutual integration (double-headed arrow) are visualised, together with indirect integration and connections to stakeholders who are not (yet) stakeholders in the regarded service innovation project.

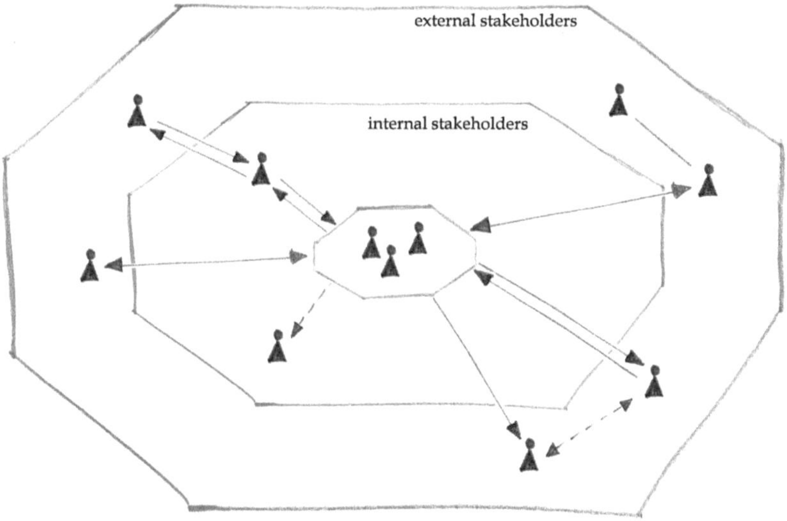

Figure 26: Example for a stakeholder map[58]

In addition to the mere mapping of stakeholders for a service innovation project, it is suggested to repeat the stakeholder mapping in the different stages of the service innovation project. The dynamics of the service system in which a service innovation is embedded in can (and most likely will) change in the course of a service innovation project. Interdependencies with other unique projects may occur, contact persons may change, and new stakeholder may become relevant as the project matures or as stakeholders may change in their attitude from earlier experiences in the project. By re-considering the stakeholder map over time, the service innovation manager can actively adjust planned stakeholder integration activities. This activity for the management of the service innovation process resembles the traditional service blueprint, coined by G. Lynn Shoestack (1984): it visualises the stakeholders for service innovation and their interrelated actions as well as decision points and needed inputs in a project, in the course of time.

---

58 Examples for stakeholder maps and some practical information are provided for instance at Servicedesigntools.org (www.servicedesigntools.org/tools/36) or at the website of the design thinkers academy (www.designthinkersacademy.com/stakeholder-mapping-at-dt-academy/).

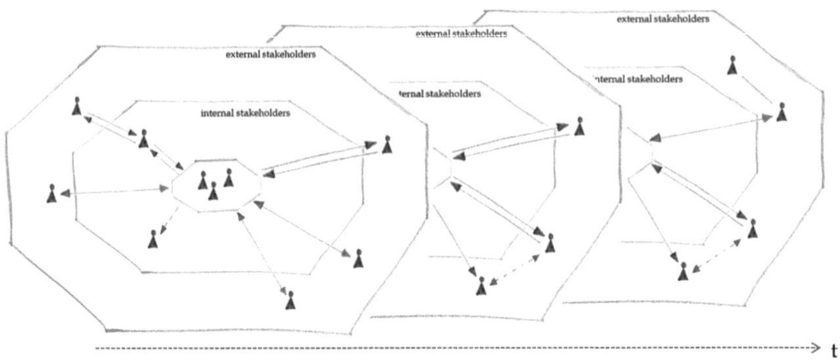

Figure 27: Exemplary stakeholder mapping for a service innovation project – adapted over time

For service innovation managers, the practice of stakeholder mapping (visualised in Figure 27) might even help as a reminder to inform earlier integrated stakeholders about the progress of the project or to allocate resources needed for later stages of the service innovation project in advance. This was evidenced in Part VI, where the integrated stakeholders wanted to receive information about the ongoing process after they had spent some time and effort for the solution of the technical challenge. With continuous stakeholder mapping, innovation managers can establish a reminder to answer the demands for information about the progress of the project, even in later steps of the innovation process, after some months or years. As stakeholder integration is embedded in a wider service system, such a sign of appreciation of the stakeholders' contribution and resource allocation has the potential to positively influence the willingness to support the innovation project, the developed service innovation or future projects of the service innovation manager in the future.

3.1.6 Stakeholder integration - modes and stages

The exploration of stakeholder integration in service innovation practices in this study is of a descriptive nature and does not lead to immediate recommendations on how stakeholder integration should be implemented. Additionally, the specific setting of a service innovation project with unique prerequisites and influencing factors prevent generalising advice for management. Still, some strong impressions from the empirical findings shall not be withheld as suggestions for management.

The integration of internal stakeholders in the mode of mutual integration for interdisciplinary idea generation was found to be a highlighted practice from the case studies. The integration of top managers, experts from other departments and potentially affected stakeholders from relevant units is emphasised since it creates unique innovations for competitive advantage, helps to have stakeholders on board and enables space for stakeholder activity. Managers can profit from mutual stakeholder integration since this mode gives room for the integrated stakeholders to give proactive recommendations regarding the innovation subject, but also about e.g. meaningful networking possibilities or future stakeholder integration.

The case studies in this thesis have discussed indirect stakeholder integration intensively. In particular, the indirect integration of customer contact employees in the idea generation stage, but also customer integration for piloting/testing are practices that can prevent access to fine-grained information, context information and tacit knowledge from experiences. Even despite scarce resources for stakeholder integration, managers are recommended to initiate direct exchange, at least in the mode of reactive integration, with customers or customer contact employees in the idea generation and in the testing stages without previous translation of filters, as already discussed above.

All empirical studies confirm that the integration of senior management throughout all stages of the service innovation process helps for the development of innovations. Their commitment, shown in resource allocation and networking, can be attained from formal and informal meetings. Whilst senior management integration is majorly implemented in a reactive mode, a number of instances showed that mutual integration for idea generation or troubleshooting during later stages is a positively evaluated practice.

3.2 Implications for service innovation research

This thesis' contribution is built upon empirical studies that align internal and external stakeholder integration (Schleimer & Schulman, 2011; Smith & Fischbacher, 2005; Perks et al., 2012). The analysis of case studies with a service-dominant logic lens contributes to service innovation research with two key issues. First, it has been put forward that stakeholder integration in service innovation includes indirect stakeholder integration. Second, this thesis has contextualised the multi-dimensionality of service innovation in IT and manufacturing. The exploration of these contexts reveals that service innovation results in a competition for resources from a management perspective, where resources for service innovation have to compete with the product-related every-day business[59]. Resources in service innovations have to be balanced for the integration of internal and external stakeholders. This adds to the complexity of stakeholder integration activities and should thus be included in the currently developing frameworks for service innovation in service systems.

3.2.1 Value creation in service systems - inclusion of multiple stakeholders for co-creating innovation

The notion of indirect and interdependent stakeholder integration in service system contributes to a more interrelated picture of multiple stakeholders in service systems. In their model of value co-creation in service systems, Vargo and Lusch (Vargo & Lusch 2008; Lusch & Vargo, 2014) show the service provider and the beneficiary as being embedded in overlapping and intersecting value creating systems (Chandler & Vargo, 2011). Thereby, the service provider and the beneficiary of the service are both seen as service systems that create a new surrounding service system. Value co-creation, and accordingly service innovation, in service systems is in Vargo and Lusch's visualisations of value creation presented with a single connection between "the organisation" and "the customer" (compare Figure 6 in Part III chapter 2).

As stakeholder integration in service innovation is herein found to be a matter of interdependent interactions with various organisational stakeholders and customers, over time, it is suggested that the single connection between "the firm" and "the customer" should be replaced with several connections between the involved stakeholders for joint value creation. This suggested adaption of the service system for value creation would reflect the multidimensionality inside and outside the organisation more clearly. Figure 28 shows the revised exemplary visualisation of a service system with several interdependent actors involved in value co-creation with the customer.

[59] This has already been put forward in the work of Christian Kowalkowski and Daniel Kindström (e.g. Kindström & Kowalkowski, 2014; Kindström et al., 2012, Kowalkowski et al., 2013) who describe the struggle for resources to innovate for services in the context of Scandinavian manufacturers. This is being confirmed in the context of the case studies of this thesis.

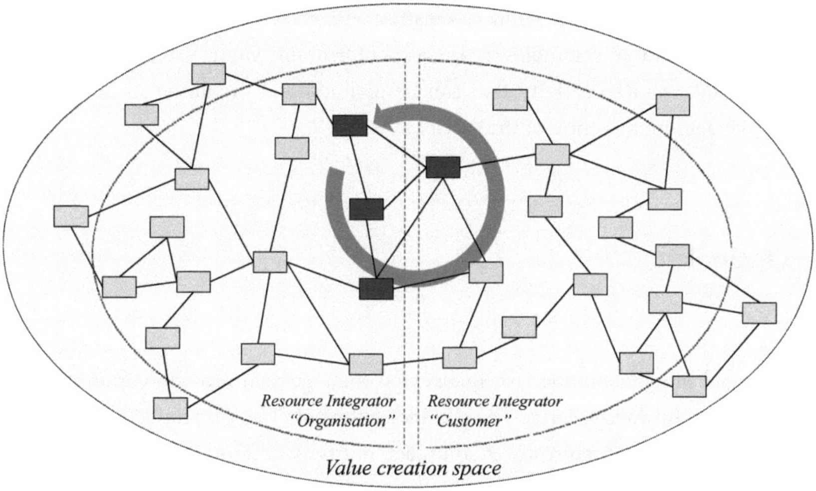

Figure 28: Value creation in service systems
- an adaption of the service-dominant logic model by Lusch and Vargo (2014)

3.2.2 Multi-sided value flows in innovating service systems

This thesis contributes further to theory development in the field of service innovation by recognising that, within these multi-sided value creation systems, the value exchange flows between contributing stakeholders (or triadic and multi-dimensional service systems) may not be reciprocal or may not stay within the service system. The service-for-service exchange in the observed innovation workshop situation happens not only between the integrating party and the integrated stakeholder, but also as an interchange between the participating stakeholders (e.g. the re-connection to former colleagues in case study of Part VI). In addition, the participating stakeholders might interact with stakeholders outside the direct service system "innovation workshop". For example, the workshop participant E-ROT reported on using a workshop-tool within his regular work unit, right after the workshop.

Whereas the paper by Kowalkowski et al. (2013) already emphasises that service innovation in a manufacturing context is enabled by value creating service systems of various forms, the findings of this thesis adds that value streams are even leading outside the core service system. Furthermore it shows that these value streams are not synchronous. The time delay for the reverse value exchange between two or multiple parties in a system makes value co-creation even more complex and difficult to track. This is where value co-creation with stakeholders in a service system for service innovation resembles more a platform for value exchange between multiple parties than an activity that can be planned and organised in detail by a steering manager in the centre of the service system.

4 Outlook

The presented implementations for theory and management provide various points of departure for further research. The specific context of IT and manufacturing in this thesis, as well as the chosen research approach of case studies to explore stakeholder integration in service innovation, enable an in-depth emergence into the selected research field. The transferability of findings to other industries and settings will have to be tested in future research by applying a broadened scope of research, through a replication of the case studies as well as an investigation of a higher number of cases.

In particular, the in-depth study of stakeholder integration in the mode of mutual integration seems worthwhile to be further investigated from the participants' viewpoint. Whereas in open innovation literature, the exploration of customer motivation to participate in e.g. open source or innovation contexts is developing (e.g. Wendelken, Danzinger, Rau, & Möslein, 2014; Lakhani & Wolf, 2005; Füller, 2010), research studies that apply a participant perspective in stakeholder integration for service innovation are still scarce. This thesis has made a start, but more research aligning multiple viewpoints on service innovation needs to be done. In an industrial setting, where the integration of customers is a matter of long-term relationship building, the further exploration of stakeholder integration for service innovation from the perspective of the integrated stakeholder seems like a promising approach for further research (Löfberg, Witell, & Gustafsson, 2010).

A starting point could also be the case company ECH, where the regional units of the international organisation were integrated as reactive and mutual stakeholders in different stages. The stakeholder integration with regional and global processes and the specific interdependencies coming along with international service innovation (suggested by Kindström and Kowalkowski, 2009) would be an interesting approach to extend knowledge on stakeholder integration in service innovation.

The facet of service systems and sub-systems being guided by institutions, as presented by Lusch and Vargo (2014), helps to clarify that every stakeholder integration activity, referring to internal or external stakeholder integration, can be seen as a new act of (re-)configuration of the shared institutions of the service system or sub-systems. This implies that service systems are developing as the service innovation process proceeds. An interesting aspect for future empirical research in service innovation will be to see how experiences, understandings and respective rules represented in institutions and the roles of stakeholders change in the course of service innovation. The further description and analysis of these dynamic changes from a service-dominant logic, applying an institutional change lens, can presumably help to better understand complexity in service systems. To find out more about the processes, variables and motives that lead to changes in the service system would be another step on the way towards a more thorough understanding of the dynamics of service innovation in service systems. Thereby, it also seems worthwhile to examine the value exchange schemes in service systems more in depth: from the in-depth case study in Part VI it was derived that value exchange in service sub-systems such as the innovation workshop, should be analysed from multiple perspectives to better understand the interdependent behaviour of stakeholders in service innovation.

Literature in open innovation as well as in service innovation proposes that all affected and interested stakeholders of a service innovation service system should be given the possibility to participate in innovation (Lee et al., 2012; Ramaswamy and Gouillart, 2010). In the settings of the observed cases in this thesis, stakeholder integration was limited to pre-selected stakeholders only. Tools and platforms such as innovation communities that invite internal and/or external stakeholders with an interest in the innovation project were not implemented. Cases ECH and EMS also showed that mutual integration of internationally based stakeholders was barely put into practice because of communication difficulties. Future research should investigate how such tools for open innovation could help to create a direct communication channel between project management and distant stakeholders (Möslein, 2013) and under which circumstances even self-selected stakeholders from outside the core service innovation system[60] take roles as contributors for innovation, in the context of service innovation in manufacturing.

Taking up the aspect of service innovation being a struggle for resources, another interesting aspect to look into are the drivers for service innovation in product-oriented settings. Literature in service innovation has discussed how service innovation does often not follow a systematic process and is highly dependent on intrapreneurs that develop and promote service innovations (Sundbo, 1997). How does this intrapreneurship show, and what are the prerequisites in the organisation to foster service innovation in circumstances where innovators have to struggle for the resources to pursue service innovation? In a product-oriented setting, it remains to be explored what the role of strategy is, when service innovations are developed with a clear commitment towards hybrid value creation or servitization, as to be found in prominent examples such as IBM, Rolls Royce or Xerox.

5 Conclusion

To create a clearer picture of the practice and dynamics of stakeholder integration in service innovation, this thesis applied a service-dominant logic perspective on service innovation by investigating interdependent processes of resource integration within a service system. With a qualitative explorative three-step approach, this thesis explores which stakeholders are integrated in service innovation, in which mode and at what stage of the service innovation process. This exploration of stakeholder integration practice evidenced that stakeholder integration is implemented in the mode of reactive integration for the majority of stakeholder groups. That is, the stakeholders like customers, partners or customer contact employees are only given the opportunity to answer to questions as impulses from the organisation, and not in the mode of mutual integration that can provide access to these stakeholders tacit knowledge.

---

60 Internal stakeholders outside the service innovations service system are called peripheral innovators by Neyer et al. (2009) if their main activity inside the organization is not related to innovation. Outside innovators are all stakeholders that are not (yet) part of the service innovations service system, but "*can act as initiator and/or participants of the innovation process*" (Neyer et al., 2009, p. 411).

Mutual integration was identified as a practice for the idea generation with internal stakeholders, to help solve problems, to create a stake in the project, and as a side effect, to establish new connections for support of the service innovation project. The two case studies further shed light on indirect and informal stakeholder integration, a responsible factor for interdependencies of stakeholder integration in service systems. The multi-dimensionality and complexity of service innovation is also illustrated through the managerial challenge to allocate and balance resources for service innovation.

According to theoretical considerations, mutual integration allows for the integration of tacit knowledge of stakeholders, including experiences and skills. The third step of this thesis provided an in-depth understanding of mutual integration with internal stakeholders and discovered influencing factors and the effects of mutual stakeholder integration. With this study it was shown that factors related to the integrator, the participant and the service system level shape stakeholder integration. By analysing the effects of mutual stakeholder integration from the multiple perspectives of the integrator, the participants and management, the multi-dimensionality and complexity of service innovation in service system is exemplified. The gained knowledge about the multi-faceted effects on the different levels of the service system contributes to a better understanding of the dynamics of service innovation, for improved managerial practice.

Next to uncovering practical implications of stakeholder integration in service innovation, this piece of research contributes to the service-dominant logic theory. The evidence of the case study analysis suggests that the multi-dimensionality of service innovation as a process of value co-creation between multiple actors should be reflected in the depiction of value co-creation in service systems. Furthermore, the findings from the case study on mutual integration of internal stakeholders shows that, on a micro level, value co-creation for service innovation is not necessarily bi-directional in its nature, but can includes return value flows from unrelated contexts of the service system, even with time delay.

6 Final notes

In the light of an increasing importance of service innovation in service systems, this thesis was designed with the motivation to explore how stakeholder integration in service innovation can be understood from a service system perspective. Measures expected to foster cost-, "sweat and tears" saving innovation processes for sustainable service innovation are the overcoming of internal challenges, the alignment of internal and external stakeholder integration activities and an optimal embedding of stakeholder integration activities in the given setting. By emerging into the research field in-depth, a first step towards understanding the dynamics of service innovation could be made. I was able to identify that stakeholder integration is not only interdependent in respect to external and internal stakeholder integration activities, but also in respect to internal and indirect stakeholder integration for service innovation.

In contrast to the suggestions of theoretical and experimental research on customer integration, the exploration of multiple cases and their organisational practices showed that customer integration in the mode of mutual integration is not widely implemented to date - this practice is regarded as too risky and resource demanding. It has also been shown that, in the context of internal stakeholder integration, dynamics caused through mutual integration have an impact on the overall system and should accordingly not be seen as processes isolated from the overall organisational business. This aspect of stakeholder integration in service systems is potentially even relevant for service innovation consultancies who design and enable stakeholder integration for their client organisations.

For managers, the derived findings can provide some guidance on how to actively steer the integration of interdependent stakeholders: to strategically plan ahead and re-adjust stakeholder integration in service innovation instead of reacting to arising issues in the service system and also to develop some leadership of stakeholder integration. This can be achieved by involving the integrated stakeholders into the planning of stakeholder integration activities and by communicating about new milestones or results of the service innovation, even some time after the stakeholder integration activity. Such management of stakeholder integration beyond the organisation of integration activities show the potential to keep the stakeholders a) on board with the project and b) motivated to set their resources free for supporting service innovation activities in the future.

My journey to explore and find out about the organisational practices of stakeholder integration in service innovation was exiting: It allowed me to get to know a variety of business settings, I met interesting people, was invited to their offices, got an idea about their corporate culture and learned a lot about the products in the German art of engineering. Following my intuitive nature as an engaged scholar, I cannot wait to get away from the desk with the completed thesis and go out, share and discuss the overall findings of this thesis with the interviewees and other interested practitioners. I am looking forward to seeing service innovation project managers derive their measures for stakeholder integration from the presented insights and to continue the research on some of the research questions that arose. Exciting research questions are waiting to be explored, as a next step on the pathway towards understanding service innovation in service systems. Foremost the creation of opportunities for mutual service innovation with customers and the exploration of value exchange with partner organisations are exciting topics for subsequent exploration. And of course, I am looking forward to further discussing the presented research implications with the community of service researchers who allowed for a really rewarding exchange in the past three years[61].

[61] Communication of the research so far includes two journal articles as well as several conference papers and presentations. An overview of related publications is provided in Annex A.

References

Adner, R. (2012). *The wide lens: What successful innovators see that others miss.* New York: Penguin Group.

Agarwal, R., & Selen, W. (2009). Dynamic Capability Building in Service Value Networks forAchieving Service Innovation. *Decision Sciences,* 40(3), 431–475.

Agarwal, R., & Selen, W. (2011). Multi-dimensional nature of service innovation: Operationalisation of the elevated service offerings construct in collaborative service organisations. *International Journal of Operations & Production Managemen,* 31(11), 1164–1192.

Akama, Y. (2009). Warts-and-all : the real practice of service design. In S. Clatworthy, R. Maziar, S. Holmlis, J.-V. Nisula, K. Virppi, & A. Amorium (Eds.), *Proceedings of The First Nordic Conference on Service Design and Service Innovation,* 61, 1-11. Oslo, Norway.

Alam, I. (2002). An Exploratory Investigation of User Involvement in New Service Development. *Journal of the Academy of Marketing Science,* 30(3), 250–261.

Alam, I. (2006a). Removing the fuzziness from the fuzzy front-end of service innovations through customer interactions. *Industrial Marketing Management,* 35(4), 468–480.

Alam, I. (2006b). Service innovation strategy and process: a cross-national comparative analysis. *International Marketing Review,* 23(3), 234–254.

Alam, I. (2011). Process of customer interaction during new service development in an emerging country. *The Service Industries Journal,* 31(16), 2741–2756.

Alam, I., & Perry, C. (2002). A customer-oriented new service development process. *Journal of Services Marketing,* 16(6), 515–534.

Andrade, A. D. (2009). Interpretive Research Aimed at Theory Building: Adopting and Adapting the Case Study Design. *The Qualitative Report,* 14(1), 42–60.

Antorini, Y. M., & Muñiz, A. M. (2013). Invited Article: The Benefits and Challenges of Collaborating with User Communities. *Research-Technology Management,* 56(3), 21–28.

Baines, T., & Lightfoot, H. W. (2014). Servitization of the manufacturing firm: Exploring the operations practices and technologies that deliver advanced services. *International Journal of Operations & Production Management,* 34(1), 2–35.

Barile, S., & Polese, F. (2010). Smart Service Systems and Viable Service Systems. *Service Science,* 2(1/2), 21–40.

Belz, F.-M., & Baumbach, W. (2010). Netnography as a method of lead user identification. *Creativity and Innovation Management,* 19(3), 304–313.

Berger, C., Möslein, K. M., Piller, F., & Reichwald, R. (2005). Co-designing modes of cooperation at the customer interface: learning from exploratory research. *European Management Review,* 2(1), 70–87.

Bessant, J., & Rush, H. (1995). Building bridges for innovation: the role of consultants in technology transfer. *Research Policy,* 24, 97–114.

Bessant, J., von Stamm, B., Möslein, K. M., & Neyer, A.-K. (2010). Backing outsiders: selection strategies for discontinuous innovation. *R&D Management*, 40(4), 345–356.

Bettencourt, L. A. (2010). *Service innovation: How to go from customer needs to breakthrough services*. London: McGraw-Hill.

Biernacki, P., & Waldorf, D. (1981). Snowball sampling. *Sociological Methods & Research*, 10(2), 141–163.

Bilgram, V., & Brem, A. (2008). User-centric innovations in new product development – systematic identification of lead users harnessing interactive and collaborative online-tools. *International Journal of Innovation Management*, 12(3), 419–458.

Blazevic, V., & Lievens, A. (2004). Learning during the new financial service innovation process - Antecedents and performance effects. *Journal of Business Research*, 57, 374–391.

Blazevic, V., & Lievens, A. (2007). Managing innovation through customer coproduced knowledge in electronic services: An exploratory study. *Journal of the Academy of Marketing Science*, 36(1), 138–151.

Blomkvist, J. (2014).*Representing Future Situations of Service: Prototyping in Service Design*. Linköping Studies in Arts and Science, Dissertation No. 618. Linköping, Sweden: Linköping

Böhmann, T., Leimeister, J. M., & Möslein, K. M. (2014). Service Systems Engineering. *Business & Information Systems Engineering*, 6(4), 73–79.

Brax, S. (2005). A manufacturer becoming service provider–challenges and a paradox. *Managing Service Quality: An International Journal*, 15(2), 142–155.

Bruins, A., Dolfsma, W., & Meijaard, J. (2003). Innovation in service firms explored : what, how and why. *EIM Business Policy Research*, Strategic Study B200205, 18., Zoetermeer.

Carbonell, P., Rodríguez-Escudero, A. I., & Pujari, D. (2009). Customer Involvement in New Service Development: An Examination of Antecedents and Outcomes. *Journal of Product Innovation Management*, 26(5), 536–550.

Carbonell, P., Rodriguez-Escudero, A. I., & Pujari, D. (2012). Performance effects of involving lead users and close customers in new service development. *Journal of Services Marketing*, 26(7), 497–509.

Carlborg, P., Kindström, D., & Kowalkowski, C. (2013). The service innovation concept: A literature review. *The Service Industries Journal*, 34(5), 373–398.

Chandler, J. D., and Vargo, S. L. (2011). Contextualization: network intersections, value-in-context, and the co-creation of markets. *Marketing Theory*, 11(1), 35-49.

Chell, E. (2012). Critical Incident Technique. In C. Cassell & G. Symon (Eds.), *Essential guide to qualitative methods in organizational research*. Sage.

Chesbrough, H. (2003). The era of open innovation. *MIT Sloan Management Review*, 40(3), 35–42.

Chesbrough, H. (2010). *Open services innovation: Rethinking your business to grow and compete in a new era*. John Wiley & Sons.

Chesbrough, H., & Brunswicker, S. (2014). A fad or a phenomenon?: The adoption of open innovation practices in large firms. *Research-Technology Management*, 57(2), 16-25.

Coffey, A. J., & Atkinson, P. A. (1996). *Making sense of qualitative data: Complementary research strategies*. Sage Publications, Incorporated.

Creswell, J. W. (2012). *Qualitative Inquiry and Research Design: Choosing Among Five Approaches*. Sage Publications.

Creswell, J. W. (2014). *Research design: Qualitative, quantitative, and mixed methods approaches*. Sage.

Dahan, E., & Hauser, J. R. (2002). The virtual customer. *Journal of Product Innovation Management*, 19(5), 332–353.

De Brentani, U. (1995). New industrial service development: Scenarios for success and failure. *Journal of Business Research*, 32(2), 93–103.

De Brentani, U. (2001). Innovative versus incremental new business services: Different keys for achieving success. *Journal of Product Innovation Management*, 18(3), 169–187.

De Brentani, U., & Ragot, E. (1996). Professional Services : What Factors Impact Performance? *Industrial Marketing Management*, 25(6), 517–530.

De Jong, J. P. J., & Vermeulen, P. A. M. (2003). Organizing successful new service development: a literature review. *Management Decision*, 41(9), 844–858.

De Vries, E. J. (2006). Innovation in services in networks of organizations and in the distribution of services. *Research Policy*, 35(7), 1037–1051.

Den Hertog, P. (2010). *Managing Service Innovation - Firm-level Dynamic Capabilities and Policy Options*. Dialogic Innovatie & Interactie, Utrecht.

Djellal, F., Gallouj, F., & Miles, I. (2013). Two decades of research on innovation in services: Which place for public services? *Structural Change and Economic Dynamics*, 27, 98–117.

Driessen, P. H., & Hillebrand, B. (2013). Integrating Multiple Stakeholder Issues in New Product Development: An Exploration. *Journal of Product Innovation Management*, 30(2), 364–379.

Droege, H., Hildebrand, D., & Forcada, M. a. H. (2009). Innovation in services: present findings, and future pathways. *Journal of Service Management*, 20(2), 131–155.

Dumbach, M. (2014). *Establishing Corporate Innovation Communities - A Social Capital Perspective*. Wiesbaden: Springer Gabler.

Edvardsson, B., Gustafsson, A., & Roos, I. (2005). Service portraits in service research: a critical review. *International Journal of Service Industry Management*, 16(1), 107–121.

Edvardsson, B., Gustafsson, A., Johnson, M. D., & Sanden, B. (2000). *New service development and innovation in the new economy*. Lund, Sweden: Studentlitteratur.

Edvardsson, B., Gustafsson, A., Kristensson, P., Witell, L. (2010). Service Innovation and Customer Co-Development. In P.P. Maglio et al. (eds.) *Handbook of Service Science: Research and Innovations in the Service Economy*. Springer Science and Business Media LLC 2010.

Edvardsson, B., Kleinaltenkamp, M., Tronvoll, B., McHugh, P., & Windahl, C. (2014). Institutional logics matter when coordinating resource integration. *Marketing Theory*, 14(3), 291-309.

Edvardsson, B., Kristensson, P., Magnusson, P., & Sundström, E. (2012). Customer integration within service development: A review of methods and an analysis of insitu and exsitu contributions. *Technovation*, 32(7-8), 419–429.

Edvardsson, B., Meiren, T., Schäfer, A., & Witell, L. (2013). Having a strategy for new service development - does it really matter? *Journal of Service Management*, 24(1), 25–44.

Edvardsson, B., & Olsson, J. (1996). Key Concepts for New Service Development. *The Service Industries Journal*, 16(2), 140–164.

Edvardsson, B., & Tronvoll, B. (2013). A new conceptualization of service innovation grounded in S-D logic and service systems. *International Journal of Quality and Service Sciences*, 5(1), 19–31.

Edvardsson, B., Tronvoll, B., & Gruber, T. (2010). Expanding understanding of service exchange and value co-creation: a social construction approach. *Journal of the Academy of Marketing Science*, 39(2), 327–339.

Eisenberg, I. (2011). Lead-user research for breakthrough innovation. *Research-Technology Management*, 50–58.

Eisenhardt, K. M. (1989). Building theories from case study research. *The Academy of Management Review*, 14(4), 532.

Eisenhardt, K. M., & Graebner, M. E. (2007). Theory Building From Cases: Opportunities and Challenges. *Academy of Management Journal*, 50(1), 25–32.

Ettlie, J. E., & Rosenthal, S. R. (2011). Service versus Manufacturing Innovation. *Journal of Product Innovation Management*, 28(2), 285–299.

Fang, E. (2008). Customer participation and the trade-off between new product innovativeness and speed to market. *Journal of Marketing*, 72(4), 90–104.

Fang, E., Palmatier, R., & Evans, K. (2008). Influence of customer participation on creating and sharing of new product value. *Journal of the Academy of Marketing*, (36) 322–336.

Faullant, R.; Krajger, I.; Zanker, M. (2012). Identification of innovative users for new service development in tourism. In *19th Conference on Information and Communication Technologies in Tourism*. Helsingborg, Sweden. Springer.

Fenton, E. M., & Pettigrew, A. M. (2000). Theoretical Perspectives on New Forms of Organizing. In E. M. Fenton & A. M. Pettigrew (Eds.), *The Innovating Organisation*. Sage Publications.

Flanagan, J. C. (1954). The critical incident technique. *Psychological Bulletin*, 51(4), 327–358.

Flick, U. (2014). *An introduction to qualitative research* (5th ed.). Los Angeles: Sage.

Freeman, C. (1982). *The economics of industrial innovation* (2nd ed.). London: Frances Pinter.

Freeman, R. E., & Reed, D. L. (1983). Stockholders and stakeholders: A new perspective in corporate governance. *California Management Review*, XXV(3), 88–106.

Frow, P., & Payne, A. (2011). A stakeholder perspective of the value proposition concept. *European Journal of Marketing*, 45(1), 223–240.

Füller, J. (2010). Refining virtual co-creation from a consumer perspective. *California Management Review*, 52(2), 98–122.

Gallouj, F., & Weinstein, O. (1997). Innovation in Services. *Research Policy*, *26*(26), 537–556.

Gann, D. M., & Salter, A. J. (2000). Innovation in project-based, service-enhanced firms: the construction of complex products and systems. *Research Policy*, 29(7-8), 955–972.

Gassmann, O. (2006). Opening up the innovation process : towards an agenda. *R&D ManagementManagement*, 36(3), 223–228.

Gebauer, H., Gustafsson, A., & Witell, L. (2011). Competitive advantage through service differentiation by manufacturing companies. *Journal of Business Research*, 64(12), 1270–1280.

Gibbert, M., & Ruigrok, W. (2010). The "What" and "How" of Case Study Rigor: Three Strategies Based on Published Work. *Organizational Research Methods*, 13(4), 710–737.

Ginzburg, I., Higgins, A., & Lichtenstein, Y. (2007). Looking for the Locus of Innovation in New Service Development. In *2007 40th Annual Hawaii International Conference on System Sciences (HICSS'07)*. IEEE.

Goodman, L. A., (1961). Snowball Sampling. *The Annals of Mathematical Statistics*.Vol. 32, No. 1 (Mar., 1961), 148-170

Gottfridsson, P. (2010). Development of personalised services in small business: an iterative learning process. *Managing Service Quality: An International Journal*, 20(4), 388–400.

Gottfridsson, P. (2011). Development of new services in smaller organisations: They do just happen. *Australian Journal of Business and Management Research*, 1(7), 91–100.

Gottfridsson, P. (2012). Joint service development - the creations of the prerequisite for the service development. *Managing Service Quality*, 22(1), 21–37.

Gottfridsson, P., & Stålhammar, A. (2014). Transforming the service idea - a communication and learning process. *International Journal of Quality and Service Sciences*, 6(1), 2–16.

Gremler, D. D. (2004). The Critical Incident Technique in Service Research. *Journal of Service Research*, 7(1), 65–89.

Gremyr, I., Löfberg, N., & Witell, L. (2010). Service innovations in manufacturing firms. *Managing Service Quality*, 20(2), 161–175.

Grönroos, C. (1982). An Applied Service Marketing Theory. *European Journal of Marketing*, 16(7), 30–41.

Grönroos, C. (1994). Quo Vadis, marketing? Toward a relationship marketing paradigm. *Journal of Marketing Management.* , 10(5), 347-360.

Grönroos, C. (2000). *Service Management and Marketing: A Customer Relationship Management Approach.* West Sussex, UK: John Wiley.

Grönroos, C. (2008). Service logic revisited: who creates value? And who co-creates? *European Business Review*, 20(4), 298–314.

Grönroos, C., & Gummerus, J. (2014). The service revolution and its marketing implications: service logic vs service-dominant logic. *Managing Service Quality*, 24(3), 206–229.

Grönroos, C., & Ravald, A. (2011). Service as business logic: implications for value creation and marketing. *Journal of Service Management*, 22(1), 5–22.

Grönroos, C., & Voima, P. (2012). Critical service logic: making sense of value creation and co-creation. *Journal of the Academy of Marketing Science*, 41(2), 133–150.

Gruner, K., & Homburg, C. (2000). Does customer interaction enhance new product success? *Journal of Business Research*, 49, 1–14.

Guba, E. G., & Lincoln, Y. S. (1994). Competing paradigms in qualitative research. *Handbook of Qualitative Research*, 2, 163–194.

Guba, E. G., & Lincoln, Y. S. (2005). Paradigmatic controversies, contradictions, and emerging confluences. In N. K. Denzin & Y. S. Lincoln (Eds.), *The Sage Handbook of Qualitative Research* (3rd ed., pp. 191–215). Sage Publications.

Gummesson, E. (1995). Relationship marketing: its role in the service economy. In W. J. Glynn, & J. G. Barnes (Eds.), *Understanding service management*. New York: Wiley.

Gupta, A. K., Raj, S. P. and Wilemon, D. (1985), The R&D-Marketing Interface in High-Technology Firms. *Journal of Product Innovation Management*, 2, 12–24.

Gustafsson, A., Ekdahl, F., & Edvardsson, B. (1999). Customer focused service development in practice–a case study at Scandinavian Airlines System (SAS). *Journal of Service Industry Management*, 10(4), 344–358.

Gustafsson, A., Kristensson, P., & Witell, L. (2012). Customer co-creation in service innovation: a matter of communication? *Journal of Service Management*, 23(3), 311-327.

Halinen, A., & Törnroos, J.-Å. (2005). Using case methods in the study of contemporary business networks. *Journal of Business Research*, 58(9), 1285–1297.

Hargadon, A. B. (1998). Firms as Knowledge Brokers:Lessons in pursuing continuous innovation. *California Management Review*, 40(3), 209–228.

Hart, S. L. (1995). A natural-resource-based view of the firm. *Academy of Management Review*, 20(4), 986–1014.

Hartley, J. (2012). Case Study Research. In C. Cassell & G. Symon (Eds.), *Essential guide to qualitative methods in organizational research*. Sage.

Havila, V., Johanson, J., & Thilenius, P. (2004). International business-relationship triads. *International Marketing Review*, 21, 172–186.

Hegarty, W. H., & Hoffman, R. C. (1990). Product/market innovations: a study of top management involvement among four cultures. *Journal of Product Innovation Management*, 7(3), 186-199.

Hill, L. A., Brandeau, G., Truelove Sal, E., & Lineback, K. (2014). Collective Genius. *Harvard Business Review*, *92*(6), 94–102.

Holopainen, M. (2010). Exploring service design in the context of architecture. *The Service Industries Journal*, 30(4), 597–608.

Howells, J. (2006). Intermediation and the role of intermediaries in innovation. *Research Policy*, 35(5), 715–728.

IfM Bonn, (2014), *Unternehmensbestand.* Retrieved from http://www.ifm-bonn.org/statistiken/unternehmensbestand/#accordion=0&tab=3; 2014-07-30.

Janssen, M., Castaldi, C., & Alexiev, A. (2014). *Dynamic capabilities for service innovation: conceptualization and measurement.* Working Paper No. 14.07. Eindhoven Centre for Innovation Studies (ECIS), Eindhoven University, The Netherlands.

Janssen, M., Castaldi, C., & den Hertog, P. (2013). Examining dimensionality and interdependencies in the design of service innovation. In *35th DRUID Celebration Conference 2013*. Barcelona, Spain.

Johne, A., & Storey, C. (1998). New service development: a review of the literature and annotated bibliography. *European Journal of Marketing*, 32(3/4), 184–251.

Johnson, M. D., Anderson, E. W., & Fornell, C. (1995). Rational and adaptive performance expectations in a customer satisfaction framework, *Journal of Consumer Research*, 21(4), 695-707.

Jonas, J. M., Möslein, K. M., & Roth, A. (2013). Passive integration or mutual co-creation? Exploring the role of stakeholders in service innovation. Paper Presented at *13th International Research Symposium on Service Excellence in Management* (QUIS13-2013), Karlstad, Sweden.

Jonas, J. M., Roth, A., & Möslein, K. M. (2014a). Stakeholder integration in service innovation - An explorative case study on healthcare solutions development. Paper presented at *Euram Annual Conference 2014*, Valencia, Spain.

Jonas, J. M., Roth, A., & Möslein, K. M. (2014b). Stakeholder integration for service innovation in German medium-sized enterprises. In *RESER Conference 2014*. Helsinki, Finland.

Jonas, J.M., Roth, A., Möslein, K.M. (2015). Co-creating innovation in service systems - exploring the effects of cross-disciplinary problem solving. Paper presented at *European Operations Management Association Conference 2015*, Neuchatel, Switzerland.

Jonas & Roth (2017). Stakeholder integration in service innovation - an exploratory case study in the healthcare industry. *International Journal of Technology Management*, 73 (1/2/3), 91-113.

Katz, R., & Allen, T. J. (1982). Investigating the not invented here (NIH) syndrome: A look at the performance, tenure, and communication patterns of 50 R&D project groups. *R&D Management*, 12(1), 7–19.

Kindström, D., & Kowalkowski, C. (2009). Development of industrial service offerings: a process framework. *Journal of Service Management*, 20(2), 156–172.

Kindström, D., & Kowalkowski C. (2014). Service innovation in product-centric firms: A multidimensional business model perspective. *Journal of Business & Industrial Marketing*, 29 (2), 96-111.

Kindström, D., Kowalkowski, C., & Sandberg, E. (2013). Enabling service innovation: A dynamic capabilities approach. *Journal of Business Research*, 66(8), 1063–1073.

King, N. (2012). Using Interviews in Qualitative Research. In C. Cassell & G. Symon (Eds.), *Essential guide to qualitative methods in organizational research*. Sage.

King, N., & Horrocks, C. (2010). *Interviews in qualitative research*. London: Sage Publications.

Koen, P., Ajamian, G., Burkart, R., Clamen, A., Davidson, J., D'Amore, R., Elkins, E., Herald, K., Incorvia, M., Johnson, A., Karol, R., Seibert, R., Slavejkov, A., Wagner, K. (2001). Providing Clarity and a Common Language to the "Fuzzy Front End." *Research-Technology Management*, 44(2), 46–55.

Kowalkowski, C., Kindström, D., & Brehmer P. O. (2011). Managing industrial service offerings in global business markets. *Journal of Business & Industrial Marketing*, 26 (3), 181-192.

Kowalkowski, C., Kindström, D., Alejandro, T. B., Brege, S., & Biggemann, S. (2012). Service infusion as agile incrementalism in action. *Journal of Business Research*, 65, 765–772.

Kowalkowski, C., Persson Ridell, O., Röndell, J. G., & Sörhammar, D. (2012). The co-creative practice of forming a value proposition. *Journal of Marketing Management*, 28(13-14), 1553–1570.

Kowalkowski, C., Witell, L., & Gustafsson, A. (2013). Any way goes: Identifying value constellations for service infusion in SMEs. *Industrial Marketing Management*, 42(1), 18–30.

Krämer, K. (2015). *What's mine, is yours? Exploring the diffusion of co-creation expertise in organizations*. Erlangen: Dissertationsschrift, Universität Erlangen-Nürnberg.

Kristensson, P., Gustafsson, A., & Archer, T. (2004). Harnessing the Creative Potential among Users. *Journal of Product Innovation Management*, 21(1), 4–14.

Kristensson, P., Magnusson, P. R., & Matthing, J. (2002). Users as a Hidden Resource for Creativity: Findings from an Experimental Study on User Involvement. *Creativity and Innovation Management*, 11(1), 55–61.

Kristensson, P., Matthing, J., & Johansson, N. (2008). Key strategies for the successful involvement of customers in the co-creation of new technology-based services. *International Journal of Service Industry Management*, 19(4), 474–491.

Lages, C. R., & Piercy, N. F. (2012). Key Drivers of Frontline Employee Generation of Ideas for Customer Service Improvement. *Journal of Service Research*, 15(2), 215–230.

Lakhani, K. R., & Wolf, R. G. (2005). Why Hackers Do What They Do: Understanding Motivation and Effort in Free/Open Source Software Projects. In J. Feller, B. Fitzgerald, S. Hissam, & K. R. Lakhani (Eds.), *Perspectives on Free and Open Source Software* (pp. 1-27). MIT Press.

Lee, A. S., & Baskerville, R. L. (2003). Generalizing Generalizability in Information Systems Research. *Information Systems Research*, 14(3), 221–243.

Lee, S. M., Olson, D. L., & Trimi, S. (2012). Co-innovation: convergenomics, collaboration, and co-creation for organizational values. *Management Decision*, 50(5), 817–831.

Leiponen, A. (2005). Skills and innovation. *International Journal of Industrial Organization*, 23(5-6), 303–323.

Leiponen, A. (2012). The benefits of R&D and breadth in innovation strategies: a comparison of Finnish service and manufacturing firms. *Industrial and Corporate Change*, 21(5), 1255–1281.

Lempinen, H., & Rajala, R. (2014). Exploring multi-actor value creation in IT service processes. *Journal of Information Technology*, 29(2), 170–185.

Lightfoot, H., & Gebauer, H. (2011). Exploring the alignment between service strategy and service innovation. *Journal of Service Management*, 22(5), 664–683.

Lilien, G. L., Morrison, P. D., Searls, K., Sonnack, M., & von Hippel, E. (2002). Performance assessment of the lead user idea-generation process for new product development. *Management Science*, 48(8), 1042–1059.

Löfberg, N., Witell, L., & Gustafsson, A. (2010). Service strategies in a supply chain. *Journal of Service Management*, *21*(4), 427–440.

Love, J. H., & Roper, S. (2009). Organizing innovation: complementarities between cross-functional teams. *Technovation*, Vol. 29, No. 3, 192-203.

Lundkvist, A., & Yakhlef, A. (2004). Customer involvement in new service development: a conversational approach. *Managing Service Quality*, *14*(2/3), 249-257.

Lusch, R. F. (2006). Service-dominant logic: reactions, reflections and refinements. *Marketing Theory*, 6(3), 281–288.

Lusch, R. F., & Vargo, S. L. (2014). *Service-Dominant Logic: Premises, Perspectives, Possibilities*. Cambridge University Press.

Lusch, R. F., Vargo, S. L., & O'Brien, M. (2007). Competing through service: Insights from service-dominant logic. *Journal of Retailing*, 83(1), 5–18.

Lusch, R. F., Vargo, S. L., & Tanniru, M. (2009). Service, value networks and learning. *Journal of the Academy of Marketing Science*, 38(1), 19–31.

Lusch, R. F., Vargo, S. L., & Wessels, G. (2008). Toward a conceptual foundation for service science: Contributions from service-dominant logic. *IBM Systems Journal*. 47, 5-14.

Lüthje, C., & Herstatt, C. (2004). The Lead User method: an outline of empirical findings and issues for future research. *R&D Management*, 34(5), 553–568.

Lüthje, C., Herstatt, C., & von Hippel, E. (2006). User-innovators and "local" information: The case of mountain biking. *Research Policy*, 34(6), 951–965.

Maglio, P. P., & Spohrer, J. (2008). Fundamentals of service science. *Journal of the Academy of Marketing Science*, 36(1), 18–20.

Maglio, P. P., Vargo, S. L., Caswell, N., & Spohrer, J. (2009). The service system is the basic abstraction of service science. *Information Systems and E-Business Management*, 7(4), 395–406.

Magnusson, P. R. (2003). Benefits of involving users in service innovation. *European Journal of Innovation Management*, 6(4), 228 - 238.

Magnusson, P. R., Matthing, J., & Kristensson, P. (2003). Managing User Involvement in Service Innovation: Experiments with Innovating End Users. *Journal of Service Research*, 6(2), 111–124.

Martin, C. R., & Horne, D. A. (1993). Services innovation: successful versus unsuccessful firms. *International Journal of Service Industry Management*, 4(1), 49–65.

Mathieu, V. (2001). Service strategies within the manufacturing sector: benefits, costs and partnership. *International Journal of Service Industry Management*, 12(5), 451–475.

Matthing, J., Kristensson, P., Gustafsson, A., & Parasuraman, A. (2006). Developing successful technology-based services: the issue of identifying and involving innovative users. *Journal of Services Marketing*, 20(5), 288–297.

Matthing, J., Sandén, B., & Edvardsson, B. (2004). New service development: Learning from and with customers. *International Journal of Service Industry Management*, 15(5), 479-498.

Mattsson, J. (2010). Developing a strategic abstraction tool for service innovation. *Journal of Strategic Marketing*, 18(2), 133–144.

Mayring, P. (2010). *Qualitative Inhaltsanalyse: Grundlagen und Techniken* (11th ed.). Weinheim, Basel: Beltz.

Mele, C. (2009). Value innovation in B2B: learning, creativity, and the provision of solutions within Service-Dominant Logic. *Journal of Customer Behaviour*, 8(3), 199–220.

Melton, H. L., & Hartline, M. D. (2010). Customer and Frontline Employee Influence on New Service Development Performance. *Journal of Service Research*, 13(4), 411–425.

Melton, H. L., & Hartline, M. D. (2012). Employee Collaboration, Learning Orientation, and New Service Development Performance. *Journal of Service Research*, 16(1), 67–81.

Menor, L. J., Tatikonda, M. V, & Sampson, S. E. (2002). New service development : areas for exploitation and exploration. *Journal of Operations Management*, 20, 135–157.

Mention, A.-L., & Asikainen, A.-L. (2012). Innovation & productivity: Investigating effects of openness in services. *International Journal of Innovation Management, 16*(3), 1240004.

Meroni, A., & Sangiorgi, D. (2011). *Design for services.* Gower Publishing.

Michel, S., Brown, S. W., & Gallan, A. S. (2007). An expanded and strategic view of discontinuous innovations: deploying a service-dominant logic. *Journal of the Academy of Marketing Science,* 36(1), 54–66.

Miles, M. B., Huberman, M. A., & Saldaña, J. (2013). *Qualitative data analysis: A methods sourcebook.* Sage Publications, Incorporated.

Mitchell, R., Agle, B., & Wood, D. (1997). Toward a theory of stakeholder identification and salience: Defining the principle of who and what really counts. *Academy of Management Review,* 22(4), 853–886.

Mohrman, S. A., & Lawler, E. (2011). *Useful research: Advancing theory and practice.* Berrett-Koehler Publishers.

Möslein, K. M. (2005). *Der Markt für Managementwissen: Wissensgenerierung im Zusammenspiel von Wirtschaftswissenschaft und Wirtschaftspraxis.* Wiesbaden: Gabler-DUV.

Möslein, K. M. (2013). Open Innovation: Actors, Tools and Tensions. In A. S. Huff, K. M. Möslein, R. Reichwald (Eds.), *Leading Open Innovation* (pp.69-85). Cambridge, Mass.: MIT Press.

Möslein, K. M. (2014). Open Innovation: Strategic Options, Actors, Tools and Tensions. In Pfeffermann, N., Minshall, T., Mortara, L. (Eds.) *Strategy and Communication for Innovations.* Heidelberg, Dordrecht, London, New York: Springer.

Möslein, K. M., Huff, A. S., & Reichwald, R. (2012). Corporate Open Innovation: Learning from Longitudinal Exploratory Research. *International Journal of Knowledge-Based Organizations,* 2(1), 1–10.

Möslein, K. M., Neyer, A.-K., & Rau, C. (2012). Rumpelstilzkin is a thing of the past: innovation practices for creating service innovations. In W. Ganz, G. Satzger, & C. Schultz (Eds.), *Methods in service innovation - current trends and future perspectives.* Stuttgart: Fraunhofer Verlag.

Nambisan, S. (2002). Designing virtual customer environments for new product development : toward a theory. *Academy of Management Review,* 27(3), 392–413.

Narver, J. C., Slater, S. F., & MacLachlan, D. L. (2004). Responsive and Proactive Market Orientation and New Product Success. *The Journal of Product Innovation Management,* 21, 334–347.

Neu, W. A., & Brown, S. W. (2005). Forming Successful Business-to-Business Services in Goods-Dominant Firms. *Journal of Service Research,* 8(3), 3–17.

Neyer, A.-K., Bullinger, A. C., & Möslein, K. M. (2009). Integrating inside and outside innovators: a sociotechnical systems perspective. *R&D Management,* 39(4), 410–419.

Ng, I. C. L., Maull, R., & Yip, N. (2009). Outcome-based contracts as a driver for systems thinking and service-dominant logic in service science: Evidence from the defence industry. *European Management Journal, 27*(6), 377–387.

Ngo, L. V., & O'Cass, A. (2013). Innovation and business success: The mediating role of customer participation. *Journal of Business Research,* 66(8), 1134–1142.

Nicolajsen, H. W., & Scupola, A. (2011). Investigating issues and challenges for customer involvement in business services innovation. *Journal of Business & Industrial Marketing,* 26(5), 368–376.

Nijssen, E. J., Hillebrand, B., Vermeulen, P. A. M., & Kemp, R. G. M. (2006). Exploring product and service innovation similarities and differences. *International Journal of Research in Marketing,* 23(3), 241–251.

Nonaka, I., & Takeuchi, H. (1995). *The Knowledge-creating Company: How Japanese Companies Create the Dynamics of Innovation.* Oxford university press.

Nordin, F., & Kowalkowski, C. (2010). Solutions offerings: a critical review and reconceptualisation. *Journal of Service Management,* 21(4), 441–459.

Normann, R. (2001). *Reframing Business: When the Map Changes the Landscape.* Chichester, UK: John Wiley & Sons.

Normann, R., & Ramirez, R. (1993). From Value Chain to Value Constellation: Designing Interactive Strategy. *Harvard Business Review,* 71(4), 65–77.

Noy, C. (2008). Sampling Knowledge: The Hermeneutics of Snowball Sampling in Qualitative Research. International *Journal of Social Research Methodology,* 11(4), 327–344.

Obstfeld, D. (2005). Social Networks , the Tertius lungens Orientation , and Involvement in Innovation. *Administrative Science Quarterly,* 50(1), 100–130.

Oliva, R., & Kallenberg, R. (2003). Managing the transition from products to services. *International Journal of Service Industry Management,* 14(2), 160–172.

Oliveira, P., & von Hippel, E. (2011). Users as service innovators: The case of banking services. *Research Policy,* 40(6), 806–818.

Ollila, S., & Elmquist, M. (2011). Managing open innovation: Exploring challenges at the interfaces of an open innovation arena. *Creativity and Innovation Management,* 20(4), 273–283.

Ordanini, A., & Parasuraman, A. (2010). Service Innovation Viewed Through a Service-Dominant Logic Lens: A Conceptual Framework and Empirical Analysis. *Journal of Service Research,* 14(1), 3–23.

Ostrom, A. L., Bitner, M. J., Brown, S. W., Burkhard, K. A., Goul, M., Smith-Daniels, V., Demirkan, H., & Rabinovich, E. (2010). Moving Forward and Making a Difference: Research Priorities for the Science of Service. *Journal of Service Research,* 13(1), 4–36.

Ostrom, A. L., Parasuraman, A., Bowen, D. E., Patricio, L., & Voss, C. A. (2015). Service Research Priorities in a Rapidly Changing Context. *Journal of Service Research, 18*(2), 127–159.

Parasuraman, A., Zeithaml, V. A., & Berry, L. L. (1985). A Conceptual Model of Service Quality and Its Implications for Future Research. *Journal of Marketing*, 49(1979), 41–50.

Parasuraman, A., Zeithaml, V. A., & Berry, L. L. (1988). Servqual. *Journal of Retailing*, 64(1), 12-40.

Patton, M. Q. (2007). *Qualitative research & evaluation methods* (3rd ed.). Thousand Oaks: Sage Publications, Incorporated.

Payne, A. F., Storbacka, K., & Frow, P. (2007). Managing the co-creation of value. *Journal of the Academy of Marketing Science*, 36(1), 83–96.

Perkmann, M., Neely, A., & Walsh, K. (2011). How should firms evaluate success in university-industry alliances? A performance measurement system. *R&D Management*, 41(2), 202-216.

Perks, H., & Riihela, N. (2004). An exploration of inter-functional integration in the new service development process. *The Service Industries Journal*, 24(6), 37-63.

Perks, H., Gruber, T., & Edvardsson, B. (2012). Co-creation in radical service innovation: A systematic analysis of microlevel processes. *Journal of Product Innovation Management*, 29(6), 935-951.

Piller, F., Ihl, C., Vossen, A., & Group, I. M. (2011). A Typology of Customer Co-creation in the Innovation Process. In H. Hanekop & V. Wittke (Eds.), *New forms of collaborative production and innovation: Economic, social, legal and technical characteristics and conditions*. Universitätsverlag Göttingen.

Pittaway, L., Robertson, M., Munir, K., Denyer, D., & Neely, A. (2004). Networking and innovation : a systematic review of the evidence. *International Journal of Management Reviews, 5*(3-4), 137–168.

Poole, M. S., van de Ven, A. H., Dooley, K., Holmes, M. E. (2000), *Organizational Change and Innovation Processes: Theory anf Methods for Research*. New York: Cambridge University Press.

Prahalad, C. K., & Ramaswamy, V. (2004a). Co-creation experiences: The next practice in value creation. *Journal of Interactive Marketing*, 18(3), 5–14.

Prahalad, C. K., & Ramaswamy, V. (2004b). Co-creating unique value with customers. *Strategy & Leadership, 32*(3), 4–9.

Raddats, C., & Kowalkowski, C. (2014). A Reconceptualization of Manufacturers' Service Strategies. *Journal of Business-to-Business Marketing*, 21, 19–34.

Ragin, C. C. (1992). "Casing" and the process of social inquiry. In C.C. Ragin & H. S. Becker (Eds.), *What Is a Case?: Exploring the Foundations of Social Inquiry* (pp. 217-226). Cambridge University Press.

Ramaswamy, V., & Gouillart, F. J. (2010). *The Power of Co-Creation: Build It with Them to Boost Growth, Productivity, and Profits*. Free Press.

Ramaswamy, V., & Ozcan, K. (2014). *The co-creation paradigm*. Stanford University Press.

Rau, C. (2012). *Innovation practices: Dissolving knowledge boundaries in innovation projects*. Erlangen: Dissertationsschrift, Universität Erlangen-Nürnberg.

Rondell, J. G., & Sorhammar, D. (2010). Functional identities, resource integrators and the service-dominant logic. *Journal of Customer Behaviour*, 9(1), 19–36.

Rubalcaba, L., Michel, S., Sundbo, J., Brown, S. W., & Reynoso, J. (2012). Shaping, organizing, and rethinking service innovation: a multidimensional framework. *Journal of Service Management*, 23(5), 696–715.

Rusanen, H., Halinen-Kaila, A., & Jaakkola, E. (2014). Accessing resources for service innovation - the critical role of network relationships. *Journal of Service Management*, 25(1), 2–29.

Russo-Spena, T., & Mele, C. (2012). "Five Co-s" in innovating: a practice-based view. *Journal of Service Management*, 23(4), 527–553.

Sandström, S., Magnusson, P., & Kristensson, P. (2009). Increased understanding of service experiences through involving users in service development. *European Journal of Innovation Management*, 12(2), 243–256.

Sangiorgi, D. (2011). Transformative Services and Transformation Design. *International Journal of Design*, 5(2).

Schilling, A., & Werr, A. (2009). *Managing and organizing for innovation in service firms: A literature review with annotated bibliography*. Stockholm School of Economics, Vinnova Report, VR 2009:06.

Schleimer, S. C., & Shulman, A. D. (2011). When Intra-Firm and Inter-Firm Collaborations Co-Occur: Comparing Their Impact Across New Services Versus New Product Innovations. *International Journal of Innovation Management*, 15(05), 869–898.

Schreier, M. (2012). *Qualitative Content Analysis in Practice*. Sage Publications.

Schulteß, P., Wegener, S., Neus, A., & Satzger, G. (2010). Innovating for and with your service customers: An assessment of the current practice of collaborative service innovation in Germany. *Procedia Social and Behavioral Sciences*, 2(4), 6503–6515.

Scott, R. W. (2001). *Institutions and Organizations*, 3rd Ed. Sage Publication Inc., Thousand Oaks, CA.

Segelström, F. (2013). *Stakeholder Engagement for Service Design, How service designers identify and communicate insights*. Doctoral dissertation, Linköping, Linköping University.

Shostack, G. L. (1984). Designing Services That Deliver. *Harvard Business Review*, 62, 133–139.

Siggelkow, N. (2007). Persuasion with case studies. *Academy of Management Journal*, 50(1), 20–24.

Skiba, F., & Herstatt, C. (2012). Users as sources of radical service innovation. In Melkas H. & Harmaakorpi V. (Eds.), *Practice-Based Innovation: Insights, Applications and Policy Implications*. Berlin, Heidelberg: Springer.

Slater, S. F., & Narver, J. C. (1998). Customer-Led and Market-Oriented: Let's Not Confuse the Two. *Strategic Management Journal*, 1006(19), 1001–1006.

Smith, A. M., & Fischbacher, M. (2002). Service design in the NHS: collaboration or conflict? *Journal of Marketing Management*, 923–951.

Smith, A. M., & Fischbacher, M. (2005). New service development: a stakeholder perspective. *European Journal of Marketing*, 39(9/10), 1025–1048.

Sonesson, O. (2007). *Tjänsteutveckling med personalmedverkan - En studie av banktjänster*. Karlstad University.

Spohrer, J., & Maglio, P. P. (2008). The Emergence of Service Science: Toward Systematic Service Innovations to Accelerate Co-Creation of Value. *Production and Operations Management*, 17(3), 238–246.

Spring, M., & Araujo, L. (2009). Service, services and products: rethinking operations strategy. *International Journal of Operations & Production Management*, 29(5), 444–467.

Stake, R. E. (2006). *Multiple case study analysis*. Guilford Press.

Steen, M., Manschot, M., & Koning, N. De. (2011). Benefits of Co-design in Service Design Projects. *International Journal of Design*, 5(2), 53–60.

Stevens, E., & Dimitriadis, S. (2005). Managing the new service development process: towards a systemic model. *European Journal of Marketing*, 39(1/2), 175–198.

Stewart, J., & Hyysalo, S. (2008). Intermediaries, Users and Social Learning in Technological Innovation. *International Journal of Innovation Management*, 12(3), 295–325.

Stickdorn, M., & Schneider, J. (2010). *This is service design thinking*. Amsterdam: bid Publisher.

Story, V., O'Malley, L., Hart, S., & Saker, J. (2008). The development of relationships and networks for successful radical innovation. *Journal of Customer Behaviour*, Vol. 7, No. 3, pp. 187–200.

Suddaby, R. (2006). What Grounded Theory is Not. *Academy of Management Journal*, 49(4), 633–642.

Sundbo, J. (1997). Management of Innovation in Services. *The Service Industries Journal*, 17(3), 432–455.

Swanborn, P. (2010). *Case study research: What, why and how?* Sage.

Symon, G., & Cassell, C. (1999). *Qualitative methods and analysis in organizational research: A practical guide* (2nd ed.). London: Sage Publications.

Syson, F., & Perks, H. (2004). New service development: a network perspective. *Journal of Services Marketing*, 18(4), 255–266.

Tether, B. S., Hipp, C., & Miles, I. (2001). Standardisation and particularisation in services: evidence from Germany. *Research Policy*, 30(7), 1115–1138.

Tether, B. S., & Tajar, A. (2008). The organisational-cooperation mode of innovation and its prominence amongst European service firms. *Research Policy*, 37(4), 720–739.

Tossavainen, P. J. (2013). Beyond sporadic actions: How to approach multi-party stakeholder collaboration in service development. *Jbm - Journal of Business Market Management*, 6(4), 171–191.

Tronvoll, B., Brown, S. W., Gremler, D. D., & Edvardsson, B. (2011). Paradigms in service research. *Journal of Service Management*, 22(5), 560–585.

Ulaga, W., & Reinartz, W. J. (2011). Hybrid Offerings : How Manufacturing Firms Combine Goods and Services Successfully. *Journal of Marketing*, 75, 5–23.

Urban, G. L., & von Hippel, E. (1988). Lead User Analyses for the Development of New Industrial Products. *Management Science*, 34(5), 569–582.

van der Boor, P., Oliveira, P., & Veloso, F. (2014). Users as innovators in developing countries: The global sources of innovation and diffusion in mobile banking services. *Research Policy*, 43(9), 1594–1607.

van de Ven, A. H. (2007). *Engaged Scholarship: A Guide for Organizational and Social Research.* Oxford University Press.

Vanhaverbeke, W., Chesbrough, H., & West, J. (2014). Surfing the new wave of open innovation research. In H. Chesbrough, W. Vanhaverbeke, J. West (Eds.), *New Frontiers in Open Innovation*, Oxford University Press.

Vargo, S. L. (2008). Customer Integration and Value Creation: Paradigmatic Traps and Perspectives. *Journal of Service Research*, 11(2), 211–215.

Vargo, S. L. (2014). Insights on Innovation from an Institutional and Ecosystem Perspective. Presentation at *RESER Conference Helsinki*, Finland,

Vargo, S. L., & Akaka, M. A. (2012). Value Cocreation and Service Systems (Re)Formation: A Service Ecosystems View. *Service Science*, 4(3), 207–217.

Vargo, S. L., & Lusch, R. F. (2004). Evolving to a New Dominant Logic for *Marketing. Journal of Marketing*, 68(1), 1–17.

Vargo, S. L., & Lusch, R. F. (2006). Service-Dominant Logic: What it is, What it is not, What it might be. In R. F. Lusch and S. L. Vargo (Eds.), *The Service-Dominant Logic of Marketing: Dialog, Debate, and Directions*, (pp. 43-56). Armonk, M.E. Sharpe.

Vargo, S. L., & Lusch, R. F. (2007). Why "service"?. *Journal of the Academy of Marketing Science*, 36(1), 25–38.

Vargo, S. L., & Lusch, R. F. (2008). Service-dominant logic: continuing the evolution. *Journal of the Academy of Marketing Science*, 36(1), 1–10.

Vargo, S. L., & Lusch, R. F. (2011). It's all B2B...and beyond: Toward a systems perspective of the market. *Industrial Marketing Management*, 40(2), 181–187.

Vargo, S. L., and Lusch, R. F. (2015). Institutions and axioms: an extension and update of service-dominant logic. *Journal of the Academy of Marketing Science.* Forthcoming (published online July 16th, 2015).

Vargo, S. L., Lusch, R. F., & Akaka, M. A. (2010). Advancing Service Science with Service- Dominant Logic Clarifications and Conceptual Development. In P. P. Maglio, C. A. Kieliszewski, & J. C. Spohrer (Eds.), *Handbook of Service Science* (pp. 133–156). New York: Springer.

Vargo, S. L., Maglio, P. P., & Akaka, M. A. (2008). On value and value co-creation: A service systems and service logic perspective. *European Management Journal*, 26(3), 145–152.

Vargo, S. L., Wieland, H., & Akaka, M. A. (2015). Innovation through institutionalization: A service ecosystems perspective. *Industrial Marketing Management*, 44, 63–72.

Velamuri, V. K., Bansemir, B., Neyer, A.-K., & Möslein, K. M. (2013). Product Service Systems As a Driver for Business Model Innovation: Lessons Learned From the Manufacturing Industry. *International Journal of Innovation Management*, 17(1), 1340004.

von Hippel, E. (1986). Lead Users: A source of novel product concepts. *Management Science*, 32(7), 791–805.

von Hippel, E. (1988). *The Sources of Innovation*. London and New York: Oxford University Press.

von Hippel, E. (1994). "Sticky information" and the locus of problem solving: Implications for innovation. *Management Science*, 40(4), 429–439.

von Hippel, E. (2001). Perspective: User toolkits for innovation. *Journal of Product Innovation Management*, 18(4), 247–257.

von Hippel, E. (2005). Democratizing innovation: The evolving phenomenon of user innovation. *Journal Für Betriebswirtschaft*, 1–26.

von Hippel, E., & Katz, R. (2002). Shifting Innovation to Users via Toolkits. *Management Science*, 48(7), 821–833.

von Hippel, E., & Riggs, W. (1997). *A lead user study of electronic home banking services: lessons from the learning curve*. Sloan School of Management, Massachusetts Institute of Technology.

Wagner, S. M., & Hoegl, M. (2006). Involving suppliers in product development: Insights from R&D directors and project managers. *Industrial Marketing Management*, 35(8), 936–943.

Wahyuni, D. (2012). The Research Design Maze : Understanding Paradigms, Cases, Methods and Methodologies. *Journal of Applied Management Accounting Research*, 10(1), 69–80.

Weber, M. (2008). Developing what customers really need: Involving customers in innovations. In *2008 4th IEEE International Conference on Management of Innovation and Technology*, 777–782.

Weinstein, O., & Gallouj, F. (1997). Innovation in Services. *Research Policy*, 26(26), 537–556.

Wendelken, A., Danzinger, F., Rau, C., & Möslein, K. M. (2014). Innovation without me: Why employees do (not) participate in organizational innovation communities. *R&D Management*, 44(2), 1–20.

Weterings, A., & Boschma, R. (2009). Does spatial proximity to customers matter for innovative performance? *Research Policy*, 38(5), 746–755.

Wetter-Edman, K. (2014). *Design for Service – A framework for articulating designers' contribution as interpreter of users' experience*. Gothenburg.

Whelan, E., Parise, S., de Valk, J., & Aalbers, R. (2011). Creating employee networks that deliver open innovation. *MIT Sloan Management Review*, 53(1), 37–44.

Witell, L., Gustafsson, A., & Johnson, M. D. (2014). The effect of customer information during new product development on profits from goods and services. *European Journal of Marketing*, 48(9/10), 1709–1730.

Witell, L., Kristensson, P., Gustafsson, A., & Löfgren, M. (2011). Idea generation: customer co-creation versus traditional market research techniques. *Journal of Service Management*, 22(2), 140–159.

Yin, R. K. (2014). *Case study research: Design and methods*. Sage Publications.

Zeithaml, V. A., Bitner, M. J., & Gremler, D. D. (1996). *Services Marketing*. Mcgraw-Hill Higher Education.

Annexes

Annex A Related publications

Parts of this thesis have been presented at international conferences and have been published in scientific journals. This applies especially for these articles:

- Jonas, J. M., Möslein, K. M., & Roth, A. (2013). Passive integration or mutual co-creation? Exploring the role of stakeholders in service innovation. Paper presented at *13th International Research Symposium on Service Excellence in Management* (QUIS13-2013), Karlstad, Sweden.

- Jonas, J. M., Roth, A., & Möslein, K. M. (2014a). Stakeholder integration in service innovation - An explorative case study on healthcare solutions development. Paper presented at *Euram Annual Conference 2014*, Valencia, Spain.

  A further developed version of this conference paper is published as

  Jonas & Roth (2017). Stakeholder integration in service innovation - an exploratory case study in the healthcare industry. *International Journal of Technology Management*. 73 (1/2/3), 91-113.

- Jonas, J. M., Roth, A., & Möslein, K. M. (2014b). Stakeholder integration for service innovation in German medium-sized enterprises. In *RESER Conference 2014*. Helsinki, Finland.

  An adapted version of the conference paper is published as

  Jonas, J. M., Roth, A., & Möslein, K. M. (2016). Stakeholder integration for service innovation in German medium-sized enterprises. *Service Science*, 8(3), 320-332.

- Jonas, J. M., Roth, A., Möslein, K. M. (2015). Actor integration in service systems - exploring effects on a micro level. Presentation held at: *The 2015 Naples Forum on Service*, Naples, Italy.

- Jonas, J. M., Roth, A., Möslein, K. M. (2015). Co-creating innovation in service systems - exploring the effects of cross-disciplinary problem solving. Paper presented at *European Operations Management Association Conference 2015*, Neuchatel, Switzerland.

These articles, co-authored by Angela Roth and Kathrin M. Möslein, are mainly conceptualized by the first author. Also data collection, the analysis of the data, and the interpretation of the results are primarily attributable to the author of this thesis. The present thesis also profited from feedback of researchers and practitioners collected at the presentation of the studies at conferences and research colloquia. Still, some parts remained unchanged and verbatim.

Earlier stages of this dissertation have been presented and discussed in the following doctoral colloquia for external feedback and discussion:

- Jonas, J. M. (2012) Investigating the practices of co-creation for service innovation - an exploratory study on the integration of external resources in service innovation projects. *7. Forschungsseminar „Innovation & Wertschöpfung" 2012,* Chemnitz, Germany. Nov 29- Dec 1, 2012.
- Jonas, J. M. (2013). Co-Creating Service Innovation - The Management of Organizational Stakeholder Integration for Service Innovation from a Service-dominant-logic Perspective. *BAM2013 Doctoral Symposium,* Liverpool, UK, Sept. 9, 2013.
- Jonas, J. M. (2013). Stakeholder integration in service innovation - An explorative case study on healthcare solutions development. *8. Forschungsseminar „Innovation & Wertschöpfung" 2013,* Hamburg, Germany, Nov 28-30, 2013.
- Jonas, J. M., Roth, A., Möslein, K. M. (2014). Co-Creating Service Innovation in Interdependent Service Systems. *Doctoral Workshop of the Forum on Markets & Marketing,* Karlstad, Sweden, June 16, 2014.
- Jonas, J. M. (2014). Co-creating service innovation. *RESER 2014 Doctoral colloquium,* Helsinki, Finland, Sept 9-10, 2014.
- Jonas, J. M. (2014). Stakeholder integration for innovation in service systems - towards a micro level model. *9th Research colloquium "Innovation & Value Creation",* Nürnberg, Germany, Nov 27-29, 2014.

Annex B

The ten foundational premises of the service-dominant logic (Vargo & Lusch, 2008)

FP 1	Service is the fundamental basis of exchange.
FP 2	Indirect exchange masks the fundamental basis of exchange.
FP 3	Goods are a distribution mechanism for service provision.
FP 4	Operant resources are the fundamental source of competitive advantage.
FP 5	All economies are service economies.
FP 6	The customer is always a co-creator of value.
FP 7	The enterprise cannot deliver value, but only offer value propositions.
FP 8	A service-centered view is inherently customer-oriented and relational.
FP 9	All social and economic actors are resource integrators.
FP 10	Value is always and uniquely and phenomenologically determined by the beneficiary.

Annex C

Frameworks for customer and stakeholder integration

Annex C 1 "The five "Co's" in innovation" by Russo-Spena and Mele (2012; p. 543)

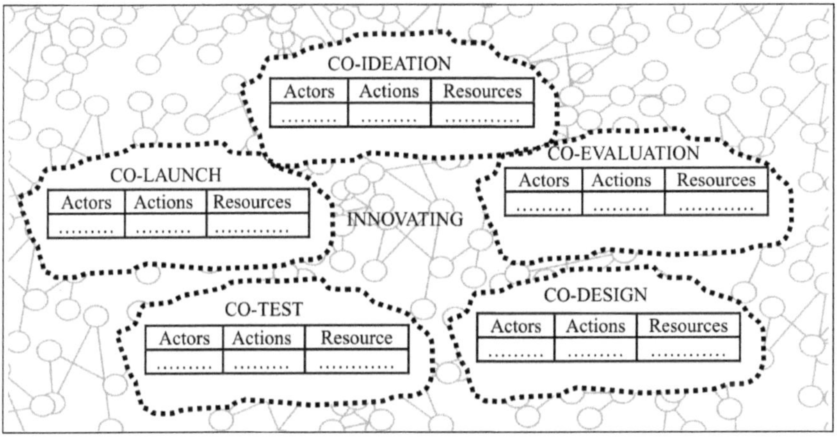

Annex C2 "The knowledge conversion process in creating extended service concepts" – presenting four roles of stakeholders in joint innovation (Gottfridsson, 2012, p.31)

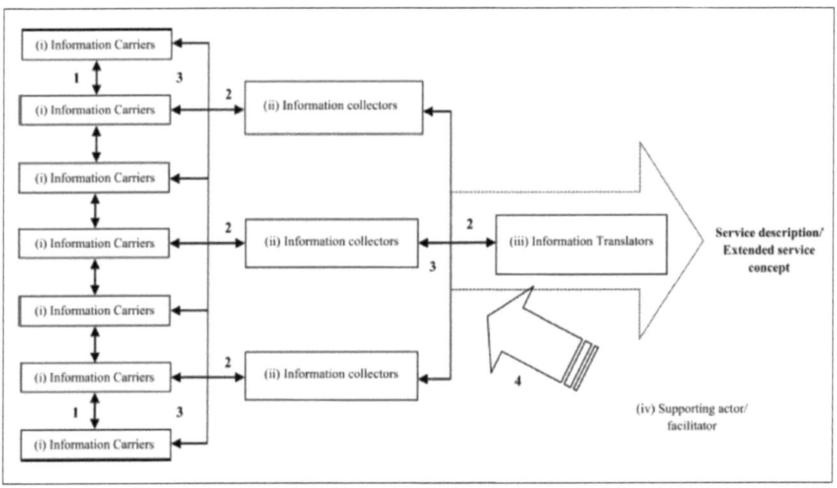

Annex C3 Framework for relating use information to methods for service development by Edvardsson et al. (2012, p. 421)

Resource context (resource constellations available to the customer)	**Use situation** (activities and interactions at a specific situation) — **Insitu**	**Exsitu**
In Context	***The correspondent***, reporting live from the situation	***The reflective practitioner*** reporting from the *armchair*
Ex Context	***The tester***, reporting from the virtual heaven	***The dreamer***, the creative who generates wild and imaginative ideas

MIX
Papier aus verantwortungsvollen Quellen
Paper from responsible sources
FSC® C105338

FSC
www.fsc.org

If you have any concerns about our products,
you can contact us on
ProductSafety@springernature.com

In case Publisher is established outside the EU,
the EU authorized representative is:
Springer Nature Customer Service Center GmbH
Europaplatz 3, 69115 Heidelberg, Germany

Printed by Libri Plureos GmbH
in Hamburg, Germany